Problems in School Media Management

. . . .

Bowker Series in
PROBLEM-CENTERED APPROACHES TO LIBRARIANSHIP
Thomas J. Galvin, Series Editor

PROBLEMS IN SCHOOL MEDIA MANAGEMENT

. . . .

by Peggy Sullivan

R. R. BOWKER COMPANY

New York & London, 1971

CONTENTS

· · · · · · · · · · ·

v

FOREWORD

. . . .

As the second title to appear in the series "Problem-Centered Approaches to Librarianship," Peggy Sullivan's *Problems in School Media Management* represents a distinguished addition to the instructional literature in the school-library, media-center field. It makes available a significant group of problem materials in case study form for use either in the library school classroom, or in workshop, institute, conference and other informal, in-service training environments for library and media personnel. These case studies reflect both the author's wide experience in the school field as a practicing librarian and as Director of the American Library Association's Knapp School Libraries Project, and her sensitivity and perceptiveness as an observer and recorder of the human condition. It is this last point—the depth and complexity of the problem situations she describes, that seems to me to distinguish Miss Sullivan's case studies most clearly from the work of other writers. These case studies ought to teach one of the most valuable of all lessons the professional has to learn: that problems often arise, not out of confrontations between "good guys" and "bad guys" in schools, but out of natural and inevitable conflicts among the honorable and the well-intentioned, often in the common pursuit of the most praiseworthy goals.

"Problem-Centered Approaches to Librarianship" is a new series designed to make case studies available for instructional use in all major areas of the library school curriculum, as well as to demonstrate the value of the case study as a vehicle for presentation and analysis of professional problems. Future volumes in this series will appear at regular intervals, and will focus on such areas as cataloging and classification, the literature of science and technology, the development of academic library book collections, computer applications, and problems of middle-management in libaries. It is the editor's hope that these will prove as useful and relevant both to the student and to the practicing librarian as the present volume surely must.

THOMAS J. GALVIN
SERIES EDITOR

PREFACE

· · · · · · · · · ·

In my own investigation into the use of case studies in education for librarianship, I have found many reasons why a collection of cases in school media management might be useful. A number of teachers of library science have told me they have adapted cases from other collections for use in courses related specifically to school media programs. One of the difficulties in using cases which apply to other kinds of libraries is that the very framework of the elementary or secondary school, and the place of the library or media program within it, changes the nature of most problems of policy and practice which arise. Thus, I have selected as the basic problems for cases presented here, the ones which occur in media programs in schools. It should be obvious that some of these programs are fairly traditional library programs, rather than unified media programs. The nature of some problems does not change when media programs are unified. The reader should understand that depiction of traditional school libraries does not indicate any bias of the author's in opposition to unified media programs.

The thirty cases in this book may be used for discussion and/or analysis by present or potential school media personnel in a teaching situation. I did not intend them to be read straight through, but rather, to be used in class to introduce problems within a specific context. The case method allows students to work from the same set of facts, thus assuring that in the discussion, all the elements of the problem will be exposed. Thus, while students' perceptions may differ, they cannot stray too far from the basic situation.

Some instructors or group leaders may choose to have the cases extended or resolved through role-playing. Although I have not used that technique myself, I am sure many of these cases are adaptable to that purpose. In that case, though, I would stress that care be taken to move toward a solution, rather than just to draw out or dramatize the problem.

Another potential use for these cases would be in in-service programs in school systems. The purpose would be to focus the attention of participants in an in-service class or meeting group on problems which might be quite similar to those which they might encounter in their own work.

The arrangement of cases in this volume is, generally, from the less difficult to the more difficult. Complexity or difficulty may, of course, be a matter of taste. Since it is important for cases to be credible, I have based these on actual incidents or situations. However, I have combined, condensed, altered, or, to be honest, have simply forgotten details on enough of these so that no one case includes a setting, characters and a problem which occurred together. To avoid coincidental use of names of actual persons or places, I have used the list of U.S. Places of 2,500 or More Population from the 1966 *World Almanac and Book of Facts* as the source of all names for persons, communities, or cities presented here.

Because I have had unusual opportunity, through my work as director of the Knapp School Libraries Project (1963 to 1968), to travel and to visit many kinds of media programs in the United States and to get to know many of the personnel working with them, I should acknowledge to all of them my indebtedness for their assistance, whether intentional or unintentional. They are many, and I may even have forgotten a few, but they probably remember the insights they offered to me.

It is customary for an author to acknowledge gratefully the assistance of his editor. When the editor has been the source of ideas, the consistent critic, and the thoughtful provider of suggestions about the book's ultimate scope, purpose, and use, gratitude is too small a thing. Tom Galvin has been all of those. Occasionally, I know, one's editor becomes one's friend. I think it is more difficult for one's friend to become one's editor, but Mr. Galvin has done that with grace and charm. For all of that, I thank him.

INTRODUCTION

· · · · · · · · · · · · · · ·

Thomas J. Galvin spoke at a conference on methods for the teaching of book selection, held at the University of Illinois in September, 1968. Although I had known his book, *Problems in Reference Service,* and, to a lesser extent, other books of cases in librarianship before that time, his talk gave me the idea of preparing a collection like this. His references to the case method and to the test of the value of specific cases were especially helpful. He pointed out that, in solving a case, there must be at least two viable solutions. I found that idea especially appealing, because I have long been bothered by the attitude that says, "This works, so this must be the only way to do it." This attitude has seemed to me to be especially widespread in school library programs, where the professional person responsible for the program has had little or no opportunity to work with others in the same field, and therefore has little sensitivity to the fact that even a good solution may not be the only one.

My opportunity to use cases in teaching first came at the University of Chicago in the summer of 1969, when I assigned one of the cases in this book to a class in Library Work with Young People. It was the first case I had written, "The Case of Extended Evenings," and in that class of students preparing for work in school and public libraries, it presented problems relating to both kinds of libraries. I used that case and nine others during two semesters of teaching at Rosary College, in the 1969–1970 academic year. The climate in the Department of Library Science at Rosary was particularly appropriate to encourage my attempting this approach, which was new to me and to the students. Sister Lauretta McCusker, chairman of the department, offers great interest and encouragement to instructors, as well as great freedom in setting directions and goals. The students in the Seminar in Library Work with Young People were, for the most part, the open, inventive thinkers and articulate discussants who make seminars the educational experience they should be.

It may be clear, by this time, that I do not employ the case method in my use of cases. Rather, I have used cases as vehicles for discussion. Instead of assigning specific students to prepare extensive analyses of cases, I have usually chosen to have the entire class discuss the case together. Sometimes, I have assigned written analyses, and sometimes, I have asked only one or two students to be prepared to lead the discussion. But that is not, strictly speaking, the case method. I believe, however, that these cases lend themselves to either kind of treatment on the part of the instructor using them. Further, although I have used some of these cases with students in a seminar class in a graduate library school, I have constructed other cases in sufficient variety and complexity to make them appropriate for less advanced graduate or undergraduate classes.

Few problems which arise in libraries would be the same in all libraries, with all publics, or for all personnel. Cases such as the ones in this volume, by placing the problems within a realistic setting, make it possible to apply policies learned in a vacuum to individual instances. A technique to be encouraged in solving or discussing these is that of treeing decisions. The student or discussant should be able to lay out the chain of decisions which were made in arriving at the crisis or problem within the case, and to indicate what options were best to follow at each of those points of decision.

When I used some of these cases, I had one student who consistently said at the opening of discussion, "Well, it's nothing but another problem of communications," and then virtually tuned out of further participation. What that student failed to realize was that "communication" can be the cause of many problems, but that the point is to find at what times and in what ways effective communications might have averted or altered the nature of problems encountered.

Instructors who use these cases will discover that some do lead to points of crisis. In others, the situation may be deteriorating or poor, but with no immediate crisis in sight. It has seemed to me that the nature of some problems causes this difference, but that students should become familiar with both kinds. I have tried to avoid endings which are such a tangle that the potential discussant will say, "Let's not do anything about it now; it's a mess." But I have also realized that unless some action is virtually demanded, the discussants of the case may simply find themselves rehashing the facts presented to them, rather than using those facts as background for their own evaluations and suggestions for action.

As an aid to initiating discussion or analysis in some cases, I have included questions or suggestions for discussion at the conclusion of some cases. The instructor or group leader may choose to prepare these for other cases. In my own teaching, I have prepared and distributed reading lists which might assist students working on cases. Since most of the readings are periodical articles dealing with specifics, the list is not included here, since it is quickly outdated.

In these cases, as in reality, there are often overlapping problems. The same case may be used for different purposes in different groups or at different times. This is especially important to note in the cases which relate generally to district-wide problems, such as "The Case of Considering a Center," or "The Case of Extended Evenings." While these may have particular relevance for individuals who are currently responsible for district programs, or are readying themselves to be supervisors or consultants, I believe that the ramifications of the decisions made at those levels are so significant for the media personnel and other faculty in any individual school that persons using these cases as part of their learning should be aware of how those decisions or practices occur. It is also possible to use a case as presented here, and to alter the course of discussion by offering alternatives to the facts as presented. For example, in "Discipline at Donora," is the problem affected by the educational background of the librarian, by the fact that she did her student teaching in that school, or by the fact that she attended that school as a child? In what ways might different circumstances affect her own actions or those of others? In some of the other cases, one might ask whether the problem would be the same regardless of level or location of the school, regardless of the race or other personal characteristics of the participants, or regardless of the size of the school.

It has been my experience that the use of case studies is much to be preferred over discussion of problems actually existing somewhere. Too often, in discussions like that, participants discover that the member of the group who is describing the situation he knows, has tended to clarify or highlight some points, while not presenting others too clearly. Thus, the value of considering a case from actual experience can be, and often is, diluted. It is hoped that these case studies in the realm of school media programs will serve as a valuable and challenging tool for library and media education.

1.
Miss Boscobel's Struggle with Skills

. . . .

"Now, this afternoon, we're going to do something just a little bit different. Usually, after you've heard a story, you know it's time for you to pick two books you would like to take with you. And we'll do that today, too. But while you're picking those books, there are some things I want you to think about. What are some of the reasons that make you decide to take one book and not another? Can we think of ten? Let's make a list and see how many we might name."

Leona Boscobel turned to the overhead projector and switched it on. She picked up a pen, ready to make notes as the third graders answered her open question.

"Ginny, I see your hand up. What's a reason you use?"

"I choose a book because I can read it myself."

"That's good. And how do you know you can read it yourself?"

"Oh, I open it up and skip through the pages."

"All right. You skip through the pages. We call that skimming sometimes, Ginny. And is there something else that skimming can tell us? Philip?"

"Well, sometimes, I skim through a book to see whether I'll like it or not. You know, I look at the pictures and I see how long it is, and I see whether there are any maps or stuff like that."

"Could we call that 'getting the feel of a book,' Philip?"

"Yes, I guess so, Miss Boscobel."

There were two points on the transparency recording the children's reactions now. Miss Boscobel gave more clues. She was attempting to get

1

the children to describe the many factors that affected what they chose to borrow. She got a few surprises, as when one boy mentioned that he chose stories that had good chapter headings to tell him what to look for, and another immediately countered with, "Not me! I don't want to know what's going to happen. You know, like in mysteries when they tell you one chapter is, 'Harry Tells All,' I don't like that. I don't want to know ahead of time who tells all." Several other children entered into this argument, and Miss Boscobel could tell by the reactions of others that the exercise was giving them an opportunity to think through some of their own reactions. The list on the transparency read:

Because I can read it.

Getting the feel of it.

I like the author.

I have to find out about the subject.

It's new.

The chapter headings tell me what happens.

I don't know what's in it.

Somebody has told me they liked it.

It's in a series about people I like.

There's no reading in it.

There had been a burst of giggles at the last suggestion, from Lester Madison, the clown of the class, who did as little reading as possible and worked harder at maintaining his image as a lazy boy than at anything else. With a straight face, Miss Boscobel wrote down his words. Then she looked back at the screen where the list was projected.

"All right. Now, we have ten things we look for in books. Some of them are really reasons why you might take one particular book, and others are reactions that give you reasons for taking the book. Do you see the difference? Getting the feel of a book is a reaction, but if you then take it because you like the feel of that book, that's your reason. Now listen carefully. I'm going to ask you, when you go to the shelves today, to remember all the things you think of as you choose your books. And then, next week, when you come again as a class, we will talk about what some of your reasons were, and whether you were right in some of the guesses you made. Do you know what I mean?"

"Yes, Miss Boscobel," came in a general chorus. Miss Boscobel dismissed the class then, and stood aside as they drifted in different directions to browse. Several went promptly to the books on the side of the charging desk, which had been checked in by Mrs. Atkinson, the clerk, while they had been listening to a story. Others sought out the fiction shelves, while others gathered around the biographies and science books, always popular with this class. Miss Boscobel, watching them, knew they were somewhat more self-conscious than usual as they handled the books. One or two, with an air of importance, walked to the card catalog, sternly studied the labels on the drawers, and pulled out drawers to flip through cards for what they wanted.

Shirley Mauston, the teacher of the class, had returned from getting a cup of coffee, and she said to Miss Boscobel, "Well, I'm glad to see that lesson on the card catalog is doing some of them some good. What did you teach them this week?"

"Well, it's funny. I'd have thought that what we talked about today might have come even before that first lesson on the catalog, but I think this may be good. We talked about what to look for when picking out a book to read. You remember, you and I put this down on that sort of vague outline we made of what to teach. I like this because it gets them thinking, and since we did it on a kind of discussion basis, they were getting ideas from each other, adding on to what one or two said. Also, there's something to follow up on next week, when I'll find out what they think they've been doing today, and see how it matches up with what we've listed as a group. See the list we made?" Miss Boscobel rolled the acetate on the overhead projector so Mrs. Mauston could review the list.

"Yes, I like that. This gives me an idea I can follow up in the classroom, too. I get tired of these paragraphs on 'Why I liked the last book I read,' and that stuff. I think I'll ask them to write their paragraph this week on 'How I picked out my book,' and we'll have the best ones ready to read when we come to the library next week. Meantime, they won't have had a chance to forget. How does that sound to you?"

"Fine," said Miss Boscobel. Noticing two of the boys scuffling near the picture book section, she began to make her way toward them, while

Mrs. Mauston turned to a girl who had come up with a book in her hand, evidently to ask her advice about it.

For some time, Miss Boscobel had been concerned about the manner of teaching library skills. Her own experience as a fourth-grade teacher had convinced her that skills had to be closely associated with other reading and study skills as taught in the classroom. She found that in practice, she seemed to omit them entirely with some classes when the teachers indicated that they would prefer to teach the skills in their classrooms. Later, she sometimes discovered that the skills were not really related to use of materials and tools in the library, and that somewhere the shortcoming either caught up with individual children, or had to be corrected in the library classes they had in other grades. Much as she herself was interested in the idea of more flexible scheduling of classes, she felt that as long as instruction in skills was an important part of her responsibility, she needed the time with classes as groups to provide it. When a teacher was quick to pick up on leads taken by the skills instruction, as Shirley Mauston had in assigning the written paragraphs, the procedure went smoothly, but Miss Boscobel was not satisfied with how things stood in other classes.

In Dorothy Barre's sixth grade, for example, it seemed to Miss Boscobel that she met one obstacle after another. When she had talked with Miss Barre at the beginning of the year about what their program of skills instruction might be, Miss Barre had said, "I have a bright group this year. I've seen their records, and I know they should, as a whole, be able to move fast. I want them to use the library extensively, but there should be no need for them to get class instruction. If you find they have deficiencies in using the library, just let me know. Our time in the library can be spent in active search for materials and in the beginnings of research."

Miss Boscobel's lips had twitched at the use of the word "research," but she knew that Miss Barre wanted the students to use the library well, and at the time, it had seemed their mutual goals could be worked out together. However, it was the librarian who received the first telephone call from the public library. It was Heather Buckley, the children's librarian, who reported almost gaily. "Say, Leona, I don't know what's going on over there at school, but all hell broke out here last night. I wasn't working, and we were short on the adult desk. A whole troop of kids came in and said they wanted to use the *Reader's Guide.* They wanted magazines that would include the 1963 issues on the Kennedy assassination, and we've been hanging on to them like they were gold bullion. Apparently the students didn't know up from down about finding what they wanted. I almost thought they couldn't be from your school, because I remembered the big effort you'd made last year to get the paperback issues of the *Reader's Guide* from us, so you could teach them how to use it, but the librarian asked them where they came from, and they're yours, all right. I really think maybe it's just one teacher who's flipped her lid, but I said I'd call you anyway. Will you look into this?"

"Sure," said Miss Boscobel. "I still have those paperback issues, and I've been wondering, for that matter, whether we should subscribe to the *Abridged Reader's Guide* here. But we're so cramped for space that we keep only about a year's worth of periodicals anyway, and we only subscribe to maybe a fourth of the ones in the index, so I just haven't pushed it. But I think I know the teacher, and I can suggest a session on the *Reader's Guide*. Thanks for letting me know what's going on."

Miss Boscobel had talked with Miss Barre after that, and the teacher had agreed it might be helpful for her to spend one of the class' library periods going over the use of the *Reader's Guide*. As part of her preparation, Miss Boscobel had made up questions that matched each of the issues. She had tried to vary the questions as much as possible, and she wanted them to be fairly relevant to the children's school work. This took more time than she had anticipated, but it was interesting.

Miss Barre accompanied her class and showed her own interest in Miss Boscobel's presentation. The librarian's opening questions and the confused or inaccurate replies of the children showed the need for this kind of instruction, and Miss Boscobel was pleased to see their interest. At the end of the class, however, Miss Barre approached her and said, "This has gone quite well, Miss Boscobel. Thank you. It does seem to me, however, that it shouldn't be necessary for you to interrogate the children about what they have been taught in the classroom. I think you place them in a difficult position. They sense that you are in some way criticizing me, and they are embarrassed by it."

"Criticizing you? Oh, Miss Barre, I'm sorry! That was certainly the farthest thing from my mind. I guess you mean my questions at the beginning about what they already knew about the *Reader's Guide*. It just seems to me that that's almost like a diagnostic test, really, or as close as I can come to one while teaching a whole class on a one-shot basis, like this. Maybe I'm sensitive about this, but I've seen too many librarians who just teach the same skills over and over, grade after grade, without finding out where the kids really stand. I don't think the children—or you, Miss Barre—should be embarrassed about that."

Miss Barre gave a thin smile. "Well, let's hope not," was all she had to say.

That incident concerned Miss Boscobel as she reviewed it later. It was small consolation that one of the girls in Miss Barre's room came to the library later in the week in the half hour before school opened in the morning, and reported, "Hey, I've got a compliment for you, Miss Boscobel. My daddy took me to the public library last night and stayed with me while I was using the *Reader's Guide* for that paper I'm writing, and he said he didn't know as much about how to use an index like that when he graduated from college, as I do now. I told him you taught me, and he said, 'How about that? A librarian who can teach! Tell her I'm all for her.' So my daddy's all for you, Miss Boscobel."

"Thank you, Lisa," Miss Boscobel acknowledged with a smile. Response like that made even Miss Barre's coolness possible to bear. The librarian was interested to note a wide range of response among the sixth-grade teachers. Two of the four teachers followed almost the same pattern, suggested little to her, made few demands on the library, were delighted when she gave the children book talks or told stories, and enjoyed the quizzes on books she made up for the children to play. Greg Williston, however, would have preempted all the time she could give either for planning together or for class time in the library, and he would have worked hard to make the most effective use of whatever services she could provide. He considered their task of teaching library skills as a joint effort, and the two of them conducted the class together, almost in a team teaching situation. The most recent class session had taken place just before the class began to write biographical sketches of famous people. Using a transparency which Miss Boscobel had prepared in advance, they had elicited from the children suggestions for names of people about whom they might write, and had placed one of the names in the lined-off space at the base of the inverted triangle. Then, in a series of questions and comments, they had pointed out ways the subject could be narrowed down, noting each of the refinements of the subject in a successively smaller lined-off space on the triangle. Finally, in the apex, they were satisfied that the topic was inclusive enough to be interesting and that there were materials available for use in writing about it. At this point, the topic was narrow enough to be workable in the preparation of a brief paper. Mr. Williston and Miss Boscobel had walked around the class then, as the children drew their own triangles on notebook paper, and they had commented on the children's progress or asked questions to prompt children who seemed stuck at some point. A typical paper had looked like this:

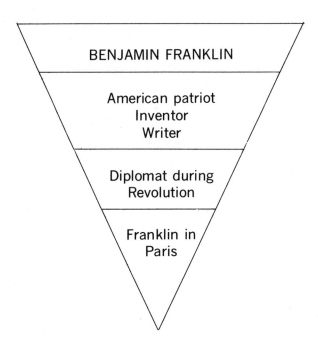

Looking at that one, Mr. Williston had commented: "Now, I think that's great. Art won't waste a lot of time when he starts reading encyclopedias and other materials in the library. He could've been lost, with all the writing there is about Franklin, but he's off to a good start already, it seems to me. If I'd had this kind of lesson in the sixth grade, it might not have taken me nine months to work out a topic for my master's thesis. I'm really convinced it's all just a matter of analysis, and I see how this all ties together. I'm really very grateful to you for working with me on this."

Miss Boscobel smiled, recalling the earlier compliment relayed from the child in Miss Barre's class. "Don't thank me," she said. "This will save us a lot of time and effort in the library, too, don't forget—and perhaps a phone call or two from the public library, for that matter. I really feel I'm getting somewhere when two of us can work out something like this so well."

"Don't you always feel you're getting somewhere?"

"No, not really, if you want me to be frank. I don't always see what needs to be done in this matter of teaching skills, for one thing, or at least not in time to really help. And, worse yet, I don't always have the opportunity. Sometimes I think I'm just wasted. After all, I'm a teacher, too, and what I can teach best is information related to the library. But I very often just miss out on really getting the information in when it would be most useful.

"The other day, for instance, Miss Laclede's third grade came in, and I was all set to teach them how to use the card catalog. I kept wondering why on earth they looked so bored and seemed so confused about the whole thing. Well, I found out. The day before, she had decided to start them on dictionary skills, and she'd been reviewing alphabetical arrangement with them. But it was just a little bit different from the way I was approaching it, so the poor kids really were just caught in the middle. Of course, we worked it out, but it really bothers me to think we could have done a bang-up job of teaching the same skills for two different purposes—using the dictionary and using the card catalog—and, doing it together, we could have taught each one better. It's the kids that concern me, of course. They must think we're working at cross purposes, and sometimes they're so polite, I have the feeling they're just humoring me about it all."

"I see your point," Mr. Williston said. "Isn't there a plan or something about what should be taught in the library program? Can't you just spread that around and follow it? Or even make up one of your own?"

"I suppose so. But the question is, does every teacher want me to be teaching a fairly structured sequence of skills? You see, it's not just individual children, it's individual teachers I have to consider."

Mr. Williston grinned. "Oh. I get it." He gestured toward Miss Barre's classroom. "You do have problems. Well, if there's anything I can do to help, let me know."

"Thanks." Miss Boscobel returned to the library, the conversation still uppermost in her mind. From her own records of class visits, she could prepare a chart of what she had been teaching to the various classes, but even without doing that, she knew that there would be great variations, not only by grade, but by class, because of the teachers' different views on skill instruction. What Miss Boscobel had to resolve first in her own mind was the extent to which the library's and the librarian's role in instruction and development of study skills should be determined by the teacher. Two ideas that were repeated again and again in the professional articles she read were the need for the librarian to be a leader in curriculum, and for library skills to be strongly coordinated with the classroom teaching of specific subjects.

Miss Boscobel had always held aloof from the discussions about library skills which went on among librarians at meetings she attended. She felt that those who were the most outspoken about exactly when and how and why they taught specific skills were really operating in a kind of vacuum, separated from the classroom teaching. She remembered a demonstration class on how to use the card catalog which a librarian had given at a state meeting. It was good, the material was clear, and the librarian presented it well. But in the question period, a young librarian had asked for what grade the class had been prepared, and the librarian had answered: "Well, I taught it just this way the other day to third graders, but you can never be sure they've learned it, so I just repeat the same thing every year to every grade, only I vary the books I use as examples."

Miss Boscobel thought to herself that that kind of repetitive teaching caused students to make excuses to stay in the classroom during the library visit, or barely tolerate the presentation they were forced to sit through for the twelfth time. She did not want to go in that direction. On the other hand, she was still sensitive after Miss Barre's questioning of the rather simple diagnostic test, if it could even be called that, which she had given so informally to the sixth graders. Would it be better to be sure that no little fish got through the net, to force every child in every class to follow some set pattern of skill so long as he came to the library with his class? She sensed that an approach like that would eliminate the creative efforts she had made with Mr. Williston, and, perhaps also, even the lukewarm cooperation of Miss Barre.

• • • • •

What is your opinion of the approach to, and work on, the teaching of library skills which Miss Boscobel has done to date? How might she proceed?

Locate and be prepared to comment critically on a statement (progress chart, article, scope and sequence, manual) prepared by a school system or school on the teaching of library skills.

What might be some of the differences between the teaching of library skills on the elementary and secondary school levels?

Locate and be prepared to comment critically on materials (transparencies, slides, filmstrips, charts, models) which are commercially available for use in the teaching of library and/or study skills.

What objectives might Miss Boscobel designate for an instructional program on library and/or study skills? With these in mind, prepare a rationale and plan for achieving them.

How might a change to more flexible scheduling of class visits affect the kind of skills instruction which Miss Boscobel gives now?

2.
A Problem
of Identity
· · · · · · · ·

Developing a consistent program under the direction of Mary Moberly, the elementary school libraries in the city of Delavan had received national attention. The seventy-five schools in the system, forty-two of them elementary schools, had school library programs that were individual, yet Miss Moberly had insisted that the same pattern should be followed throughout the system in such matters as general arrangement of the facilities, charging of fines, and purchase of equipment. In recent months, however, the elementary librarians in schools of the inner city had begun to feel some conflict between the recommendations for the library program as such and the freer atmosphere being cultivated in the administration of schools.

The principals of inner city schools, some of them working closely with citizens' advisory committees for the first time, were anxious to try more ways to individualize their programs. A collection of paperback books was provided in each school; students were encouraged to swap one book for another, with no record kept of losses or loans. Stirred by the report that forty-five percent of the children in these areas came to school with no breakfast, one task force of planners in the school system had inaugurated a plan to provide a free breakfast for every child. Response to this was enthusiastic. Another fairly recent plan had been to employ students from the nearby high schools as aides in the cafeteria and library. The announced purpose of this was not only to provide the high school students with spending money, but to stimulate their sense of responsibility and to give them status among the elementary children who would see them working capably and being paid for their efforts. As Hal Versailles, a sixth-grade teacher at Lincoln Elementary School, commented to the librarian, Fiona Joseph: "When I think of the kids in my class who are the second or third generation of families where no one is working full-time and earning a minimum wage, I realize what a boost it should give them to see high school kids working and getting paid for it. Why, when Jimmy Jefferson came in, after we had completed that unit on work a few weeks ago, and told me he'd decided to be a bagger at the supermarket, I thought, 'Hallelujah!' Do you realize what it must mean to have even that much ambition in a family where the father is a carwasher on the days when the weather is good enough for it?"

Mrs. Joseph was pleased with this feedback. The social studies unit on work was one that had been added to the curriculum within the past year, largely because of Mr. Versailles' enthusiasm and persistence. It had required the use of many new library materials, including pictures and clippings about jobs from newspapers, in addition to the slim collection of books and other materials on the subject. Largely as a result of that experience, Mrs. Joseph had begun a more concentrated effort to add clippings to the vertical file. The assistance of Susan Hickman, the high school aide, was especially useful in this task. Susan had learned to mount clippings on the drymount press and she had also learned to letter them with the appropriate subject headings. Mrs. Joseph's feeling that the vertical file collection would be much richer as a result of these efforts was somewhat shaken when she went to it one day and discovered that scarcely any of the folders on kinds of occupations were there. She assumed they were in use, but as she looked around the library, she did not see them. It occurred to her that Mr. Versailles might have taken them all to note for the bibliography of materials which he was preparing for the new district curriculum guide, but there was no record of the loan.

Her attention was distracted from this problem when Helen Gladstone, a fourth-grade teacher, hurried in, saying, "Oh, Fiona, am I glad you're here! I'm all set to show that film on birds that Marge showed while our class was having physical education, but there's no lens in the projector. Do you have an extra?"

"No lens!" Mrs. Joseph had not encountered this emergency before. She was more accustomed to sudden calls for bulbs, screens, or even films, but not lenses. "I'm sure we don't, because all we keep here are the less expensive supplies, but one of the other projectors was just returned. Why don't you take it?"

"Well, I'd rather not take it, because it's harder to thread, and I've got the other one all set up and ready to go. I did that before the kids came back to the room, and before I noticed that anything was missing. But if this is the best you can do, O.K." Miss Gladstone left with the second projector, wheeling it on a cart to her classroom. When she returned both projectors about forty minutes later, Mrs. Joseph looked at the one with the missing lens.

"Wow!" she said. "This must've happened between classes. You said Marge used it in her room, didn't you? So the lens must've been taken in the few minutes between her using it and your starting to thread it. Where was it?"

"Well, Fiona, you know how tightly we schedule equipment. I knew she was on your sheet just ahead of me, so I went down to her room to get the film and the projector on the cart while the kids were still coming back. She'd used it at about ten o'clock, she said, so I suppose it could've stood in the corridor about half an hour before I picked it up."

"Half an hour! Anything could've happened in that length of time! Why didn't she keep it in her room?"

"Well, we used to do that, but it's a big distraction for the kids when somebody opens the door and comes in to pick up equipment like that, so most of us have gotten into the habit of leaving the cart outside the door of the room. I suppose it is a little riskier, because anyone could make off with something, but with all the necessary interruptions there are during the day, I'm for avoiding the unnecessary ones. I'll be more careful another time."

It seemed to Mrs. Joseph that this was not the time to go into the problem of replacement of the lens, which would be expensive in terms of their limited budget for supplies and equipment, and which would also be time-consuming. She would remember to bring up the matter at a meeting of the teachers, when they might discuss the general problem of pilfering, and what troubled her more, the lack of respect for community property.

Before the day was over, she had heard of another example of the problem. Mr. Versailles had come in to show her slides he had taken of several student projects which had grown out of the unit on work. She looked closely at the display of pictures and cutouts shown in one of the slides, and looked up from the viewer to say, "But Hal, I think these cutouts of airline pilots and bus drivers came from the study prints on transportation workers that you borrowed from our vertical file."

"Sure, they did. That's why I thought you'd be interested in all this. Don't you remember? I'd invited you down for the last day of the unit, to see all the stuff we had on display, when one of the fathers talked about his job as a mail carrier? It was the day you were home sick."

"Yes, I remember," she said weakly. "But the study prints were a set. They weren't supposed to be cut up to make a display out of. We won't be able to use them again. And think of the information on the back of them. That's really all lost now."

"Oh, Fiona, you're the one who's always going around saying that materials are here to be used. These were used, and used well. What more could you want? Why, I spend lots of money out of my own pocket to bring in things the kids can use. Surely the library can afford to give something."

"That's not the point," Mrs. Joseph started to say, but interrupted herself to ask, "Hal, is it your class that has all the vertical file folders on work? What are they doing with them—making scrapbooks?"

Mr. Versailles missed the note of sarcasm in her voice. "Something like that," he said. "Jimmy Jefferson told me he'd tacked that picture of the supermarket bagger at work up above his bed. That guy's like a hero to him, but a believable hero, because Jimmy thinks that's something he can do for sure. You know what that does for a kid?"

"Of course, I know what that does for a kid, but I also know what it does for a library to have its material just given away. Look, Hal, you'll be teaching this unit year after year. Do you want us to start from scratch every year in assembling materials for it?"

"Why, I have such faith in you, that wouldn't bother me at all. Look at all you came up with this year! But give me credit—I brought a lot of it in myself and the clerk drymounted it. I'll be saving things all year long, and I'll bring them in from time to time so there won't be the big rush we had this year. It'll be another great unit."

"Mrs. Joseph," Susan Hickman broke in, "could you step over to the desk? Naomi has lost a book or something, and she's really close to having hysterics."

"Go ahead and bully the poor kid, who probably doesn't have a bed of her own, let alone a room of her own, in that housing development where she lives. Remember how important your materials are," said Mr. Versailles, as he scooped up the slides and walked out of the library, without giving her a chance to reply.

While handling the incident of the lost book, Mrs. Joseph became more and more troubled. She drew Naomi away from the two other girls who had come to the library with her, but they stood and looked through the glass window of the workroom as she tried to get the child to remember where she had last seen the book, what the name of it was, and to ask her to look for it again. Mrs. Joseph was uncomfortably aware that to the two girls she might indeed look like a bully, as she spoke calmly but firmly to the child, whose eyes were still wet, but who simply stared sulkily at her as though too tried of thinking about the book to listen.

Mrs. Joseph felt that the last straw was added to the day when the telephone rang as she was ready to leave that afternoon. It was Mary Moberly.

"Hello, Fiona," she began. "I'm sorry to be so late reaching you, but I've been at an all-day meeting and I wasn't able to get to a phone. We're having a small group meet tomorrow to discuss the policies we'd need to allow children to borrow filmstrip projectors and other equipment to take home overnight. You remember that we discussed this briefly after seeing *Project Discovery* at our last meeting of librarians, and agreed to consider it. Hedy Gallatin has been trying it at her school, and she has a report to give us. I hate to ask you at the last minute, but I think it's important that we all do the same thing, and also that we get the point of view of someone from one of the ghetto schools. I've cleared it with Mr. Rolla, and he says it's okay with him if you leave early to attend. He's a great principal, isn't he?"

"Yes, he is," Mrs. Joseph agreed. "To tell you the truth, Miss Moberly, right at this minute, I'm beginning to think it's a mistake to let anything out of the library if I ever intend to see it again. Maybe I'll feel different tomorrow, and, of course, I'll be glad to come, but I warn you, I'll have some ammunition for the other side."

"Well, it's late. Let's not go into all that now. But I hope you'll speak up tomorrow. See you here in the office about 3:30 then. And thanks for being so nice about coming on such short notice."

That evening, Mrs. Joseph really began to wonder what her own position should be. She talked for a few minutes with Mr. Rolla in the morning, but he asked whether they might discuss whatever the problem was over lunch instead. Walking through the lunch line ahead of him, Mrs. Joseph was not sure whether to begin by mentioning some of the recent losses in the library, which in themselves were not major items, but which seemed to her to indicate a lack of concern for community property, or whether to introduce the idea Miss Moberly had presented about lending out equipment. Mr. Rolla settled it by saying, as they sat down at a small table in the teachers' lunchroom, "Well, I hear that Mary Moberly is willing to let us have a go at letting kids take equipment home. Several of us have been pushing for that for some time. I've heard how well it's been going at Hart School, and I'm anxious to try it here."

"And what if we lose all the projectors and tape recorders in a week?" Mrs. Joseph asked. "I brought along a list of the pieces of equipment that have had to be replaced since the beginning of the school year."

Mrs. Joseph handed the principal a list she had made hastily on half a sheet of paper:

> Lens of 16mm film projector
> 2 bulbs, filmstrip projector
> 4 plugs, tape recorder (cut off end of cord with sharp knife)
> 2 headphones, tape recorder
> 1 extension cord

"I'm sure that if I could even get a similar count of materials, it would shock you," she continued. "With the equipment, the loss of time is as important as the cost. I found out today, for example, that it will be Tuesday before anyone comes out from the district office to put in a new lens to replace the one that was stolen yesterday."

" 'Stolen' is a pretty strong word to use," the principal remarked.

"Yes, it is, but I don't know what else you can call it when a lens is taken out of a projector when there must've been nobody but our own students in the corridors during a twenty-minute period in the morning."

"Look, Mrs. Joseph, what we're trying to do for these kids in every way we know is to increase their sense of self-respect, and yet to make them feel a part of society. Every activity we've taken on has been geared to this, just as I think our curriculum has been geared to this. And—"

Mrs. Joseph broke in to say, "I'm all for self-respect, but doesn't respect for community property come in there somewhere? On the days the cleaning woman comes to my home, I'm careful not to leave any money around, because I pay her a fair amount, and I don't want to be responsible for tempting her to take money that isn't hers. By the same token, why keep saying to these kids, 'Look! Look! We have all these great things in this school. Help yourself!'? I guess, Mr. Rolla, it depends on whether you think you increase their sense of community property by limiting their privileges until they understand their responsibility, or by letting them help themselves, and then trying to convince them that what they've taken or misused or damaged belongs to everybody, and that its loss hurts everybody. It's a complex attitude we're trying to teach them."

"Oh, I realize it's not simple. I see now that some of the things we've done may work against some of the things you do in the library. For example, if a child can borrow a paperback in his classroom and just replace it with another one he's already read, or not even swap for it, he probably wonders why he has to bring back a library book at all, let alone on a specific day."

"Yes, and one of the things we've discussed, Mr. Rolla, is the problem of giving these children a sense of time. I've seen a great improvement over the years, but that may be because many of the children are now living in high-rise housing, where Sunday is a different day because the schedule for the elevator and the guards is different. When they were all in those awful old tenements that've been torn down, every day was like every other. We used to laugh about it then—about the children who came to school on Saturday and were surprised to find the school closed. And, of course, I was always especially interested, because all that affects how children know when to return books."

"That's terribly important to you—that the children return the books on time, isn't it?" The quizzical look Mr. Rolla gave her made Mrs. Joseph feel like some kind of an ogre.

"Of course, it's important, but not just to me! Mr. Rolla, we have about 7,000 books in this library, if that's the example you want to use, and we have almost 1,000 children in this school, and if every child took a book home with him every day and decided not to bring it back, our collection would be gone in seven days. I know that's ridiculous, but I also know that when Mr. Versailles, for example, wants his sixth graders to use the *World Almanac*, he wouldn't be very happy if I told him that the art teacher had torn it up to make papier-mâché. I'm concerned about the children, too, but I hope we have something for next year's children, not just this year's."

Mrs. Joseph had been aware, by the lowered voices of the teachers at the other tables, that their conversation was attracting attention. She was sure some of the teachers would agree with her, others with the principal, but she was also sure that there must be some right on both sides. She wanted the library to reflect the spirit of the school in its freedom and respect for the individual, but the library also depended on everyone's cooperation and interest. If borrowing and using materials became too difficult, there were teachers who would just stop using materials. And she did not feel too free to suggest changes, since Miss Moberly kept a firm line on changes of policy and procedure in all the schools. She was not even sure what position Miss Moberly might take, but she thought uncomfortably of other times when she felt she had been unable to convey to the library supervisor some of the problems which she felt were unique to an inner-city school. Perhaps, this time, all that was coming to a head. Mr. Rolla was saying, "When you attend that meeting this afternoon, you will be representing the school. I would like to know now what point of view you intend to present. What will you say, specifically about the home loan of projectors—or about related problems which may come up?"

3.
Sylvester ...
Meets the Press
· · · · · · · · · · ·

Fleur Wilmette had been the first elementary school librarian hired by the Baileys Crossroads School District five years earlier, and she had been responsible for building the collections in schools where the libraries came rapidly to life with federal funds, as the result of the Elementary and Secondary Education Act of 1965. Since six of the nine elementary schools in the district received Title I funds, she had done a good deal of work with community groups to stimulate interest in the programs of tutoring, community responsibility, and preschool programs, which had received most emphasis from the school district in the use of Title I funds.

When the Newbery and Caldecott Award winners of 1969 were announced, Todd Evans, the associate editor of *Baileys Daily*, the local paper, called her to ask for an interview. Fleur immediately said she would be delighted to talk of her experiences, but she would clear the interview with Mr. Duluth, the superintendent of schools.

"Okay, you do that," Mr. Evans said. "But I'm sure that it's fine with him. He was telling me at Kiwanis the other day that we should give more feature space to the schools, and when I saw this press release on the award books, I thought it would be a good feature for our women's page."

Fleur set a date for the appointment. Mr. Duluth was, as she had expected, very pleased that she had been asked for the interview.

When Mr. Evans arrived for the interview, he brought with him the press release announcing the winners of the awards. He was pleased to see that Miss Wilmette also had copies of the books available for him to see. He asked to borrow them, and she agreed.

19

"I was really interested to see this guy Steig win an award for art. I know his cartoons from *The New Yorker,* and I wouldn't have called them art. Of course, they're good."

"One of the important things about the Caldecott Award," Fleur said, "is that the drawings should really illustrate the story. They're not always great art, but they have to be good as illustrations. In picture books, that means they really have to tell the story."

"Oh, I see," the editor said with a smile. He put the books aside and asked, "Okay with you if we run an illustration or two from these along with the story on you? Of course, we'd like to run your picture, too, and I've brought my camera."

When he was ready to take pictures of her, Mr. Evans suggested that her desk be piled with books. There were a number of them available from the processing room, and they stacked them on the desk so that the librarian herself was visible between the books that were as high as her head.

The picture and article appeared in the Thursday edition of the paper, and Fleur's telephone rang all evening with congratulations and comments from friends. Fleur could tell that Mr. Evans had read the books himself, because he gave brief synopses of each, in his own words. Then he quoted her comment that the committee had realized there might be reactions to Armstrong's *Sounder,* the Newbery Award winner, because of its strong message about the dignity of man and the need for racial understanding, but that they had felt the selection of Steig's *Sylvester and the Magic Pebble* would be a highly popular choice, with no controversial possibilities. Just as she did in book talks, Fleur had also mentioned some of the titles which were favorites of hers, and ones which appeared on the list of notable children's books of the year. Mr. Evans had included these, with the comment that the libraries in the elementary schools were growing rapidly, and that many more good books, as well as other materials, were available there. The two other pictures with the story featured the jacket illustration from *Sounder* and the illustration from *Sylvester . . .,* in which a tearful mother and father donkey were pleading with the police for help in finding their son.

At her office the next morning, Miss Wilmette received five copies of the clipping "for your scrapbook and boy friends," according to Mr. Evans' note, along with the books he had borrowed. She wrote him a note of thanks during the midst of a hectic morning, with several more interruptions occasioned by the feature write-up. She took time to eat a sandwich lunch at her desk about one o'clock, and had scarcely finished when her telephone rang again.

"Fleur?" It was Mr. Duluth. "I wonder if you'd come down to my office and bring that clipping from last night's paper, and a copy of that book about the mule, if you have one on hand."

"Yes, sir, of course," Miss Wilmette answered, adding almost automatically, "but it's about a donkey, not a mule."

"The point is, it's also about pigs who are police. But come down and we'll discuss it."

Somewhat mystified, Miss Wilmette went to the superintendent's office. He leaned back in his chair and scanned the clipping rapidly, saying, "Well, it's one newspaper photograph that's pretty good. The one of you, that is. I'm sorry about this, Fleur, but it seems to have touched off something." He leaned forward and picked up *Sylvester . . .*, which she had left on the desk. He flipped quickly through the pages, and continued, "I had a call this morning from the chief of police. They're very angry about this picture. Now, mind you, they're not angry with you, and I want you to understand that this is not a personal attack. They even liked the fact that you said in the paper you had other favorites among the books being considered. But what Chief Groton wants to know now is where the school system stands on this book."

"Wait a minute, Mr. Duluth! Are you saying that because there's an illustration of pigs in this book, the police are taking it as some kind of personal insult?"

Mr. Duluth held up the book open to the illustration which had appeared in the newspaper. Two donkeys stood before a desk like a magistrate's desk, and two pigs wearing policemen's uniforms were interrogating them.

"Well, there's no doubt that these are policemen, and that they are pigs, is there? I may be mistaken about donkeys and mules, but not this. Right?"

"Of course, they're pigs dressed as policemen, but all through the book—"

"I know what you're going to say. All through the book, other characters are animals too, but this is the only offensive one—or at least, the only one that seems so to me. And the chief was on the phone to me first thing this morning about it. I was out, but when I returned his call, he was still wild. Now, you know, Fleur, we've spent a lot of effort, especially in our Title I schools, in cooperative programs with the police in this town. It seems to me it would be a shame for it all to go down the drain because of this little incident. I'm not sure yet just how to handle it, but in the meantime, I'm asking you to round up all the copies we have of this book in the elementary schools and hold them at your desk."

"Why, Mr. Duluth, that's censorship!"

"No, I'm just trying to get to the bottom of this. By the way, do you know how many copies we have?"

"Yes, I know exactly in this case. We have five subscriptions with a book club which offered that as a selection. Not all the schools wanted it, so we kept just those five."

"What was that about a subscription?"

"You know, a subscription to a club, just like one you might have at home. Several years ago, it seemed like a good way to get things going, and we started five subscriptions. That usually is about how many copies we buy among the nine schools since there are differences in each community, and we've kept it up. When we have a full-time librarian selecting for each school—"

Mr. Duluth broke in again, holding up his hand in a familiar gesture. "Hold it, Fleur. I know that theme of yours, and we will get them some day. But meanwhile, the fact that librarians did not just sit down and read and review this and buy it, may be in our favor. I'm glad we had this little talk. But I do want those books at your desk no later than Monday afternoon. I think you'd better call the librarians, and ask them to put them in the pouch to be picked up first thing Monday."

"They just might be in circulation, you know."

"In that case, the librarians can ask whoever has them to return them by Monday morning, and they could still be here by Monday afternoon, Tuesday at the latest."

Miss Wilmette was getting more disturbed at the trend of the conversation, and she realized Mr. Duluth was deciding what the direction was. She took a deep breath and made one more effort.

"Mr. Duluth, I really think the police chief is wrong. Even if he is right to protest, why doesn't he do it like anybody else in this community would have to? We have a policy which says he has to come in, or somehow pick up a form to make his complaint. But you know all this. How come all he has to do is pick up the phone and he gets all the copies withdrawn?"

"The copies will not be withdrawn without the usual procedure, Fleur. But, since the chief functions virtually as a member of our staff in planning the community responsibility program in our curriculum, I intend to extend to him the same courtesy I would to any member of the staff. We will hold the books for review. After all, your librarians are able to review and to decide yes or no about books. Are they always one hundred percent right? You know they're not, but I support them, because the responsibility is mine—repeat, mine."

The superintendent was speaking more firmly than Miss Wilmette had ever heard him, outside of some staff or board meetings when controversies had raged. She decided this was not the time to try to discuss the matter further, and she left his office. She placed calls to the several libraries which, according to the district union shelflist, had the book in their collections. The librarian was away from one of the libraries, and the principal agreed to find the book and send it in. When librarians asked Miss Wilmette about the action, she tried to explain with as few details as possible, and with no reference to her own negative reaction.

Four of the books came in the delivery from schools shortly after noon on Monday, along with a note from Irene Proctor, saying the fifth copy would be sent as soon as she could retrieve it from the second-grade child who had borrowed it. Miss Wilmette stacked the copies together, laid the note on top, and set them on one side of her desk. About thirty minutes later, she looked up when a familiar voice said, "Hi, there, just thought I'd have a look at the celebrity on my way to see your boss."

Todd Evans stood at the door of her office, and she returned his smile. He came in and quickly spotted the pile of plastic-jacketed books. "Oh, what have we here? Our squeamish superintendent has knuckled under to the pigs?"

Instinctively, Miss Wilmette came to Mr. Duluth's defense. "No, these are just here to be looked over."

"You're a good, loyal little gal. More credit to you. But I'm off to see the dragon. I heard about Groton's scream on *Sylvester . . .*, so I asked for an appointment. Lots of luck." He walked out and down the hall to the superintendent's office.

Curious as Fleur Wilmette was about that interview, she heard nothing more directly, but the next day's paper ran another feature, with quotes from the superintendent, the chief of police, and, reportedly, several of the librarians, but the article noted that the school employees interviewed, with the exception of the superintendent, had asked not to be identified. It also reported that no copy of the book could be obtained in any of the elementary school libraries at this time, and quoted somewhat ironically from the glowing comments made about the book by a representative of the American Library Association on the occasion of its receiving the award. Another point made was that the book had been purchased on a subscription basis, without the usual careful review given to new titles by the librarians. Miss Wilmette was certain that information had come from the superintendent, who had seemed to regard the means of purchase as a reasonable defense of having acquired the book in the first place.

Miss Wilmette's first reaction, in her conversation with the superintendent the preceding Friday, had been that he was being highhanded and acting as a censor. Now, she felt a certain sympathy for him, and her loyalty to him and to the school system made her somewhat disgusted with the newspaper treatment. And there was more to come.

In the letters column of the paper on Thursday, the retired librarian from the public library wrote to inform everyone that she had checked in there Tuesday evening, and could proudly report that several copies of *Sylvester* . . . were available in the picture book section, one was already set aside in the collection of first editions of Caldecott Award winners, and several others were probably out. She concluded with: "Since the public library has never given in to any other public agency in its concern for the reading available to the citizens of this community, it can now supply the needs and interests of children unable to obtain this prizewinning book elsewhere." To Miss Wilmette, the letter seemed likely to do more harm than good, perhaps even eventually to the public library, whose present director would not have made such a comment. She was sure that many readers would scarcely notice the word "Retired" after the librarian's title, and would credit the public library with a kind of open-mindedness not operating in the schools.

A less inflammatory letter followed that one. A reader in a suburban community wrote to say that the most distressing feature in the Tuesday article was the report that the school librarians refused to give their names. He stated that their fear for their jobs, if that was their motivation, was based on unreasonable concern. He lamented the fact that children were sent to school to learn uprightness and honesty, in addition to reading, writing, and arithmetic, while school personnel were, as he put it, " . . . allowed to cop out (no harm intended, Chief Groton, sir), when a public issue of this kind presents itself."

Miss Wilmette, who had scarcely seen the superintendent since their conversation on Friday, now wondered whether the next move was up to her. She recalled her conversation with the librarians, and thought perhaps she should have cautioned them about making comments to the newspaper. Yet now they were being criticized for being too cautious about being quoted. Any of them who might call her for advice, if Todd Evans should ask for more comment, would expect her to know the superintendent's view, but she felt at this point she scarcely understood his position. She was unsure whether to call him or to hope the whole affair might blow over.

4.
Sid Creates
a Dilemma
· · · · · · · · ·

"I thought there was a filmstrip on the Shakespearean theater in that series about drama through the ages," Jim Tucumcari said to Glenda Sherrill as he came into the media center workroom to check the shelflist.

"Yes, I'm sure there is," Miss Sherrill replied. "I remember how pleased Dennis Premont was when that series came. He used it with the juniors last year, and they put on that great program of readings from Shakespearean plays. Remember? They used those recordings of recorder music and did such a good job of creating an atmosphere."

"Sure, I remember, although I can't be as sure as you that that means there was a strip in this series about the Shakespearean theater." But as Mr. Tucumcari was talking, he was looking through the shelflist, and he raised his head and read from a card: " 'Drama for all times . . .' Here it is. And strip number seven is entitled 'Shakespeare's Theater.' I suppose it could be that I was looking under Shakespearean instead, but I even opened the filmstrip cabinet and looked through the 800's and didn't find anything. Maybe it's in the number for world drama, as a series. I'll try that." He walked out of the workroom.

Sid Mandan had been working quietly in the corner of the workroom, checking in magazines. He looked over at Miss Sherrill, seemed to be about to speak, but said nothing. Miss Sherrill smiled at him. "Yes, Sid?" she said.

"Oh, nothing," he answered.

It was good to see Sid smile. He was a loner among the high school students, and was the kind of boy Miss Sherrill was almost sorry to see on the library squad. He was tall and thin, and acutely aware of his own awkwardness. When he was on duty at the desk, he dissolved in shyness when a girl came up to ask for information or to check something out. Working in the library was obviously one of his few pleasures, and he did his work slowly but well. Once started on a routine job, he seemed to forget his own clumsiness and to concentrate on doing the task as well as he could. He was excellent at something like checking in the magazines, because he approached the task methodically and carefully. He cared little for reading, and he never interrupted his work to skim the pages, as most of the students did at some time or other.

The period ended in a few minutes, and Sid left a careful note about how far he had gone, gathered up his books and left. Miss Sherrill felt that something was still on his mind. She went out on the floor to relieve Mr. Tucumcari who had been at the desk helping students.

"Well, did you find the filmstrip all right?" she asked.

"No, and it's the darnedest thing. There really isn't a card in the catalog for that title. There are cards for the others in the series, which I checked, but that one's gone. And I checked the filmstrip drawer again, to be sure. Nothing there. I'm almost positive it's not out in circulation, but I didn't go so far as to check for it. I just set Mike to work on some books instead."

Miss Sherrill looked at the students working at tables near the desk, and saw Mike Burnham poring over an oversize volume. She could see plates of the Globe Theater, and Mike was busy sketching from the illustration.

"Well, he looks like he's doing all right," Miss Sherrill said.

"Oh, yes, but I'd like to know what became of that filmstrip. It seems to have vanished without a trace! Well, I guess there are more important things to worry about." Mr. Tucumcari gathered up some work he had with him and left to get coffee in the faculty lounge.

Mr. Tucumcari had been gone only a few minutes when Mike Burnham came up to the desk and spoke to Miss Sherrill.

"Gosh, Miss Sherrill, I hate to bother you some more, when Mr. Tucumcari took so much time helping me find what I needed for my senior honors project, but would you happen to have another copy of this book?" He held the illustrated text on the age of Shakespeare open and ran his finger down the smooth stubs of several pages, which had been neatly cut out of the book. "See, somebody's cut these pages out. I could hardly tell, and I kept thinking the pages were put in wrong or something, but then I opened the book flat, and I saw where the pages had been cut."

"Oh, what a shame!" Miss Sherrill said. "I've never seen such a neat job of mutilating a book, but it always makes me sick. Mike, I'm sure that's our only copy of that rather expensive book, but let's check."

After a futile search for another copy, or for similar material that Mike could use, Miss Sherrill left him using an encyclopedia as a poor substitute. In a few minutes, Mr. Tucumcari returned.

"You'd better get down there for coffee while everybody's still talking about it. Dennis Premont has just won a great international fellowship. It's got everything—lots of travel, time for research, no particular tie to a university. It's just right for him."

"But we'll hate to lose him. How long does it last? A year?"

"Yes. But he says he won't take leave; he'll just resign. After that, I'm sure he'll have a chance to go on and work for a doctorate, and then maybe move up to college teaching. I'm sure that's what he's had in mind. Our great principal is down in the lounge now, saying this is one of the greatest honors ever to come to the school, and he always knew Dennis was one of the most gifted young teachers, and he's proud of all of us, and all that. But go on down and get in on it yourself." Miss Sherrill left.

When she had left, Mr. Tucumcari stopped by the table where Mike Burnham was working. "How goes it?" he asked.

"Oh, fine, thanks. Miss Sherrill found me this encyclopedia with some good pictures. But I just remembered that once in Mr. Premont's class, we had some transparencies that were cross-sectional views of the Globe. Do you remember them? On an overlay, they even showed where people in the audience were, and how many parts of the stage the actors and musicians could use. I'd like to use those. Will they be in the transparency file under Theater?"

"Yes, I'd think so. Or if they're not there, try Shakespeare, or Globe, or English Drama. Do you think you'll have time to use them before the end of the period?"

"Oh, sure. I'm really just checking my memory anyway." Mike went to the file of pamphlets and pictures, and Mr. Tucumcari turned to help a girl who had just come in.

Mr. Tucumcari was standing near the door when students left at the end of the period. He spoke to Mike. "Did the transparencies help?"

"No," the boy answered. "They weren't there. But I've got lots of stuff. Thanks, Mr. Tucumcari."

Sid Mandan was entering the library for his second work period of the day, and he overheard this conversation. He stopped in front of Mr. Tucumcari and said, "Do you think I could talk to you—in the workroom, maybe—sometime?"

"Why, of course. I'll be right in, Sid. Just as soon as things get under way for the fourth period. Okay?"

When Mr. Tucumcari entered the workroom, Miss Sherrill and Sid were working together, checking in magazines. Sid looked up and said, "I guess I might as well tell you this while you're both here. I don't know whether to say anything or not, but I guess if I'm a responsible assistant in the library, I have to, don't I?"

"That depends on whatever is on your mind, Sid," Mr. Tucumcari said.

"That Burnham guy was looking for stuff on Shakespeare, right?" Sid asked.

"Yes."

"And a lot of it was missing, right?"

"Right."

"I think I know where it is. Mr. Premont has a whole lot of stuff from the library in the trunk of his car. They're mostly books, and I know he's had them a long time, maybe a couple of years, because I looked at some of them once when I was helping him load an overhead into the car to take to that state meeting. I think he's been taking stuff for a long time, maybe on those afternoons when his play-reading group meets in the conference room, and they leave after the library's closed. I just know he has a lot of stuff—transparencies, slides, filmstrips, books, everything."

"Of course, he might have a lot of things like that, and they might not be from the library at all," Miss Sherrill said.

"Oh, sure. But I work here, Miss Sherrill. I know how things are marked, and I really recognized some of the things. I might be wrong about some of them, but even so, he has a lot. I didn't want to have to tell on him, but when you found out about that missing filmstrip this morning, and when Mike said those transparencies were gone, and I knew those were things Mr. Premont was interested in, I just knew he was the one. What will you do now?"

Miss Sherrill spoke again. "Sid, I don't know whether you realize how serious the things you are saying are. It could well be that Mr. Premont, or any other teacher, could have library material for some time, but to suggest he's taken it purposely, without checking it out, and is intending to keep it—well, that's a big accusation. Why don't you think about this, Sid, and we'll discuss it again tomorrow?"

Sid looked sulky. "Mr. Tucumcari, is that what you think, too?" The man nodded. "Okay. I'll think about it, Miss Sherrill. But if a teacher accused a student of having a whole trunkful of library materials, I wonder if you'd let it go like this."

Sid turned back to his work, and the two librarians felt rebuffed. Sid, who was so often ill at ease, seemed very sure of himself now. The librarians exchanged glances before Mr. Tucumcari returned to the desk, where two students were waiting for help.

It was late afternoon before Miss Sherrill and Mr. Tucumcari were alone again. Miss Sherrill brought up Sid's accusation. "You were mighty quiet when Sid was sounding off today," she said.

"That's because I was thinking. He could be right. It's crazy, but Premont does use the library a lot, and he could have stolen us blind, and we wouldn't know it."

"Say, you are jumping to conclusions. Why would you take the word of a nice boy, who desperately wants attention, but who is kind of strange, when he accuses one of our prize teachers?"

"Well, as Sid says, if a teacher accused a student of the same thing, we'd have the student down here in no time flat. We'd hear his side, of course, but we'd almost accuse him on the basis of what a teacher said. I hadn't realized before what a difference there is in how we handle these things. Of course, nothing quite like this has come up before."

"And it would have to be the day that Dennis has said he's leaving! If there is a chance of his having those materials, and if we want them back, we'll have to move fast."

"But on the other hand, it could look like we're trying to take the wind out of his sails, just when this big award has come through. Maybe we should check out our suspicions with the principal?"

"Oh, no," Miss Sherrill demurred. "That just increases the seriousness of the whole thing. Besides, how can we accuse him to someone else, when we haven't faced him yet? And I suppose the principal could think we're just trying to take the tarnish off the glow of Dennis' good luck."

"Now you're being harsh. Why should anyone think that? We could just go to Premont and tell him the story."

"And involve Sid?"

"I suppose we'd have to. Why?"

"Because Sid flunked Mr. Premont's sophomore literature class, and had to take it in summer school from another teacher. Premont would say right away that we're crazy to listen to a kid who's carrying a grudge against him."

Unexpectedly, Mr. Tucumcari chuckled. "You know what we are really saying to each other, Glenda? We do half believe what Sid has told us, and we're just afriad to find out for sure that he may be right. Well, whatever else, there isn't much for us to do until Sid comes in tomorrow. But then what? For that matter, let's say for some reason or other he says the whole thing was a mistake, and to forget it. Can we do that? Or would we have to check out our own suspicions?"

5.
Fly on the Wall
at Capitol Heights

· · · · · · · · · · · · ·

Christine Milo, media specialist at the Capitol Heights Elementary School, often said she wished she could be a fly on the wall in various classrooms, to hear how teachers prepared students to visit the center, to know how they presented media in classes, and to understand better the various ways that media entered naturally into their instruction. On her rare visits to classrooms, she was more likely to be observing the conclusion of a unit, the presentation of a program, or some specially programmed use of media. She thought, however, that the more she knew about how teachers used media, either effectively or ineffectively, the better she might be able to arrange for its good use by others. For that matter, knowing what had led to a reference question from a class might enable her to give better assistance to the student seeking the information.

The following are accounts of actual incidents or conversations in classrooms which she might have observed:

Bart Fulton's fourth-grade class studied trees in October. Mr. Fulton had worked out a schedule with the other fourth grades so that no two would be competing for the limited number of materials about trees. This was a unit popular with the children, and, when taught in October, it allowed them to bring in leaves and display them, which often led to friendly competition among the students in trying to find the most unusual or the most perfect leaves.

The unit lasted two weeks. On Wednesday of the first week, Mr. Fulton announced that if the children continued to work well on their reports, he would have a surprise for them on Friday. On Thursday, he assured them the surprise would come. Friday afternoon, at the beginning of the science period, he told the children that they would not need papers or books on their desks. The surprise was to be a filmstrip about some of the trees and leaves they had studied. As he began the filmstrip, he called on children to read the captions under each frame. When it was Brendan Cheverly's turn, he read, "The elm tree blight in North America is killing many of our most beautiful trees. This is one of them." Then he added, "Hey, Mr. Fulton! That's the way the one outside school used to look when I was little. And today, there are men out there cutting it down. I saw them at lunchtime."

There was a buzz among the children. Mr. Fulton spoke. "Thank you, Brendan. The rest of you, who may not be as observant as Brendan, may see the men working on the tree after school. Next frame—Sarah?"

When Anne Yarmouth read the caption which described the difference between deciduous and nondeciduous trees, Mr. Fulton flicked the projector off, gestured to one of the children to turn on the light in the room, and said, "You may need your notebooks for this. I'd like to know whether the tree on which you are writing a report for next week is deciduous or nondeciduous. Let's start with Jack."

"Mine's a fir. It's deciduous," said Jack.

"Poplar. Nondeciduous," Jane Fenton reported. When it was Paul Corunna's turn, he hesitated. "Mine's an ash. I've never seen one. I don't know. Deciduous?"

"When there are only two possibilities, there's no guessing, Paul. Does anyone else know?" Mr. Fulton saw no hand go up, so he said, "Go to the media center and look it up, Paul. Then come back and tell us. And what's yours, Billie?"

The door had scarcely closed behind Paul when Charlie Pelham, who sat in the row nearest the window, reached for a volume of the encyclo-edia near him, opened it, and raised his hand. Mr. Fulton called on him.

"I found it! The ash is a deciduous tree, Mr. Fulton. It says so right here."

Mr. Fulton was somewhat annoyed. "We have asked Paul to report to the class on the ash, Charlie. He will be back in a few minutes. Now put the encyclopedia back, please. We'll see whether you know what your own tree is."

The teacher continued to ask the students to identify their trees as

deciduous or nondeciduous, then darkened the room again for the conclusion of the filmstrip. When there were a few minutes left at the end,
he suggested that they work on their individual reports. Paul Corunna
did not return to the room until Mr. Fulton was dictating spelling words
to be studied over the weekend. The boy quietly slipped into his seat,
pulled out notebook and pencil, and hurried to catch up with the rest of
the class. He had the answer now, and he was somewhat deflated when he
did not have a chance to share it. He was more disappointed later, when
he hurried out to see the men working on the big old elm tree in front of
the school. There was nothing left, not even a stump. The men had dug it
out, filled the hole, packed up the limbs of the tree and their tools, and
gone on. Paul wondered why they had to get rid of every bit of the old
tree, but he was sure that if he asked Mr. Fulton, he would be sent to the
media center again on Monday. Miss Milo would be busy, as she had been
today, and he would miss out on something else in the classroom. He decided he would try to remember to find out for himself some other time.

Cecelia York had taught a sixth-grade class at Capitol Heights for
seven years, and her students were known, at the neighboring junior high
school, to have an unusually strong background in reading, and the ability
to adjust quickly to the pace and pattern of junior high school scheduling.
Christine Milo herself had marveled at Miss York's ability to make readers
out of students. Miss York considered reading a habit which could be
developed by regular book reports. At the beginning of the year, she provided her students with forms that all reports should follow, and with a
chart on which they were to indicate by categories what they had read.
Her objective was to encourage them to read widely and in various fields,
and she kept a check on how well they filled in the charts. When Bobby
Kalispell read straight through all the L. M. Boston stories about Green
Knowe, he was penalized by not being allowed to count reports that he
made on the last two. In a struggle to catch up and to keep his reading
chart on a level with the rest of the class, Bobby borrowed two biographies
from the "Childhood of Famous Americans" series and read them over one
weekend, to keep the biography section of his chart filled in.

The only time that Miss Milo and Miss York had anything close to a
disagreement had been at the close of a school year, when Miss York's
class had visited the media center the day before Miss Milo was beginning
the inventory of the collection. Miss Milo had announced that she had de-

cided this would be a day to relax and have fun, to reminisce about books they had read before.

"You know, boys and girls, when you get to junior high, you will not be able to find some of your old favorite books in the library. So I thought today it would be fun for you to see some old friends from the Capitol Heights Library. This month, when you're leaving our school, you will be making note of many things to remember. I hope that the media center is one place you will remember with pleasure. Today I am going to tell you a story that I'm sure most of you remember, and on all the tables I've put books that you may have enjoyed several years ago. There may even be some that you wanted to read, and never had a chance to read. John, what are some of the books at your table?"

John Wyckoff held up a fresh copy of Beverly Cleary's *Henry Huggins*. "Here's one Mrs. Herkimer read to us in the third grade. *Henry Huggins*. And here's *Anatole*, and *Tale of Peter Rabbit*, and *The Three Billy Goats Gruff*, and—"

"Thank you, John," Miss Milo broke in. "I just wanted to give you all an idea of what you will find. Today, instead of looking on the shelves for your books to borrow, I thought you might like to choose from this group. But, of course, you can get them from wherever you like. And the story I have to tell you is the same one I told to a second grade this morning. I'm sure you've heard it. I just wonder who can guess what it is?"

"*The Five Hundred Hats?*" Bobby Kalispell asked hopefully.

"No, but that's a good guess," Miss Milo said. "This isn't about a hero quite like Bartholomew Cubbins. It's a hero of little brain."

"I know! I know! Winnie-the-Pooh!" Ginny Sloan called out.

"That's right. Now, settle back, and I'll tell you about the day Winnie met some bees."

Miss Milo enjoyed telling the story and seeing the class take pleasure in it so much that she did not notice Miss York's look of disapproval. But when it was time for the children to select books, Miss York's voice broke in. "For those of you who still have books to read to complete your charts, just remember that the story books will not do. If you want them also, that's fine, but remember—we will have all the charts up on the bulletin board for your parents to see on the last day of school, and we want to have those charts filled, don't we?"

As the children moved around the room, Miss Milo went over to

Miss York and said, "Goodness, I thought all the kids in your room had done enough reading for the next couple of years! They certainly wipe out the media center every time they visit!"

"Oh, you know how it is. Some of them slack off toward the end. And I am sorry to see you encouraging them to do so. They will have fun with those baby books, but at this time of year, I think they need to be pushed every minute."

Because her own pleasure in the day's visit had been so keen, and the children's response so enthusiastic, Miss Milo felt rebuffed and hurt, but she let the remark pass. She made it a point not to program the same kind of activity in Miss York's class in other years.

One of the points on which Miss York insisted was that her students should use the school media center for all the books they read for reports. This sometimes led to the making of some underground bestsellers, as when Jerry Ewen brought in the paperback edition of *The Double Helix.*

"Can I read this for a report, Miss York?" he asked. "My dad bought it, and he laughed and laughed when he read it. It's really a serious book, you know, but my dad says it tells about science just the way it is, down at the lab where he works. I'll read it anyway, but I just wonder whether it'd be okay to report on it."

"Well, I suppose you may read the paperback edition to report on, Jerry, but only if there's a copy of the book in the media center. If not, you'll have to find another book."

When Miss Milo confirmed Jerry's own search of the center by saying she had not ordered *The Double Helix,* although she had read it and liked it herself, Jerry borrowed one of the Golden Nature Guides for his book report. And when he had read the paperback, he circulated it widely among his friends. It was a little difficult for some, but the ones who read it talked about it so much that the others felt they knew it too.

One class about which Miss Milo was especially curious was Rose Massillon's second grade. Mrs. Massillon used the media center in fits and starts. She was likely to book several films and filmstrips, and to borrow transparencies and recordings during one week, use nothing for a month or longer, and then use a great variety of media during one week again. She was evasive about how she intended to use the materials, but, from the children's comments in the center, Miss Milo knew the materials were shown to them.

Mrs. Massillon believed that all media were intended for the original presentation of information. She tried to time her teaching so that she would be at the point of introducing several new topics in different subjects at approximately the same time. This often coincided with the end of a marking period, when she had a number of conferences to schedule with parents. What she liked about the arrangement was that it provided a way to get the children started on something new, without tying her as closely to them as she would have been if she had presented the material herself. She was able to talk with parents in the back of the room while children were occupied with recordings or films in the front. She recognized the importance of knowing what they would see, and allowed time to preview the materials herself. That was easier than to arrange for a series of evening or late afternoon meetings with parents, as some of the teachers had agreed to do.

One medium which Mrs. Massillon used consistently was the television set which had been installed in her class. She made careful notes of programs that might be of major interest, and she saw to it that her children never missed one. Each day, she also remembered to have the children stop whatever they were doing to watch *Sesame Street.* This was one they all loved. Mrs. Massillon made use of this time to cut out materials for their art classes, to change the bulletin boards, and to do many of the things which seemed never to get done otherwise. Usually, she stayed at her desk, where she could keep an eye on the children, who watched the television set at the side of the room above her desk. Occasionally, one of them would be distracted from the program and she would see him watching her. A word or two usually brought his attention back to the set. Sometimes the activities suggested by the program made the children restless, and it would take her a few minutes to calm them down when the program was over. Since there were about forty minutes between the end of the program and their outdoor play period, she did not wish to give them opportunity to get out of hand.

• • • • •

Even if Miss Milo had sometimes been able to visit classrooms, she might have missed seeing some of the activities indicated here. Do you consider them to be things she should know about or change? How might knowledge of them help her in her work with other teachers and students, if not with the ones described here?

6.
Dr. Wooster
Makes a Visit

· · · · · · · · · · ·

When visitors came to the East Conemaugh Community Schools, Edith Boyer, the district library supervisor, frequently took them to visit the Freedom Elementary School. Gwen Walters had been librarian there for eight years, and as a former teacher in the school, her rapport with the teachers and with the principal, Glenn Purcell, was exceptionally good. Mrs. Boyer realized that Mrs. Walters was only giving lip service to the concept of the school library as a materials center, but the excitement of the program, the interest of the children, the support of the parent volunteers who assisted in the library, and the strong tie between the library and classroom instruction were such assets, that she considered the school well worth a visit.

When Jim Wooster, a faculty member from a nearby state college, had asked to visit several schools with her, Mrs. Boyer naturally included Freedom among them. She telephoned the school and talked with both Mr. Purcell and Mrs. Walters. Mrs. Walters asked whether there was anything Dr. Wooster would especially like to see, and Mrs. Boyer replied, "Oh, I don't think so, Gwen. He's visited several of the schools in the district before, but now he's going to serve on a program dealing with the teaching of literature in the elementary schools, and he just wants to see what the role of the library is in that. I don't like to impose on you all the time with visitors, but I think he'll just want to see things as they are. He's a very nice guy, so there shouldn't be any problems about that."

Mr. Purcell was attending a principals' meeting at the administration building when Mrs. Boyer and Dr. Wooster arrived at the school, but the secretary greeted them cordially. She took their coats, and said, "Mr. Purcell said he'd be back in time to have coffee with you in his office, and since I know you know your way to the library, Mrs. Boyer, perhaps you wouldn't mind going on alone? I have to stick around here to answer the phone."

"This school has a nice atmosphere," Dr. Wooster commented as they walked past a line of kindergarteners waiting in line at a drinking fountain in the hall.

"Yes," Mrs. Boyer agreed. "It's a pleasant community, too. The parents want the best for their children, but they don't spoil them. This is one of our older schools, and it has a kind of stability. Mr. Purcell helps there, too. He's young, but my guess is that he's the kind of person who will be content to stay principal at this school for his whole career."

"I can see why," Dr. Wooster agreed with a smile. "I never had it so good as when I was an elementary school principal a hundred years ago. But tell me again, how does this school compare with others in your district? Did you bring me because it's typical, or because it's so good?"

"Well, I think it's much better than average—and you understand the library program is the only part of the school I'm really qualified to judge. Mrs. Walters is an unusually competent and thorough librarian, very well organized. When we can manage it, I like to have our new librarians visit her to see how things go. On the other hand, we have some programs that are more innovative, but they are working to get the kinks out of those, so for a VIP visitor like you, I thought this would be a good choice. Of course, I'm hoping we can stop by some of the other schools this morning, too."

"And how many schools do you have altogether?"

"This year, thirty-seven elementary schools. Four schools came into the district when Ellwood finally gave up its own district, and we built one new school in Red Bank, which opened this fall. And there are nine secondary schools. The elementary schools of this same vintage are all pretty much on the same plan, as you probably know, and were designed with a library that is half again as large as a classroom. Mr. Purcell has managed to add a small room to be used for reference by the fifth and sixth graders, too, so it probably has more room than any of the others on this plan. But I warn you, it won't look it. Gwen Walters is a packrat, and if she has one fault, it's her tendency to let things get cluttered."

They entered the library then, and stopped inside the door as Mrs.

Walters spoke to them from across the room. "Well, good morning, Mrs. Boyer. Good morning, Dr. Wooster. We're glad to have you at the Freedom School Library. We have been choosing our books, but now we are going to sit down on the storytelling magic rug and listen to our story for the day. Who will get chairs for Mrs. Boyer and Dr. Wooster? And what do we say to them?"

"Good morning, Mrs. Boyer. Good morning, Dr. Wooster." It was a fairly ragged chorus from the second graders, who were looking at books spread on the tables or kneeling in front of the picture book shelves, searching for books. Two boys, bursting with importance, carried chairs from one of the tables to the edge of the green rug. The children sat down on the rug, their eyes on Mrs. Walters, who sat on a low bench facing them.

"Now, I want to see every eye," Mrs. Walters said. "And now, weathervanes." She held her right arm up at shoulder level, straight in front of her, saying, "North," turned it to the right, saying, "East," swiveled around with the arm still out saying, "South," and faced front again as she pointed to her left, saying, "West." The children imitated every movement, and scooted forward, backward, or sideways to leave space among themselves. It was a means of spreading them out on the large carpet, and one Mrs. Boyer had not seen before. Dr. Wooster smiled at how smoothly it worked.

"I am going to begin," Mrs. Walters said, in a lower voice. "I will tell the story just like this, and you will be able to hear me, because you are such good sitters and such good listeners. This is a story about a boy who is looking for something, and I think it will remind you of some other stories you know. I am going to ask you about that later."

Mrs. Walters was obviously conscious of the visitors, and they both sensed it, but the children, seated in front of them, quickly became interested in the story and seemed to pay no attention to the visitors.

". . . and there was his cap, right under the chair where he had left it that morning!" Mrs. Walters ended the story. The children relaxed, and a few of them held up their hands.

"Please, Mrs. Walters! I know a story that's like that one," a boy near the back said.

"All right, George. What is it?"

"It's *Lost on Luna*. The men go all over the solar system looking for something that will keep their pet monkey alive, and they find it's the atmosphere right here on earth that he needs."

"*Lost on Luna.* I don't think we have that book in the library," Mrs. Walters said reflectively.

"No, Mrs. Walters. I don't think it is a book. It's a movie I saw last Saturday, but the story is just like the one you told. You know, they look all over in funny places, and when they finish, what they want is right in front of them."

"All right, George. Thank you. And, Michael, you have your hand up."

"Yes, Mrs. Walters. Miss Rotan read us a story just like that last week. It's about this funny old dog who goes all over looking for his bone, and he can't remember where he buried it, and then he finds it right in his own dish. He had forgotten to bury it. We all laughed at him." There was an echo of the laughter as the children recalled the story.

"Very good, Michael!" Mrs. Walters said. "I can see that many of you remember that, and I think that this week Miss Rotan will tell you a story about the same boy who's in the story we heard today. How would you like that?"

"Oh, we'd like that, Mrs. Walters!" It was almost a chorus, and Mrs. Walters picked up another tall picture book from the bench where she was sitting, took the card out of the pocket, and said, "Now, I am writing Miss Rotan's name on this card, just the way you write your names on the cards for the books you want to borrow, so Miss Rotan will have this book to read to you this week. And who will carry it to her?"

"Please!" "I will!" "May I?" Several children raised their hands or reached for the book, but Mrs. Walters held it over their heads to a girl almost in the middle of the group.

"Sabra is such a good listener, I think she will be a good carrier," Mrs. Walters said. "And now, children, there is just time for you to check out your books before the next class will be coming in. And my helpers can straighten the books and chairs and see that the pencils are back in the baskets."

"There's just a minute or two between classes," Mrs. Walters said breathlessly. "Is there anything you'd especially like to know—or anything you'd like to see while you're here, Dr. Wooster?"

"No, I think not, thank you. This next class—what grade is it, and what will they be doing?"

"It's a fifth grade, and the slowest of the three fifth grades. They've had a substitute teacher for most of the year, and Mr. Silsbee is just getting back on his feet after an illness. It certainly isn't the class I'd choose to have for visitors, but I took you at your word, Mrs. Boyer, and I didn't try to juggle the schedule or anything. Oh, there is one thing I'd like you to see while you're in the building. I've been giving Mr. Silsbee a little extra help, and I put up a bulletin board on favorite book characters in his room Tuesday after school. He's very pleased with it, and I think they'd love to have you stop by."

"Thank you. I'd like to do that," Dr. Wooster said. "And what will you be doing with the class this period?"

"With all the fifth graders, we're studying folk tales this month. It's one of my favorite units. Today I'll tell most of one of the Jack tales, and we'll talk a bit about heroes and the exaggerated tales that grow up around them. I have some books on the truck that go nicely with this."

"Will you be telling a story at the end of the period, as you did with the second graders?" Dr. Wooster asked.

"Oh, no. I just arranged it that way because I knew you were coming, and I thought that's what you'd like to hear. With this class, I'll have the story first, then give them a chance to browse. They're accustomed to things being switched around occasionally, but usually I like to have the story or the lesson first, then leave them free to look for books."

The class came in then, and Mr. Silsbee greeted the visitors and sat with them behind the children as Mrs. Walters launched into her introduction of Jack, the mountain boy who could trick even giants. The straight-faced humor delighted the children, and at the end of the story, they had a string of "But what if—" kinds of questions, to ask about how Jack might have gotten himself into and out of other predicaments. When Mrs. Walters dismissed them, they went eagerly to the book truck to look for more tall tales.

Mr. Silsbee turned to Mrs. Boyer and said, "Oh, she's a wonder, isn't she? You know, I've heard her tell that same story every year for several years, and I enjoy it every bit as much this time as the first time."

Dr. Wooster leaned forward to ask. "And what kind of follow-up do you have about folk tales in your room, Mr. Silsbee?"

"Oh, not too much. There are a couple of tall tales in the reader we use, but two or three of the children are beyond the reader." He lowered his voice. "It's actually a fourth-grade reader, but it's about right for about a third of the class. The others need more work on drill and vocabulary, and they just need to do lots of reading. That's why it's great to have someone like Mrs. Walters who can help them get just the books they need. I don't mind telling you, I rely on her a great deal for the whole reading program."

"Yes," Dr. Wooster said thoughtfully. "I can see where that might happen."

Mrs. Walters, followed by one of the girls in the class, came over just then to say, "I hope you'll feel free to look around as you like, and to talk with the children. They're very accustomed to visitors, and I don't want you to miss anything. If you have any questions, just let me know."

Dr. Wooster stood up and walked over to a table where children were looking at recent issues of a news magazine. He sat down at a vacant place and began to talk with them. Edith Boyer chatted with Mr. Silsbee for another minute or two, then walked around the room, keeping an eye and an ear on the children as they examined books at the shelves. She smiled to herself at the clutter, remembering that when she had once commented to Mrs. Walters on it, there had been obvious feverish attempts to clear it up before her visits. But in recent years, as each of them felt more sure of herself, that kind of panic had died down. Now, there was a small box of paper slips on top of the card catalog, with a note suggesting that children use them to suggest books they would like to have in the library or to jot down numbers of cards they were looking up. An easel poster beside it was a guide to how to find books in the catalog. A teleidoscope labeled, "See through me" stood beside the box of slips. On one of the window sills, Mrs. Boyer counted five items: a box in which children could leave slips with jokes they especially enjoyed, a plant in a wooden shoe, a list of classics in a plastic folder, a color wheel suggesting a variety of kinds of books to read, and a metal file box marked "Community Resources."

Mrs. Boyer opened the box and was interested in what she found. There were cards with names, addresses, and telephone numbers of people in the community who would give talks or demonstrations, lend exhibits, or conduct tours. Originally typed, some of the cards had penciled notes of changes—on one, for example: "No longer will lend doll collection unless kept in locked case." Mrs. Boyer made a mental note to discuss this file with Mrs. Walters another time, as she turned away from the crowded window sill at the sound of the class leaving the library.

Mr. Purcell was standing in the doorway, chatting with Dr. Wooster. Mrs. Boyer walked over to them, and Mr. Silsbee stopped on his way out to say he'd be glad to have them visit the classroom, especially to see Mrs.

Walters' poster. As they said goodbye to Mrs. Walters, she glanced at Mr. Purcell and said, "As soon as I get this next class started on some things, I'll be down to have coffee with you."

Dr. Wooster walked ahead with Mr. Silsbee and Mrs. Boyer fell into step with Mr. Purcell, who was talking enthusiastically of Mrs. Walters' work.

"There are times," he said, "when I'd like to have her in the classroom again. But we need her in the library. She's really the sparkplug of this school."

It was pleasant to hear this kind of comment, for in Mrs. Boyer's job, many of her conversations with principals centered on problems caused or represented by the librarians. She basked in this praise. It continued as they paused in Mr. Silsbee's classroom and went on to Mr. Purcell's office. The secretary had brought in a plate of fresh buns from the cafeteria, and there was fresh coffee in Mr. Purcell's percolator. Mrs. Boyer was conscious that they were making an effort to welcome herself and Dr. Wooster to the school.

Gwen Walters came to the office to join them, and said, "I wish you could have seen those fourth graders tear into that card catalog. I just gave them enough to get them started. Now, each one of them is looking up a book, and they'll have the books ready for me to check when I go back. I can just stay a minute, but I want you to know how happy we are to have had you visit us, Dr. Wooster."

Dr. Wooster smiled and chatted, but Mrs. Boyer sensed a coolness in his manner that surprised her. He asked several questions about the library, the number of books, the use of indexes, the plans for the future, the idea of its becoming a materials center.

"There was a time when that might have been a sore point, Dr. Wooster," Mrs. Walters said. "But we're coming along. I keep some filmstrips for the teachers to use, and you may have noticed that community resources file we have. The teachers really appreciate it."

"Yes, I'd like to ask you some more questions about that," Mrs. Boyer said, but Mrs. Walters was standing up to go.

"Well, it was nice seeing you again, but I don't want to impose on Miss Slater by staying away too long. She's helping the children, but she'll want to get her break while the class is in the library." Mrs. Walters turned to Mr. Purcell and added, "You'll be glad to know that little situation seems to be working itself out. I keep an eye on the classroom, since it's right next to the library, and there seem to be no problems of discipline lately."

"That's good to know," Mr. Purcell said, rising as the visitors stood to leave. He walked to the door with them, and said, "You can see how much I rely on Mrs. Walters. She is almost like an assistant principal for me. The teachers go to her for help which they would not ask me for, and she helps them in ways I really have neither the time nor the ability to do. We just couldn't get along without her. I hope there are lots more librarians like her coming along, but from what I hear from the other principals, there aren't many, if any."

Mrs. Boyer smiled and said, "Well, some of them have different styles, but we have some very good ones—'coming along,' as you say."

Dr. Wooster was pleasant as they said goodbye, but silent for the first few minutes in the car. Then he turned to Mrs. Boyer and said, "Do you have any more librarians like that?"

"Well, none exactly, of course, but Gwen has a strong following among the younger librarians, and I'm sure she's a model for some of them."

"I'm sorry to hear that."

"Really? Why?" Mrs. Boyer listened intently as she drove.

"Because she's virtually running that school. She's telling the teachers what to read to their classes, she's going out and trying to run their class-rooms, and, incidentally, reporting them to the principal when things aren't going well. She's like his spy in that building. I'm being terribly out-spoken, but I was really upset by that whole business. You realize, of course, she staged everything for us. She held up the story so we could see her perform, she had set up that poster in Mr. Silsbee's room mostly for our benefit, but it's all worse than that. She's upstaging the teachers. A man like Silsbee needs help, perhaps from your language arts or reading supervisor, but Mrs. Walters just calmly does a big chunk of his job for him, so he leans back and lets her. All of this makes me wonder about school libraries—at least when they get out of hand."

Mrs. Boyer respected Dr. Wooster's opinion too much to break in, and she found her own reactions running a gamut from automatic support of one of the librarians to astonishment at his outburst and realization that there was some truth in what he said. Perhaps because her own loyalties and interests were so much with the library program, she wondered whether she was blind when it seemed to take over other parts of the school, or when the librarians usurped responsibility. Or had she been swayed by Mr. Purcell's great confidence in Mrs. Walters? Might even that mean that he was interested in having a member of his own staff helping the teachers rather than calling in a supervisor for assistance when it might be needed? She would have to answer Dr. Wooster in some way.

• • • • •

In Mrs. Boyer's position, how would you respond to Dr. Wooster now?

In what respects, if any, do you agree with Dr. Wooster's estimate of this situation?

Do you consider that any change or action relating to Freedom Elementary School is desirable on Mrs. Boyer's part?

Dr. Wooster has mentioned the possible need for a reading or language arts supervisor. Assuming there is one in the district, would you suggest that Mrs. Boyer communicate with him about some of her own, or Dr. Wooster's, reactions? In what ways?

Assume that at the next meeting of the supervisory and administrative staff, Mr. Purcell approached Mrs. Boyer to ask her what she thought of her recent visit and what Dr. Wooster's opinion was of the school library. How would you respond to him, if you were Mrs. Boyer?

7

The Committee and
the Community Resources File

· ·

For some weeks after her visit to Freedom Elementary School with Dr. Wooster, Edith Boyer had had in the back of her mind the idea of doing something with the community resources file that Gwen Walters, the librarian, had developed. When the speaker for the in-service meeting of librarians scheduled for the third Wednesday of the month telephoned on Monday to say he was unable to come, Mrs. Boyer thought she could accomplish two things—consideration of a similar file for the district, and a worthwhile focus for the meeting—by asking Mrs. Walters to bring her file and introduce it to the other librarians.

Mrs. Walters was obviously delighted to be asked. "I've done a lot of show-and-tell with that file, Edith, and it does impress people. Every librarian in this district could build up the same sort of thing, if she'd just put a little effort into it. I'll really give them a boost."

Mrs. Walters not only brought the file; she had duplicated samples of the form used on the five-by-seven-inch cards, and she had these ready to distribute. She had also made notes to use in her introduction, in which she mentioned specific uses for the file and ways in which it had grown.

"We've had this file for several years now, and it's grown enormously. You can see how often we've added more information, and once we'd gotten started, and the teachers began to use the file, I began to make notes on the backs of the cards about which of the resources were especially good ones, and that sort of thing. This keeps us from using the same materials over and over, and that's a help to the people or organizations who are the resources. Sometimes, too, when it's a matter of a classroom presentation, it helps to remind teachers they may combine classes if they're studying the same thing at the same time."

Louise Cresco, librarian at one of the high schools, spoke up. "I'm sure that having the name of the local fire station and that sort of thing is helpful in a grade school, but I don't see much point in a file of this kind for us. Our teachers usually go to some other teacher in their department if they want an idea or a suggestion, and it just doesn't seem to me that it's any of the library's business. Heaven knows, I don't need to go around looking for little projects—or more files to keep!"

Dorothy Scituate, as usual, disagreed. "I don't see where there'd be much effort involved, and Gwen's file looks handy enough to keep around somewhere. I'd be glad to have it at Whitman, where we have a lot of new teachers who often spend too much time spinning their wheels when they might get help from something like this."

At that, Gwen Walters looked surprised. "Oh, this isn't the sort of thing you can just hand out from one school to another. Each of you would have to develop your own, I'm sure. For one thing, there are a number of our school's patrons who probably wouldn't want to go to other neighborhoods or to lend their materials, but on the other hand, you all probably have people right in your own community who would be glad to be listed. When we first started this, we had just a small note in the parent-teachers bulletin, then an announcement at a meeting, and then a form the children could take home for their parents to fill out, and that got us just the results we wanted. After that, as different people were asked to do things, the word got around to those who had missed hearing about it. Why, we get many more offers of assistance than we can really use."

"It sounds to me like more of the same old stuff, and I'm already sick of that," Wanda Wellesley spoke up. Miss Wellesley was half-time librarian at two schools which were on the far north side of the district, and the closest thing to rural schools in the district. "Here, I've got kids living in places that aren't good enough to be chicken coops any more, and you think if I'd ask their parents, they'd be willing to come up and give us a little talk on soil conservation or something! Well, you can forget it as far as I'm concerned!"

Edith Boyer was always concerned at Wanda's growing cynicism, perhaps more so because she realized there was good reason for it, but she was also aware that Wanda's attitude increased her isolation from the other librarians. She thought this was a good time to break in on the discussion, but just then, Ward Barrington looked over at Mrs. Walters and said: "Actually, we're all talking in a vacuum anyway. Before we get to any opinions or decisions, I'd like to know more about what's really in your file. How's it arranged?"

"Alphabetically by subject," Mrs. Walters said. "That makes it just like the card catalog, and as easy to use."

"Then why not interfile it in the card catalog?" Ward asked.

"Well, because it's really different, and it's used by teachers. It would just confuse things to have these cards in the catalog. Then, too, even though I keep it out in full view, remember I do make those notes on it about which talks or exhibits were especially good, and I wouldn't want those notes where the children could have access to them."

"How about reading us what's in the file under a couple of headings, say, safety or pets?"

"Okay." Gwen Walters held up one of the cards. "Now, you all have this form, so I trust it's clear to you. And I'll read you exactly what's on one of these, so you may want to be looking at your own. Okay?"

TOPIC:	
SOURCE:	
ADDRESS:	
TELEPHONE:	
KIND OF MATERIALS:	
EQUIPMENT NEEDED:	NOTICE NEEDED:
LENGTH OF TIME:	GRADE LEVEL:
DATE USED:	BY WHOM USED:

"Now, under Safety, I have four cards. The first one is Safety, Household, and there's a reference to our local fire station, with its address, telephone number, and the name of the station captain. That's been changed within the last few months, and so I've added the new man's name with the date when he came there. And the card tells us they will lend out full uniforms, boots, overcoat, hat, all for three days, and that two firemen will also come to the school to give a talk or to show a film about safety—really, fire prevention. They have to have a week's notice to do that, and, as you can guess, they sometimes have to cancel out if there's an emergency. The presentation takes thirty-five minutes, and it's best for the fourth-grade unit on safety. The last time we used them at Freedom was October 10, last year, and they were invited by one of the fourth-grade teachers. Oh, and I also made a note on the back that the younger of the two firemen really wasn't very good. He was very gruff with the children, and they just didn't respond. When we ask them again, we'll try, in some tactful way, to get somebody else.''

Miss Wellesley had listened intently to all this, and she said, ''Maybe this isn't as complicated as it sounds. I could tell you most of that about the fire stations near my two schools. I just don't have it all written down and filed.''

''That's true,'' Mr. Barrington said thoughtfully. ''How about giving us an example of something we wouldn't all be so likely to know about? But before you do, what other places do you have under Safety?''

''I have the telephone company, for that film we previewed at one of our meetings last year. We've used that several times, and it's excellent. An one of the mothers in our community is on another card. She's Evelyn Galveston; you've probably read about her. She was blinded in that terrible accident at the hospital several years ago, but she still works as a lab technician. She really impresses the children, because she not only tells them how senseless accidents like that could be prevented, but she brings things along to show them how she has to have things organized at her home and in her lab, so she can take care of things herself. The last card is for a motorcycle salesman in our community who'll give demonstrations of safety on bikes and motorcycles. Now, that's one that might be even more useful in the secondary schools than the elementary.''

Mrs. Walters went on to mention some of the more unusual items on the cards—rare pets available for brief loans, a lawyer who would talk on local government, a banker who accompanied his coin and currency collection to talk about the history of money. Mrs. Boyer sensed a growing interest on the part of the group. Even if not all of them were interested, she thought there was good reason to have some of them work on the idea and develop items for a file that could be used in all the schools. When she suggested this, however, Gwen Walters looked indignant.

''Why, Mrs. Boyer, I had no idea that's what you had in mind. I'd be sorry to see this simple little thing exploded into some big, complicated project. It's not that I'm not willing to help other people, as I think I have this afternoon, but to just multiply this file for use all over the district— why, that won't be much good for anyone. And besides, we've gone to a great deal of effort to check on our resources and not to impose on them. Now, you'd have forty schools calling them up all the time to ask for assistance. I'd hate to see that happen."

Using every bit of diplomacy she possessed, Mrs. Boyer pressed her point. She acknowledged that many of the items in the Freedom School file were unique to that community, but she was sure that many would be as useful, or more useful, as Mrs. Walters herself had said about the motorcycle salesman, in other schools in the district. In any case, she was most anxious that Mrs. Walters should serve on the small committee which would be a study or feasibility committee, really, and which would recommend to the group as a whole how they might proceed. Still somewhat reluctantly, Mrs. Walters was willing to serve under these circumstances. When Wanda Wellesley volunteered to work with her, Mrs. Boyer accepted quickly; it was the first time she could remember Wanda's volunteering to do anything. Ward Barrington, as a secondary school librarian, seemed a logical choice for the third member of the committee, with Mrs. Walters acting as chairman.

The three librarians met twice within the next month and then asked to meet again with Mrs. Boyer. Their meetings had been at one of Miss Wellesley's schools and at the junior high where Mr. Barrington was librarian. Apparently the visit to Osawatomie, Miss Wellesley's school, had convinced Mrs. Walters of the value of more sharing of materials. She had realized for the first time the different duties of a librarian responsible for two schools where assistance from parents was limited and where the needs of many children reading at greatly varying grade levels were overwhelming. With the other two librarians, she had worked out a sample form that could be duplicated for use in a community resources file. They were agreed that each individual or organization listed should be sent a form letter to ask whether they wished to be included in a listing for all the schools, and the committee had also constructed this form letter. It read:

> The East Conemaugh Community Schools rely on all the resources of the community in conducting programs of educational value for the children of this district. We are asking your cooperation in

making these resources more generally available. In our schools, the libraries will maintain a record of exhibits, speakers, free materials, demonstrations, and other resources. From time to time, a teacher may call or write to ask for the program or resource included in the file. At that time, the individual or organization listed may determine whether or not it is feasible or convenient to offer the service that is requested. Being included on this list does not mean that all requests must be honored.

We understand that you represent a resource that could be valuable in this project. May we have your permission to include you in the listing? At the end of this letter, we have indicated the special resource which we understand you can make available. If this information is correct, please complete the enclosed postcard with information about how and with whom we should communicate to make use of this resource. If you have other resources which you can make available, we would appreciate receiving information about them as well.

The purpose of this letter is to clarify the means of asking for assistance from the community, and to relieve the burden of participation which may, heretofore, have rested more on some groups in the community than on others. We shall appreciate your assistance.

The three librarians were silent as Mrs. Boyer read the letter. When she looked up, Mr. Barrington leaned forward and said, "See, then we'd put down here in the left corner what we know, or think the group has, and enclose a post card made out pretty much along the lines of the resource file card—we have a sample of that, too—and that way, we'd get everything on one sheet. How does it look to you, Mrs. Boyer?"

"I must say it looks good. You've done a good job. There are a few minor things I'd change in the letters, but we can come to that. Now, how about sending it? Do you have a list of who should receive it? Are you prepared to explain and defend your recommendation to the other librarians? About how many copies of the letter will we need to send?"

Gwen Walters spoke first. "I think the librarians will be delighted with this. Some of them will probably have names to add, but just among ourselves, using my list and adding some names that Mr. Barrington and Miss Wellesley have come up with, we have about 150 names. Some of those, like the fire department, are general ones for the district, so we'll want to enclose another letter—and we have a draft of that, too—to get them to name the place in each community which should be included in the file. That'll be a sorting job, when the replies come in, because each school should have the fire station, for example, that's handiest for them."

"There is a good deal to this," Mrs. Boyer agreed. "More than I thought when I brought up the subject. For one thing, there's the cost of duplicating and mailing out the letters and cards. I suppose I can squeeze out money for that somewhere, but I guess we shouldn't impose the typing on any school, so that will have to be done here, too. Everything does always turn out to be more complicated than I think it will in the beginning!"

"I hope you aren't backing off, now that you've got us all fired up about this," Wanda Wellesley said quietly. "Just being on the committee and working with these two, I've gotten some good ideas, and I've already passed them on to some of our teachers. I can see that this would really be something practical and helpful for most of us."

"Oh, no, I'm not backing off—just thinking out loud, I guess," said Mrs. Boyer. "This looks worthwhile to me, and I'm game. I think we may also be able to get some library publicity out of this, as teachers use the file the first few times. And that, in turn, may lead to more offers and suggestions from resources in the community we don't even know about yet."

"That's something I've thought of, too," Mr. Barrington said. "What are we going to do if the ball really gets rolling, and we get people asking to be put on the list, and for one reason or another, we don't want them?"

"Why would that be?" Miss Wellesley asked.

"Oh, you know, they might really have more of a commercial interest or want to use this as a way to get names of kids to use in selling products to their parents. Even that motorcycle salesman who talks safety is a borderline case, as far as his being a commercial interest is concerned, if you ask me. The school district has always been so strict about that sort of thing, we don't want to stir up something."

"Thanks for calling this to my attention, Ward. There are some things to think through. One thing I want to do is to discuss this in the administrative council meeting, and call the whole project to Dr. Spokane's attention. I think it would be a good idea for him to sign the letter, too. That makes it clear this is a project for the entire district, and it might carry a lot of weight with some of the people whom we're asking to supply some pretty valuable resources."

Miss Wellesley's sullen expression was returning. "Well, here we go

again! We've got a nice simple little thing here, and before we can begin
to do it, the people we want will all be dead! More red tape! Anyway, I'm
glad I was on this committee. This way, I've got the ideas, and I guess
there's no law against my using them without asking two dozen people
whether or not it's okay."

All of them were somewhat startled at Miss Wellesley's bitterness,
and Mrs. Boyer, aware of some of the things to be done, let their meeting
end in the next few minutes. As they left, she realized the committee members felt they had put great effort into something which might be dropped
or which might very slowly be completed. For her part, she was conscious
of how much of her own and other staff time would have to be invested
from this point on, if the resource files were to work.

At the next in-service meeting of the librarians, the group heartily
endorsed the progress made to date and encouraged more work on the
compilation of a file. Several had remembered to bring names that might
be added to the list of resources, and others said they would send them
along later. It turned out that all but one or two of these new resources
were already in the list compiled by the committee, which made Mrs.
Boyer wonder whether there would be more duplication of effort before
the compilation was complete. Even checking the listings took time.

Mrs. Boyer presented the idea at a meeting of the administrative
council, and the group acknowledged it with little comment. Dr. Spokane
agreed to sign what he called "the begging letter," and he asked to be kept
informed of what kinds of responses came in, since the responses were
directed to Mrs. Boyer. These were generally favorable. The typing and
duplication of the cards proceeded smoothly, and Mrs. Boyer was proud
when the stacks of duplicated three-by-five-inch cards began to spread out
in the workroom near her office. Recalling a time when cards for new
films at the district office had been sent out to the schools for inclusion
in the card catalog, Mrs. Boyer had recommended that, this time, the cards
should be alphabetized first, so that the task of interfiling them in the card
catalogs could be that much simpler. She remembered the librarians' bitterness about having to alphabetize the film cards, and realized it was something that might have been done easily at the district office, but was just
one of those things she had not been alert enough to catch. The decision
to have the cards made to go into the card catalogs had been made at the
in-service meeting, with Gwen Walters adamantly opposed to the end. The
majority had decided the material would be better used, even if only by

teachers, if it were in its logical place in the card catalog, and Gwen had finally admitted defeat.

It was with some feeling of anticipation that Mrs. Boyer planned to take a visiting foreign librarian to the Freedom Elementary School later that spring. Mr. Pasco had asked many intelligent questions during his visit to the office, and she thought he would enjoy seeing the program at Freedom. He quite evidently did, and he walked over to the window sill during a class's browsing period to examine the several items there. To her surprise, Mrs. Boyer saw that he was looking through the community resources file, still in its accustomed place and format.

"And what is this?" Mr. Pasco asked Mrs. Walters.

"That's a very useful listing of resources right here in our community. You can see, there's a card for the stamp collection which you may have seen on display as you came through the main corridor. We borrow or ask for these things when we need them."

"I see. And how do you know about all these?"

"Oh, mostly, I've built that up myself. We worked on getting more items for the school district as a whole, too, but when those cards came through, I had to retype them so they'd be the right size, and they generally aren't too useful."

Mrs. Boyer felt sure the last comment was directed to her rather than to Mr. Pasco, but she chose not to respond.

• • • • •

Analyze the reasons for a district-wide community resource file, as described here. Are there reasons for such a file to be developed by individual schools rather than by the district?

Mrs. Boyer indicated she would make some minor changes in the letter drafted by the committee. Do you have any to suggest?

What is your opinion of Mrs. Boyer's handling of this activity? Of her leadership of the librarians, as indicated here? Of her decision to have a committee carry out the first steps of this project?

8.
Explosive Potential
at Nitro High School

· · · · · · · · · · · · · · · ·

In setting up departmental media centers at Nitro High School, Roy Mills had given careful consideration to the potential problem of communications among the members of the media staff. The high school covered one square block of the city, and the centers, located near the teaching areas of departments which they served, were to draw staff in all directions. As he organized the plans, he thought of the plastic sets on which one played three-dimensional tic-tac-toe. Although staff members were assigned responsibilities according to their own subject specialization, he hoped to stress their responsibilities as general staff members by having them work designated periods in the center itself.

The departmental centers were small, two of them converted classrooms, and the third a portion of the old auditorium, which had become the art department. The decision about which departments should have centers had been made on the basis of the interest of the department faculty in having their own center. Although the art department was small, the teachers pointed out that a picture was often needed for just a few minutes, to use as a pattern, and that few of the titles most vital to them overlapped with those in the general collection. The English department, which had been most enthusiastic about the prospect of a departmental center, had withdrawn the idea after discussion, when they began to realize how many of the general reference materials would have to be duplicated for a departmental center, and how much overlap there would be with titles for general reading and the contemporary novels and collections that would be essential in a departmental collection. The foreign language teachers, using the same measures, had been insistent in their demand for a center, and its location across the hall from the language laboratory made it ideal in many respects. The foreign language periodicals, which had often been lost in the general periodicals shelves in the center downstairs, were especially read and appreciated by the students.

The third departmental collection was in science. Here, there had been more difficult decisions to make about what was appropriate for the departmental center and what belonged in the main center. Mr. Mills remembered his own reaction, as he had supervised the transfer of materials, the marking of cards in the catalog to indicate location, and the tightening of the materials left on the shelves in the center. What remained were some good readings in science—Cousteau, Carson, Storer, and others. He wondered whether the users of the science media center might miss popular titles like these which often gave insights rather than just information. Although many were duplicated in both centers, he realized that it would be harder to locate the more enjoyable, well written books in the science center than it would be in the main center.

The specialists who would work with each center had all been a part of the planning. Ione Hahn had been delighted with the prospect of devoting herself primarily to the science collection. Because her undergraduate major in biology was unique on the center staff, she had been responsible for selection in the sciences for the two years she had been at Nitro. Mike Monroe was well fitted to work with the art materials, since, in his own words, he was the kind of artistic person who had a little talent and a lot of interest, so this proximity to the art teacher and students gave him a toehold on his favorite field. For Adrienne Rogers, the foreign language assignment was a natural. On her summer trips to Europe, she had always returned with materials that were excellent for the library and hard to obtain in this country. She was struggling to learn Russian, since that was the only language taught at Nitro with which she was totally at a loss.

Mr. Mills felt that since the collections varied so greatly in size, as did the departments, the allocation of the specialists' time should be proportional. Mr. Monroe would have several periods each day in the main center, Miss Hahn and Mrs. Rogers one or two periods, with a schedule varying through the week. It seemed that this kind of schedule would help the specialists feel like a part of the media team. Their assistance in the busy main center was essential. In this school of 2,000 students, there were often one hundred in the media center at one time, even when the departmental centers were heavily used. In addition to himself, Mr. Mills had Lud Calvert, who assumed major responsibility for nonprint materials, and Sally Hart, whose two big jobs were the technical processing, and the training and supervision of clerical and student assistants. Although he was concerned that Mr. Calvert and Mrs. Hart should also have some knowledge and concern for the departmental centers, he had not yet worked out a way to schedule them there for set periods. In the beginning, he had thought it was important to have students and faculty get in the habit of seeing the same person on duty in the departmental center, so students would accept him as the person in charge and faculty in the department would consider him a colleague. Although the staff members had been in the school in other years, Mr. Mills had worried that teachers, who were accustomed to coming to him directly, might be slow to accept the departmental media specialist with the same respect. He had considered the first month's department meetings a good test. It was his practice to rotate his own attendance at these meetings, always checking in advance with the department head, but he was pleased when he heard that Miss Hahn and Mr. Monroe had been invited by their respective departments, and that when Mrs. Rogers had offered to come to the foreign language teachers meeting to ask for suggestions for additional periodical subscriptions, her offer had been warmly accepted.

The difficulty was that the center staff members themselves were unable to meet together. While Mr. Mills thought there was probably little need to report on specific points which might have come up at the departmental meetings, for example, he realized that the separate locations of the staff and the differences in their hours of arrival and leaving virtually precluded their getting together at any time. He found himself telling the same thing to one person twice, and discovering the next day he had missed telling someone else who needed to know about it. He posted notes and memos on a bulletin board which each member of the staff was to check

One problem was the professional or review journals. Mr. Mills knew that the staff members looked forward not only to the reviews, but to the articles, and he wanted them to be informed. Yet, when a large department like the English department was limited to no more than two copies of a professional periodical because of the budget, he did not see how he could duplicate periodical titles of primary interest to the media staff. The departmentalization of the collection affected this in two ways; not only were staff members more keenly aware of their responsibilities for suggesting purchases in their respective subject areas, but they were geographically more separated and thus less likely to be able to share titles among themselves. Even the assignment of staff members to the main center did little to relieve this situation. As Ione Hahn remarked to him one day, after spending two periods in the main center, "Really, sometimes I feel like a snail, crawling along with my house on my back. By the time I bring down here the things I want to check on or look up in the reference section or catalog and the stuff I want to photocopy, and then carry back what I've found or copied, and spend the time in between trying to gallop through and make notes on *Library Journal* and *Choice*, for example, I begin to have the feeling I'm not very much good to you at all—at least as an assistant on the floor."

Mr. Mills made no comment, but he shared her concern. He himself was spending more and more time assisting students and faculty directly, and he was sure there were things he was letting go in the areas of planning and supervision, which would eventually catch up with him. He did not know how to avoid that problem. He also sometimes heard students say to Mrs. Rogers or Miss Hahn, especially, "Say, what're you doing here? I thought you worked in the departmental center!"

The problem of the disappearance of materials from the various centers was growing, too. Even with a part-time clerical assistant at each center, with the specialists taking their allotted times in the main center and leaving to visit classes or have lunch, there were many occasions when the centers were unsupervised. In a community like Nitro, discipline at those times was not too much of a problem, although Mr. Mills tried to stagger and vary the schedules so students could not assume there were regular, unsupervised periods. He realized that this also meant that students, and teachers, too, could not count on having someone available when they needed and wanted help in the departmental center; that seemed to be an advantage they could not offer in their present setup. No one on the staff wanted to have the centers locked when the specialists were away, but if a decision to do that became necessary, it would doubtless be because of the growing problem of theft of materials. Mr. Mills' former conviction that an active, well-used media center would be bound to have some loss and that it might be predicted as some percentage of the circulation, rising as the circulation figures rose, was being disproved. The departmental specialists agreed that their total circulation was undoubtedly lower than the circulation of those same subject categories in other years, but they cited several reasons for this which seemed valid enough to Mr. Mills when he considered them. With materials in a sense preselected in the centers, students did not borrow half a dozen titles hastily, and then sort out later the ones which were really useful. Even with the relatively small size of the departmental centers, there was space for a student or teacher to sit down and consult or read materials without checking them out to hurry back to the departmental teaching area. By the same token, the specialists felt that much of the assistance to students lay in helping them make better selections in the first place, so that circulation might be controlled by that. Mr. Mills gathered these reactions in his chats with the specialists, and he almost regretted the emphasis he seemed to be placing on circulation, but the question had arisen from this plaguing problem of loss. He began to wonder whether the informality of the rooms where departmental collections were housed encouraged students simply to walk out with materials without thinking to check them out. If that were the case, they would probably reappear eventually.

It seemed ironic to Mr. Mills that it was in the course of this first year of the departmental centers that a new member of the school board adopted a campaign to have the high school materials be available on evenings and Saturdays. The question had not been raised at Nitro before. The school drew from a fairly densely populated community, so that more than ninety percent of the students walked to school, and it was a long-standing tradition that no activities directly related to school were scheduled after the evening dinner hour. Debate practice, play rehearsals, club meetings, were all scheduled in the afternoons after school, and the community reactions had been placid. However, Ignatius Newberry had made this an issue in his campaign for the school board, saying the needs of the students called for a twenty-four-hour school, and that the first step toward that would be to open the library at night. Since Mr. Newberry had toured the school only once, he was not aware of the division of the media into departmental collections. When a reporter had asked how he would take care of that problem, he had responded promptly, "I'd have them all open! They're our materials, aren't they? Twenty-four hours a day—that's the way we pay for them, and that's the way we should be able to get them."

The board had reacted coolly at first to this newcomer, but when he continued to cite examples of other communities, more or less similar to their own, which had evening hours in their materials centers, they had asked for a report from the school staff on what might be involved in providing this kind of service. Mr. Mills was asked to estimate how much staff, including professional, clerical, and custodial, might be required to keep all four of the centers open three evenings a week, and when he had done so, he was horrified at the costs that would be involved, in terms of personnel only. When the report had been presented to the board by the superintendent, with Mr. Mills on hand to answer questions, even Mr. Newberry had indicated his concern at what an investment this would be. He addressed his next question: "Let's say, Mills, that it is too expensive to keep all these little places open. Would it cost, say, a fourth of this to have the main center open?"

"Yes, sir, I'd say a fourth or perhaps a little more, since there'd still be the minimal cost for the custodial help, and when you get into things like lighting and so forth, the cost of operating the main center is surely more than one fourth of the total."

"And would it seem feasible to you to have that be the only one of the centers that would be open at night?"

"Ye-es, I'd think so. For one thing, the main center has copies of a lot of the things that are in the departmental centers, and there would certainly be ample space for any students who might come at night. And even though the smaller centers serve individual departments, much of that material is available in the main center, too. I think something like that might be a good compromise."

"Compromise! You sound as though you think this is some kind of controversy between us. I want the best for the kids of this town, just as you do. There is no room for compromise." Mr. Newberry was nettled, to say the least.

"I'm sorry, Mr. Newberry. I guess that was a poor term to use, but keeping the main center open at night might be a good way to try out the idea, as you suggest."

Mr. Newberry was somewhat mollified, but before Mr. Mills was dismissed, he had one more thing to say. "What I'd like to know, then, Mr. Mills, is why we must have departmental centers anyway. They tie up classroom space, they evidently aren't necessary—or you wouldn't be so willing to go without them in this evening hours plan, and I, for one, didn't even know they were in operation. They evidently don't affect many of the kids, and I wonder if it's just a way to keep that big staff of yours occupied."

Mr. Mills felt that this more direct attack had been provoked by his own inept handling of the earlier question, but he was immediately defensive. Before he could speak, however, the superintendent broke in smoothly to say: "Now, Iggie, let's tackle one thing at a time. If there are no more questions about evening hours, let's leave it to Mr. Mills to work out a schedule for keeping the main center open several evenings a week. The matter of the departmental centers is a new item, and I can see where we might wish to have a report on their success sometime later. Let's ask Mr. Mills to come in with that the meeting after next. But now, it seems to me we can go on to something else." And Mr. Mills left at that point.

The delay was a temporary one, Mr. Mills was sure, and even before the principal's note came to remind him of the need to prepare a report on the centers, he was determined to get some facts and reactions together. He posted a note asking staff members to come to a special meeting to discuss and evaluate the success of the departmental centers. He was interested in the first reaction he heard. Lud Calvert turned around, after having read the note on the bulletin board, and commented: "Well, swell. I'll be there to discuss and evaluate their success. Will you have another meeting later where we can discuss and evaluate their failure?"

"Do you think we'll need that?" Mr. Mills asked, taking the question as a joke.

"Yes, I do. I used to think it was a drag to run all over this building repairing equipment and delivering extra cords and that sort of thing, and I had the idea the centers might help cut down on that—that people would repair or do whatever needed to be done closer to the scene. Instead, I find that it just increases by three the number of stops I have to make, and the number of places I have to go to look for things. But I'm not just thinking of myself. It seems to me, Mr. Mills, that the really bad thing is that everything in the curriculum is taking us away from this kind of development, and here we are, the media people, perpetuating an old-hat idea."

"Hey, hold on there! I didn't want to have this evaluation session turn into a rose-colored report, and I'll change that notice right now. Let's make this a kind of brainstorming session about the centers. I don't want to get all your reactions now—save them for the meeting, so we all can hear—but I'm really not sure I follow you about 'perpetuating an old-hat idea.'"

"Well, I was thinking of how we're really categorizing things and people. Just because there are departmental centers for three of the departments and no others, in a way that seems to indicate that there's a closer relationship between media and those departments than any other. You and I both know that's not true, but I can see that, at least on the face of it, people could get that impression. But, more important, we're kind of freezing ideas into departments. The feeling I have is that media are getting to be less tied to individual subjects—you know, like that new film we previewed last week on art treasures at the Hermitage. As we discussed it then, we were trying to decide whether it would go in the foreign language collection as background for Russia, or in the art center. And you know it could perfectly well go into the main center as part of the general social sciences. Yet as long as we have these centers, we seem to be saying that it is possible to divide materials up in neat little categories."

"Yes, I see. Of course, some of these points were discussed before we began the centers. We were certainly aware of the pitfalls."

"Sure, Mr. Mills, but I haven't even gotten to the other side of the squeeze. That's the curriculum, which is saying more and more that the artificial divisions in learning should be erased. Why, look at every new thing we've tried. Black studies, the humanities, advanced level science mixed in with math—all of these are cutting across the old department lines. Probably nobody realizes that more than I do, because I go all over this building rounding up what teachers want. The teachers themselves sometimes don't think of the overlap with other areas, so they don't even bother to look. I really believe we're bucking a trend. But I'll speak my piece again at our meeting."

"Do, Lud. We'll count on you." Mr. Mills had more things to mull over, but what really struck him forcibly as Lud Calvert had been talking was that there really had been very little of this free-and-easy, open discussion between them since the centers had opened. When the staff gathered to discuss this issue, it would be the first time in four months—since before school opened—that all the specialists would be together. Finding that Mr. Calvert had such strong feelings, of which Mills himself was completely unaware, confused and concerned him, because it made him realize that it was, in some respects, a group of strangers who would meet.

It could well be, he continued to think, that he would have reason to be grateful to Ignatius Newberry for causing this meeting and for challenging the present organization. Sorting out his own reactions, Mr. Mills realized that many of Mr. Calvert's negative reactions were based on problems with films. It could be a relatively simple matter to recall the films in the various centers and administer them from the main center. In their eagerness to get everything out to departments, they had perhaps gone overboard. He realized that he might have assumed that the early enthusiasm of the staff had remained as high as it had been at the beginning, while he was actually misreading their reactions because of this nagging lack of opportunity to communicate among themselves. Although he realized that a first priority at the staff meeting would be to stimulate the most provocative and helpful comments, he believed his own responsibility would be more concerned with working out a way to keep the line of communication open on a two-way basis, if the departmental centers were continued. The preparation of the report to the school board might well turn out to be more complex, and to include more varied views, than he had at first envisioned.

9.
All Kinds
of Copying

· · · · · · · ·

When the Ottawa Hills High School built a new addition, a materials center was one of the major improvements. The formerly overcrowded library facility was replaced by a spacious suite, including space for seating 130 persons at one time, equipment for use with the growing collection of nonprint materials, microfilm readers and printers, which made it possible to reduce the large area formerly reserved for back issues of periodicals, a production area for transparencies and other materials, and adequate shelving for the collection of 12,500 books. Jason Charles, who planned the new facility, felt that the result was worthy of the months of effort he had spent on plans, reading, visits to other libraries, discussions with other librarians, and conferences with the architect and other members of the school's planning team. He welcomed many of the people whom he had formerly visited who were curious to see his new facility. He was proud of the care that students and faculty took of its many new features. The school newspaper featured the new materials center and used it to call for cooperation and pride in the school. The 1,500 students of the school entered enthusiastically and thoughtfully into use of most of its offerings.

The photoduplicating unit, installed on a lease basis, was a novelty in a school where students were not at all hesitant to spend ten cents a page to photoduplicate several pages of a periodical article or encyclopedia article, rather than to miss the school bus while making notes or hastily scanning the item which interested them. When all the equipment in the materials center was new, students used the photoduplicator extensively to photoduplicate their own hands and to reproduce abstract designs made by spreading paper clips, rubber bands, and crumpled gum wrappers on the glass plate of the machine. But as the novelty wore off, they still used it often, but sensibly. As word of its availability spread, the faculty also put it to heavy use. Mr. Charles attached a small notebook to the machine so that users would record the kinds of material copied and the number of copies.

Mr. Charles hoped that the discreet sign supplied by the company which leased the machine to the school was protection enough about violation of copyright. It stated: "Copying of certain material is legally prohibited. Respect for the copyright law encourages creative authorship." But when the director of the madrigal singers photoduplicated fourteen copies of a song sheet, Mr. Charles spoke to him about this large number of copies.

"I tell you, that machine's a godsend. I don't know how we've done without it all these years. Sure, I ran fourteen copies, but do you know how long it would've taken me to copy those off by hand for any other kind of duplication? And I don't really care about copyright. For one thing, nobody's going to come after a teacher like me—right? For another, I think there's something in the law that says the librarian takes the rap if the library machine is misused. We'd hate to lose you, of course, Jason." At that, Ken Delmer knocked him with a friendly fist. "Seriously, though, if the publishers want to sell copies of things, they have the responsibility for making them available. We wanted to use this song last year, couldn't get it locally, and by the time we sent to New York for copies and got word back that it was out of stock or something, it was too late to try to copy it for the Christmas carol program. So this year, thanks to you, we've got it."

Another of the services of the new center, with its enlarged staff, was the assignment of a technician who was responsible, among other things, for the public address system in the auditorium. At the assembly before Veterans Day, he had, as usual, attached the tape recorder to the microphone before the local congressman began his speech. During the coffee break in the lounge adjacent to the auditorium, the principal was congratulating the speaker on an impressive speech alerting the student body to some national issues.

"One of the great features of this, Mr. Aberdeen," Dr. Seymour began, "is that the students will get something out of your remarks for weeks to come. I was sorry that some of the top-notch seniors, who might've asked you some pretty perceptive questions, were away today at a science fair in the city, but they'll be able to listen to the tape tomorrow in our new materials center. Now, I hope you have time to visit the center with me."

"Of course," the congressman replied, setting his coffee cup down, and following the principal out the door. Mr. Charles followed along and heard him continue. "Did you say the talk was taped?"

"Yes, I'm sure it was. I saw the technician up on the stage before the assembly began. Would you like to have a copy?"

"I'd like to have *the* copy," Mr. Aberdeen said. "No one asked me for permission to tape the talk, and if they had, I probably would have said no. As far as I'm concerned, I'll be glad to come back and talk to your students from time to time, when we can work it out on our schedules. After all, I'm their servant, too. But I don't want comments taken out of context or confused as they may have been in being taped in that crowded auditorium."

The principal was being ingratiating. "Well, I'm sure we can take care of that, can't we, Charles?" he said, turning to the center director. "You round up the tape from your assistant, and we'll just turn it back to Mr. Aberdeen. Now what I want to point out to you, sir, is—"

Mr. Charles left them as the principal was pointing out some of the center's better features and returned a few minutes later with the tape. He had been distressed to find that Larry Hopkins, the technician, had already placed it on the tapeduplicator.

"But, gosh, Mr. Charles, that's just standard procedure, as far as I'm concerned. When you've only got one copy of a tape that's likely to be used as much as this one, you make a copy right away. For that matter, we've got lots of blank tapes, and I usually copy every tape and reserve the original as a kind of master copy. If we didn't do that, they'd be torn or split so often that we wouldn't be doing anything but repairing them."

"I know, Larry, how easy it is to do all this. But right now, I'm beginning to wonder just how much copying of all kinds goes on around here. If you have your own idea of 'standard procedure,' as you put it, maybe I'd better know what it is. I'd like you to keep track, for the next week, of the amount and kind of duplicating of anything that you do."

"Do you mean just the audio stuff, Mr. Charles, or the slides, too?"

"This time, I mean everything. Okay?"

"Okay, but that's a big order. That's a big part of my job, you know."

Larry turned the report in within eight days. He had noted the items he had duplicated by format. Mr. Charles read:

*Slides: 35mm—2 sets, 2 copies each—19 in set for Miss Winnfield—23 in set for Mr. Joplin (original + 1 set of dups. returned to teachers; 1 set of dups. kept in center)

Transparencies for use on overhead: 17, 2 copies each (original and one transparency returned to teachers requesting, 1 transparency kept in center)

Tapes: 5, 2 copies each of three; 7 copies of one (for use of Mrs. Alton and cast of senior play); 3 copies of one (for use of debate teams)

Photographs: 7 enlarged for use on bulletin board

*Sent out to Slidecraft for reproduction

Mr. Charles noted that the technician had included items which he sent to a commercial firm for duplication. One set of slides had been brought in by a social studies teacher; the slides had been taken on his seminar and study trip behind the Iron Curtain the summer before, and he wanted a set to keep at school for class showings. Larry Hopkins had had two sets duplicated, one to be returned to the teacher with the originals, and the other to be filed in the center's growing slide collection, where it would be available for other teachers. The other request for duplication of slides had come from the home economics teacher, who had taken pictures of the participants in a national chicken cookery contest to which she had been invited. Technically, her slides were not too good, and several of them featured the reflection of the flash on her inexpensive camera, but Mr. Charles saw that there were now three sets, the teacher's own, the second set assigned to her, and the third which would be kept at the center.

It was a coincidence that during the same week, Mr. Charles was walking through the center as Larry Hopkins was giving a teacher five transparencies he had requested for his physics class. Larry was sorting the transparencies which a student aide had duplicated and mounted. The teacher, George Quincy, watched him making up the sets, then asked: "What's that other set for?"

"That's for our file, Mr. Quincy," Larry replied. "See, we keep a set here, and then if you should lose yours or something, we'd have another one all ready to go for you."

"I'm not likely to lose any of these, after all the trouble I've gone to to make up the set in the first place. I've sweat blood over these, and they're unique. They are going to be great to have in that honors physics class, I can tell you. Why don't you just give me that other set now, and I'll keep them on hand and lend them to a student if he should want to review on his own or something?"

Larry Hopkins smiled as he answered, "Oh, you'd be surprised what people lose, Mr. Quincy. Here in the center, we hear about it all the time. But even so, we'd have to have a set for our master file here. It's a record of what we've made, and it's also a set to have for another teacher who may want to use one or more of the transparencies in his class."

"Now, wait a minute, young man!" George Quincy raised his voice. "*I* had the idea for these transparencies, didn't I? I combed this center and the college library for the material, didn't I? I spent hours combining stuff into new graphs and making it all make sense for my kids, didn't I? And you're going to stand there and tell me you'll hand it out to any teacher who happens to come across it in the file? Why, for one thing, there isn't another class in this school that could handle the material, except for my senior honors group, so any other use would be ridiculous."

"But we're here to help everybody, Mr. Quincy!" Hopkins' tone was almost pleading.

"I don't call it helping anybody to hand out one guy's hard work to somebody else who's too lazy to do it himself, and who will undoubtedly misuse it if he gets his hands on it. Let's just settle this by having you give me both of those sets. This isn't the end of it, either. It seems to me this is something the union should look into, but for now, just give me both sets, and we'll see about the rest of this later."

Mr. Charles was aware that Quincy was probably being more high-handed than he would have been with one of the professional staff members of the center, but he let the conversation go this far before he broke in. He felt it was important to support Hopkins in front of the teacher, although he was unsure himself of how good a plan it was to keep copies of all transparencies. But Quincy's mention of the union meant he would not let the matter rest here. Mr. Charles stepped forward and said, "George, I think you're putting your finger on something that's been bothering me, too. If this is your preparation period, maybe we could have a cup of coffee in my office and talk this over. Larry, I'd like to see those transparencies, because I should be more in touch with the kind of stuff we're turning out here in the center."

Mr. Charles and Mr. Quincy settled themselves in the director's office, and Mr. Charles turned the conversation back to the issue.

"George, you've walked right into the middle of something that's been bothering me lately. I see more and more the potential we have here to provide service of a kind and quality that nobody's ever thought about before, but right now, we're at a stage where we're like an army at the start of a war. We don't know the strength of our weapons, and we haven't thought through all the problems that may be associated with them."

"I'll say you haven't! Now, I don't want to be a sorehead, Jason, but I'm not going to stand around and have other people take over the best of what I've produced. As far as I'm concerned, this thing about the transparencies is just like the issue about the televised instruction that the union took care of for us. You remember that? It was when that bright guy who only stayed here a couple of years had done a series of videotapes on the new humanities program. He caught on to the fact that he was just being bled for his brains and talent, and that the tapes could be used over and over, while he was put back to teaching diagraming to ninth graders. So the union got something set up in contracts that says teachers have residual rights to use of themselves on T.V. We need some kind of protection like that for our ideas, like mine for these transparencies."

"But, George, what's the difference whether you share your idea by leaving a set of these transparencies for the center, or by taking part in your department meetings or curriculum committees? Everybody's got you pegged as one of the most helpful people here at Ottawa Hills. I see how the new teachers in science pick up ideas from you and use them. Do you have some kind of grudge against the media center?"

"Oh, no, it's not that. But when I share my ideas, I want to know I'm sharing them, and I want to decide with whom to share them. I don't want to just leave them lying around in a drawer for someone else to use. Or, in this case, for someone else to misuse. Look, Jason, I know this school, I know these teachers, and I know the science course of study like the palm of my hand. Nobody, but nobody, would have any reason to use this stuff in a class, except me. So be a good guy and give me what belongs to me anyway. Okay?"

Mr. Quincy had his hand out for the transparencies lying on Mr.

Charles' desk. Before he handed him the transparencies, Mr. Charles said, "Look, I've got a lot to think through about this. I'm not sure you see all the dimensions of this problem, and I'm darned sure I don't. I can see where we could get into all kinds of trouble, with the best intentions in the world, and I think no one of us wants that to happen. But if I outline some of the stuff I see tying in with this, would you sit down and go over it with me? Why, when you were teaching biology last year, you were crazy about that videotape of your cutting up the cat, and we've used it a lot since, and will probably use it a lot more. I realize the union's policy on that makes it easy, but, as you pointed out at the time, videotaping that one good dissection saved a lot of supplies and, for all I know, it saved a lot of cats. It also means that every kid has a front seat when he sees the tape of the dissection. There must be some logical way we can handle this thing, too, but if you give me a week or so, I'll have enough other examples laid out for you so you can see it's a matter of all kinds of duplication, and, perhaps, all kinds of in-service work with teachers, like maybe even offering a photography class here in the center. Will you help?"

"Well, sure," said Mr. Quincy, picking up the transparencies. "Just say when and where. Thanks for the coffee." He stood up and left.

Larry Hopkins had apparently been watching the door, because he tapped and opened it almost before it had closed behind Mr. Quincy.

"All set, Mr. Charles? Did you set him straight?"

"Larry, I'm not sure I'm set straight myself. But don't worry about those transparencies. Mr. Quincy has them, but I'm pretty sure there'll be no calls for them from anybody else, and if there are, we can get in touch with him again."

One look at Hopkins' face was all Jason Charles needed to realize he had given the impression of failing to support his own staff member. Seeing the sullen look come into Hopkins' eyes, he was embarrassed, and he spoke more brusquely than he had intended. "This is a ticklish problem, Larry, and because it involves school policy for personnel, among other things, I'm not sure I can explain it to you. But for the time being, I'd like to see and okay all requests for orders like this. Let me see the material and the request before you go to work on it. O.K?"

"O.K., Mr. Charles. If that's the way you want it, that's it." Hopkins closed the door and went back to his work area. Jason Charles felt confused at his own reactions and at the tempest that seemed ready to form.

He was concerned at his failure to get across to Hopkins the dimensions of the problem. He wondered where to begin in identifying the need for firmer policies and clearer procedures. He was sure the problem was not exclusive to the media center, but he was also sure that before he could discuss it with either principal or vice-principal, he would have to identify as many aspects of it as possible, and also some of the steps toward solution.

On a yellow pad, he wrote:

PROBLEMS OF USE OF REPRODUCTION SERVICES

1. Teachers' rights to *ideas* in materials duplicated by request—difference if material is developed by teacher or simply copied from another source?
2. Standard handling of requests—number of copies made, reserve of copies for center.
3. Taping (video, audio) of teacher presentations.
4. Taping (video, audio) of student presentations.
5. Form needed for release of taped presentations?
6. Taping (video, audio) of presentations by visiting speakers, etc.
7. Decision *re* duplication of material that is technically poor by department head? By center director?
8. Difference between formats—e.g., charts reproduced as transparencies different from slides reproduced as slides?
9. Center policy *re* number of copies of any item—different maximums, depending on formats, etc.?

10.
The Case
of Staff Selection

· · · · · · · · · · · · ·

Herb Lowell was fond of saying that, for an administrator, there were days and days of tedium and triviality, relieved only by the occasional day when he had to make a decision—and it was on that day he earned his pay. His position as assistant superintendent for instruction in the Frontenac School District followed that pattern. Dell Dexter, principal-designate of the Florissant High School, had reminded him in a memorandum earlier in the week that all department heads had been chosen except for the director of the school's media center. This was the time for Dr. Lowell to meet with the district consultants for libraries and for audiovisual programs and with Dr. Dexter to make that selection.

The plans for the new high school were on the table in Dr. Lowell's office. They included the district's first unified media center, and he hoped that the plan on which they had worked so long would prove to be a prototype for other centers. Although the older high school had a fairly new addition which housed the library, the facility had not been planned as a media center. The problems with that building had led to many of the decisions made for Florissant. Dexter had been the administrative assistant to Dr. Lamar, the principal, when that addition was planned, and had participated in many of the decisions. His experience in that, and in working with the new plans, would be major assets in his administration of the new high school.

One of the reasons for making the plans for Florissant as innovative as possible was the resistance that had been expressed in the school district for many years toward the idea of a new high school. In a period when the population had remained fairly static, the enrollment of the one high school had seemed to stabilize at approximately 3,500, but as some of the large suburban homes were torn down and replaced by apartment buildings or converted into several units, the steady rise of enrollment had forced the planning of a new high school. The interest of the community was high; it was essential that every step taken should be the right step.

Dr. Lowell bent over the blueprint page which showed what the media center would be like. Planned for an eventual enrollment of 2,500 students, the area included carrels around the walls of the largest room in the suite. When the tables, which each seated six students, and the carrels were filled to capacity, there was seating for 130 students. There were sixteen tables and thirty-four individual carrels. Seventeen of the carrels had electrical outlets and seventeen, no outlets. The arrangement of the carrels had intrigued them all in the planning, and the four of them most concerned had been delighted when Rob Kinloch, the district consultant for libraries, had suggested their location on the periphery of the large area, with islands of low shelving for the book collection and one long section of high shelving against one wall. Kinloch had thought at first that such a situation was unworkable, but he had visited a high school where the shelving was tight and controlled like this, with a turnstile near the charging desk, and he had been impressed with its efficiency.

There were other areas for seating in conference rooms and in an honors study hall, to be reserved for seniors with high rankings for academic subjects and citizenship. The students at Frontenac High who knew they would be transferring to Florissant had been enthusiastic about these features, which were lacking in the older facility.

The part of the plan which had been entirely new for all of them was the area for production, screening, and maintenance of the nonprint materials. Dr. Lowell remembered when this part of the plan, fully one third of the entire media center, had been marked in large letters, A-V, with no indication of contents or uses. That was before Jim Lees had come to head up the district's audiovisual program. It had become increasingly clear that Kinloch could not supervise all of the librarians, run the processing center, and carry any major responsibility for nonprint materials, so the appointment of Lees had been a wise decision. Within weeks, he had come up with plans for the installation of a small viewing area, of the drymounting press and other equipment he considered essential for the work area, and for plans for the storage and control of projectors and other equipment of greatest use in classrooms. To Dr. Lowell, who had no experience with this kind of facility in a high school, the plan looked good. But he realized that much of its effectiveness would have to depend on the person who would have final responsibility for the media center in the new high school.

In a system like Frontenac, where the three junior highs had funnelled their students into the one senior high, and where there were nine elementary schools, there was no formal way for teachers to apply for transfers or other changes of assignment. Dr. Lowell and the superintendent had prided themselves on the fact that they would interview any teacher on request. Their head of personnel, who also handled public relations for the school system, was also easily available to talk with teachers who were interested in a change. Because the community was pretty homogeneous, and because the schools were of fairly uniform size, there was little transferring from one school to another. The planned opening of the Florissant High School seemed about to change all that.

Lionel McComb, science teacher at one of the junior highs, had written from the university where he was on leave for a year to get a master's degree in educational media, to ask to be considered as director of the media center in the new high school. Dexter had virtually promised Martha Malden, the assistant librarian at Frontenac, that she could move with him to the new high school. His loyalty to the old school, as well as Dr. Lamar's anxiety to hold on to as many of his own leaders among that faculty as he could, had meant he was usually taking the second level of leadership in many of the departments with him, and Martha was one of these.

Unlike some of the other department heads, neither Lionel nor Martha had participated in any of the planning for facilities for the media center. When McComb had left for his year's study, there had been much speculation that he might not return to the district, and there seemed no point to keep him informed of plans for the new building, even though his appointment to that staff in some capacity could be virtually assured. As for Miss Malden, she had looked at some of the early blueprints and declared she had not yet found a library where she couldn't work, but that she also had not yet found a blueprint of one in which she could visualize herself working—or anything else happening. She would have to see the facility before she could get a good idea of how the staff of four media specialists, four technicians, and two clerks could be assigned, and how materials could be arranged.

Dr. Lowell thought that the decision to be made would have to be between these two staff members. The final decision was his, but he wanted to know the views of Dexter, Kinloch, and Lees. He had set up this meeting with the other three after Dexter's reminder earlier in the week. He thought he had a pretty good idea of the stand each would take and of what his own decision would be, but he was eager to lay the facts out on the table. For that reason, he had invited Laurel Christian, the personnel officer, to come and to bring the personnel folders of the two possible appointees.

"In a way, I'm sorry that this decision has been delayed for so long," Dr. Lowell said as he opened the meeting. "As you realize, one reason for this has been the pressure of the many other decisions to be made in connection with the new building. Another is that we have gotten so much extra mileage out of the library staff at the high school, who have worked up a basic list for purchase for Florissant, and out of Jim here, who has made all the recommendations for purchase of equipment and such for the nonprint materials. But, I think, in fairness to whoever will be in charge, and, for that matter, to whoever will not, we have to decide now on personnel. It might be best to review some of the facts that Mrs. Christian has about Mr. McComb and Miss Malden. Mrs. Christian?"

"Well, I brought their personnel folders with me. I hope I have what you want. Mr. Dexter has worked with Miss Malden, so he probably knows all this. She has been at Frontenac High for seven years, and has been the assistant to Mrs. Clinton all that time. We have annual recommendations from Mrs. Clinton about her—'highly reliable,' 'key member of the staff,' 'indispensable during my recent illness,' 'works well with others,'—you can imagine the sort of thing."

"And did she have teaching experience before that?" Mr. Lees asked.

"Oh, yes, in the Okolon schools. Apparently she wasn't too successful, because she was taken on probation here, even though she had taught junior high school English for two years there. There were discipline problems, which were noted on the rather restrained recommendation form from the principal there."

"I had forgotten about that," Mr. Kinloch said thoughtfully. "My impression is that her work with students and teachers has been excellent at Frontenac, but if she couldn't handle discipline in a classroom, what might happen in a large, open center like this one, where even the supervision of staff involves some ability to discipline and direct? I guess we all know more about McComb. He's considered to be one of the leading lights at Marks Junior, isn't he?"

"Oh, yes. There've been three different principals there in the nine years he's taught at Marks, but they all have great praise for him. They say he's imaginative, keenly interested in science, and a leader among the faculty. In fact, Mr. Belzoni, the principal there, told me last spring that he was trying to talk McComb out of taking this course in media in favor of going into general administration, where he thought he'd be able to contribute more. But, as those of you who know Mr. McComb can imagine, once he makes up his mind to do something, he's not likely to change it."

"All of those sound like admirable qualities for the director of our first media center, I'd say," Mr. Lees pointed out.

"There's something I think I should mention," Mrs. Christian began somewhat tentatively. "We've been getting several inquiries about Mr. Mc-comb from other school systems. I don't know whether he's really applied for other jobs for next year or not, because it could be that, with the need there is for people in media, the graduate program in which he's enrolled could be suggesting him, but it's safe to say he's getting some pretty promising offers."

"And if I know Lionel, he's not likely to come back here to play second chair to some gal," Mr. Dexter said.

"That kind of consideration should not enter into our discussions," Dr. Lowell said.

"Sure, but you know darned well it does. We don't want to lose a good man, especially if we can keep him *and* our other candidate, by naming him the head," Mr. Dexter said with a chuckle. "One thing I don't know too well about either of them is their academic background. I don't mean grades so much as their undergraduate majors, what courses they've taken since they began to teach, and so forth."

Mrs. Christian thumbed through the folders again and pulled out several sheets. "We're a little behind in recording recent credits, and of course we have no records on Mr. McComb's studies this year, but his letter requesting leave states that he will obtain a master's degree in educational media and will have all the requirements for the state certificate as a media specialist. Miss Malden, of course, already has that certificate, and her most recent graduate work was in a Higher Education Act institute, where the theme was Administering Media Programs in Secondary Schools. Her undergraduate major was English, and she has a master's in librarianship. Mr. McComb, as you'd guess, had a biology major in college and a master's degree in science education. So this will be his second master's degree."

"They're both about the same age, too, aren't they?" Dr. Lowell asked.

"Yes, sir. Mr. McComb will be thirty-five in September, and Miss Malden was thirty-six last May."

"Does either of them have any special work in administration, supervision, something like that?" Mr. Dexter wondered.

"Let me see. It doesn't look like it. Oh, the note on Miss Malden's folder about attendance at that institute says she was especially good in planning for the work assignments of others and that she exercised leadership within the group of participants in the institute."

"Of course, you never know what that means—in a fairly artificial, summer school situation like an institute," Mr. Kinloch observed.

"One of the things I want to know is—what does either one of them know about the specialty of the other? Let's assume that McComb comes back to us with all the answers about nonprint materials, and Miss Malden really knows the operation of the library at Frontenac. I still think that to be in charge of a center like this, the head guy would have to know something of the other's specialty. Isn't that true?" Mr. Dexter asked. Dr. Lowell listened with special interest for the replies from Kinloch and Lees.

"Well, I think it's only fair to say that, all things being equal, someone like Miss Malden, who's taken library science courses, has been forced to pick up something about nonprint materials. I'm sure it isn't one of her big interests, but she'd know one end of a projector from another, at least," Mr. Kinloch said.

Mr. Lees chuckled. "You've got something there. One of the things that makes it hard for someone with a background like Lionel's to pick up something about cataloging of books, for example, is that so many of the courses in librarianship are geared to liberal arts graduates, and library science programs have requirements about foreign languages and such which virtually rule out someone like Lionel before he even begins. I know, because I discussed this very thing with him before he left. I think it's a safe bet that he won't have had much about print materials. But what you should keep in mind is his subject background. It's rare to find someone who is interested in media in general who has the science background that Lionel has."

"That makes me wonder about something I probably should have checked earlier." Dr. Lowell turned to Mrs. Christian. "We don't have any other good bets around, do we? Someone on the staff who might be interested or qualified, or any applicants who've come in?"

"I think you know the answer to that as well as I do, Dr. Lowell. It seems to be these two or nobody. Unless you want to do something like transfer Mrs. Clinton from Frontenac."

"Heaven forbid!" said Mr. Dexter with feeling. "She's two years from retirement, and has almost no interest in the media center concept. We'd be better off with no head than with her."

"Now, that's an interesting statement, coming from you," Dr. Lowell said. "I'd just been turning all this over in my mind, and I wonder—. Maybe, at least at the beginning, we're not ready to name anyone as director of the media center. Maybe we just need a very good librarian, and a very good nonprint specialist, because it seems to me that's what we really have here. After all, we've gotten along with an arrangement something like that at Frontenac for all these years. Maybe after you have a good estimate of the relative strengths of these two people—or of anyone else, for that matter—it will be easier to decide on a director. What would you think of that, Dell?"

Mr. Dexter was obviously nonplussed. "I think I'd like to think it over. It just didn't occur to me we wouldn't come up today with a pretty good indication of what we want for next year. What do the rest of you think? Could we take a straw vote?"

"Fine," said Dr. Lowell with some heartiness. "Let's all five of us say what we think should be done this first year. Shall we start with you, Mrs. Christian?"

"Oh, I didn't think you'd put me on the spot like that, but since you have—all things being equal—and they seem to be in this case—I tend to prefer a man as supervisor or administrator. If I really had to vote, I'd vote for Mr. McComb. I guess that's partly because I think he might leave if he doesn't get this appointment, and in my job, that's an important consideration."

"So you're for McComb. I can't say I have much respect for your reasons, but they're interesting. And you, Rob?" By asking the library consultant next, Dr. Lowell thought he might be getting a balancing vote.

"I guess this is really unfair. I'd like to know, for example, what would happen depending on which appointment we made. In terms of the library program, I'd hate to see Miss Malden leave the district if she didn't get this job, but she just might. For that matter, I suppose if she were not to be director of the center, she might prefer to stick out two years at Frontenac and take over when Mrs. Clinton retires. Of course, I know her better than I do McComb, and for that reason, I'd choose her."

"And you, Jim?" Dr. Lowell shifted in his chair to look at Mr. Lees.

"Oh, I find myself in a dilemma, too. I've sweated over those plans, I guess, as much or more than anybody else, and I just don't want to see the whole thing turned into a kind of no man's land. I guess what I'd hate most would be to have nobody be named in charge, because that would make the program seem unimportant. I almost wish there were an outsider we could bring in, who might very well develop into what we want at the head of this kind of program. You know, there are districts where they have a curriculum person or administrator at the head of the media program, and that seems to work, with the people whose prime interest is libraries and those whose prime interest is audiovisual materials, both happy under such an arrangement. You see, one of my problems is I don't know just what McComb is learning this year. He may come back here far ahead of me in educational technology, or he could come back having just discovered the flannel board and the overhead projector. Those are extremes, of course, but the fact of the matter is we just don't know how skillful he'll be with nonprint materials, especially in making decisions about production, and here we're talking about putting him in charge of a center, where he knows even less about the library end of it."

"Now, let me get this straight," Dr. Lowell broke in. "Do I hear you saying, maybe, that we should keep these programs separate?"

"I think you're teasing us with that kind of talk, Herb," Mr. Dexter answered. "We've sold this community on the idea of a media center, not a twin operation of library and audiovisual center. We can't go back on that. Besides, there are a lot of practical problems. I grant you the first year will be touchy. Who'd interview possible staff for the center? Both of them? Who'd come to department head meetings? Both of them? Who'd get the extra salary for being department head? Both of them? Come off it! We may be able to work out some compromise, but that's not the answer."

"And as for me, Dr. Lowell," Mr. Lees said, "I hate to go on record at all, but if I must, I guess I'm for Mr. McComb."

"I don't see that this kind of discussion is getting us anywhere," Mr. Dexter said. "After all, it's your decision, Herb, and we'll all have to live with it. I suppose I'll have to live with it more intimately than anyone, but we have faith in you. We have lots of questions we can't answer, I grant you, and since I'll have to work with either person, I'd rather not express an opinion."

"Fair enough, Dell. I guess there's not much point in going on with this, since we seem not to be able to settle anything. It's at times like this

I wish for a point system or some kind of schedule of interviews and recommendations like some of the larger systems have—though I wouldn't want their headaches, either."

"Is that it?" Mr. Lees asked, and, at Dr. Lowell's nod, the four rose to go.

"Oh, Dell, I'd like to see you another minute," Dr. Lowell said, and Dexter turned back to his desk. "See how this idea strikes you. It just came to me, and it may be wild, but it almost fits with my other one. How would it be if we asked Lees to go to Florissant, just for one year, and get things going as director of the center? He knows the plan for the audiovisual part of it better than anybody, and he could keep an eye on both Miss Malden and Mr. McComb and recommend one of them by the end of the year, perhaps. I have the feeling he could make it swing. And, of course, he could still be the district consultant, just have his headquarters there. What would you think of that?"

"Well, this is something I'd have to think through. I have great respect for him, of course. But how would he feel being responsible to me as a department head—as I assume he would be? Might that shortchange some of his services to the other schools? And would this look like we really just couldn't make up our minds, and so we just let things ride? Oh, I appreciate your asking me my reaction, but I'll need time."

"Fine, good! Tomorrow at ten?" Dr. Lowell asked with a grin.

11.
Plans for Friday Freak-Outs

· · · · · · · · · · · · ·

"Yes, Mrs. Wheeling?" said Mr. Dearborn, head of the social studies department, as the teacher came into his office. He did not look up from the catalog on his desk. "How are things going?"

"Oh, pretty good, I think, thank you. This is the period when that tough class of tenth graders is answering a questionnaire about how they would change the world, so I'm supposed to be somewhere else, and I thought this would be as good a time as any to see you."

"Yes, of course. I just want to finish noting some of these titles from this catalog. Mr. Pilot has told me the senior class came to him as principal and told him they had voted their entire class gift—usually something like 300 dollars—to be in memory of Jason Jekyll. Since he was in the social studies department, we can get something appropriate for the social studies classes with the money. And that, of course, made me think of all the times poor Jason used to come in, practically screaming for materials to use in classes. I'm working now on some recordings in black history, which he was teaching, as you know, before he was killed. And I think there'll be enough for some slide sets on different sections of the country. He really loved to travel, and he brought his own slides to school often, to show to his classes. I feel these will be really appropriate memorials to him."

"They sound like it," Mrs. Wheeling agreed. "Actually, I was thinking of Jason today, too, when I asked to see you. Do you remember that meeting we had early in the school year, when he talked about his 'Friday Freak-Outs'?"

"Yes," Mr. Dearborn chuckled. "That was a good old Jekyll expression, wasn't it? I wonder if word of that ever got back to Warren Street."

"Oh, I imagine the things Jason Jekyll did with these kids were talked about by everybody at some time or other. It must have reached the administration building. But, as usual, he was overdramatizing things. His 'Friday Freak-Outs' were really just 'doing your own thing.' Of course, Jason had the gift of making it all seem different and exciting. That's what made me want to try it."

"Well, good, I'm glad to hear that. What do you have in mind?"

"You remember one of his points was that these Fridays were to be set up on a different basis from regular classes. There'd be no testing, no follow-up as such, but some good background given so the kids would be ready to discuss whatever the topic was. And the topics would all be as relevant as we could find. That's why I don't even want to plan them too far ahead. I thought I'd try to set up five—five Friday Freak-Outs—which also keeps the whole thing alliterative. I'm not even sure how they'll go, or whether I'll want to continue them, but I'd like your okay to start."

"I see no problem at all. One thing that did cross my mind when Jason was so enthusiastic about these was that Friday seemed like a poor day, because we have so many more absentees on a Friday."

"Yes, I'd thought of that. And I still don't understand why that is."

"Oh, I think in an inner-city area like this it's related to the reasons why offices and factories are hardest hit before and after weekends. Kids just take off. Or they have chances at jobs as busboys or carwashers, and those build around the weekend. I've gotten used to it, of course, but on the other hand, it could mean that if the idea of your Fridays really caught on, it would draw some of these kids back, or it might mean they won't have missed so much when they do come back, at least as far as the regular class topics are concerned. So I suppose it might work both ways. But what topics did you have in mind, to start off with?"

"My husband tells me they sound like cocktail conversation topics, but the thing is, if they're relevant and they fit, that's what we want, isn't it? Anyway, I've made notes on the problems of cities—housing, pollution, health, protection agencies; the control of knowledge—censorship in libraries, bookstores, television, that whole scene; the value of life—problems of old age, overpopulation, abortion; responsibility in the family—planning for the future, sharing responsibility, that sort of thing; and, finally, civic responsibility. But here, I want to put the emphasis on their responsibilities to each other, to the school, the responsibility which is acquired by the opportunity for education."

"Is that *all?*" Mr. Dearborn asked with a smile. "It seems to me, my dear, you have tackled some things that might keep a United Nations or a federal commission going for years—and you're going to do it on five Fridays with some of the most academically disinclined students imaginable! Even if they're your best classes, they'd still be low for the district as a whole. But go to it! Maybe, somehow, you'll reach some of them who need this. But what's your real plan? Will you just kick around ideas, give them readings, present something in advance and expect them to come in with reactions? What?"

"That's a big reason why I'm here. I've really been thinking about this for several weeks, but when I went to the library to round up some material, Mrs. Anderson really told me off. She said that if I'd wanted to do this, I should have thought of it last year, when she was begging teachers to submit suggestions for materials to be ordered. You remember when there was that confusion on Warren Street, and we suddenly had money for library materials, and she had to hustle to get it all spent? Besides, when she looked over my notes, she said these were all things that were in demand a lot anyway, and that, while the library might have something about them, much of it would be in magazines, which wear out quickly because the kids generally like them, and use them for many different kinds of assignments, and for recreational reading, too."

"Mm, I was afraid there might be a response like that. I know she's not going to be happy, either, when I appear with this list of materials we'd like to get. Even though the funds will come from the seniors, she'll have to make up the orders, and I know she'll double check every item I've put down so carefully that I might as well let her do it in the first place. It does seem the only alternative is for us to order these materials separately, and just keep them here in the department office, where the teachers will know about them, and get them as they need them. But, if I did that, I'd practically be running a library in competition with hers, and heaven knows, I'd rather not get into that. Anyway, we depend on her too much to offend her by trying to go around her—although I must admit I haven't entirely given up the idea of asking Mr. Pilot about that possibility. But here, now—none of this helps your situation, does it?"

"No, except that it's nice to know you more or less share my reaction. I'd begun to wonder whether maybe I was just thinking up things that would complicate life for other people. But then, I thought there might be other ways to handle this. I'm only going to try out the idea with my three top classes, so I could sort of pace them against each other—start each one on a different topic, on which I'd do the groundwork, and then use debates one class might have, or even tapes from their discussions, to get something going in the other classes. It would make it sort of a round robin, because it's obvious that whatever I do, there isn't going to be enough material to go around, and this way, we could get the most mileage from it. I can bring my tape recorder from home. The last time I borrowed one from the library, it arrived five minutes after class had started, and it was missing a cord, so I'd have lost another ten minutes tracking that down and getting it set up to use."

"Ah, the joys of media!" Mr. Dearborn said with a grin.

Mrs. Wheeling smiled back at him. "Look, if I were against media, I wouldn't be going out of my way to use it, would I? It's just the administrative tie-ups that bother me. Media would be fine, if I knew that in every classroom there'd be materials to use, and that the equipment would all be plugged in and just waiting for me to flip a switch. But it's not like that."

"No, that's true. That's how we've gotten into this bind of storing overhead projectors here in the department office. When the unit on drugs was news, and we were using lots of homemade materials, everyone seemed to have charts on transparencies, but there was no reliable way to project them. And at the time, everyone was so keen on warning high school students about drug absue that the Kiwanis presented these to us. They aren't used as much, I notice, as they were at first, which reminds me that perhaps I should mention them again to the new teachers. But at any rate, they're here, and they serve the purpose. Will you want to use them, by the way?"

"Probably, but I don't have all my materials in mind yet. When I do, do I have your okay to have some transparencies made in the library? And to get some things copied, too? They would be giveaways, for the kids to take home. I see this as the kind of classroom activity which would have a lot of carryover into the homes. If I were laying out more formal goals for it, one would be the enrichment of family discussions, even family reading that might grow out of it. So, since we don't have textbooks that hit on this, I'd like to be sure the kids have something to take home to keep the ball rolling there. Are you saying okay?"

"Yes, I am. In fact, since I want to encourage you on all this, I'd say just keep producing and asking for what you need until the funds run out. Someone will be sure to tell us when that happens. And then, you'll have to quit. But the trick is to get in first with what you want. There is never enough to sit down with all the teachers and sort out, around a table, who will get what. You have this idea, and it's been tried, to some extent, by Mr. Jekyll before. It calls for materials immediately, and if you waited a year to do it, there'd probably be different topics and different materials anyway, so you might as well go ahead now. Keep me posted about how it goes, though, won't you?"

"Of course, Mr. Dearborn. I appreciate your faith in me. Oh, there is one other thing. I hate to do this, but you know, we received information in our mailboxes the other day about the new Sunday supplement which will be directed to teenagers. It's going to start with next Sunday's paper, but that promotional piece for teachers pointed out how helpful it would be in classes just like this one. In fact, every topic on my list was included, in some form, in the list of topics they said would be covered in the first month. They offered bulk rates, four issues for a quarter, for high school students. Would you have any objection to my asking the kids to sign up and pay a quarter for four issues? It seemed to me they might not only get some of the material that seems to be hard to lay hands on otherwise, but they'll also get introduced to this new feature in the newspaper. That should be a good thing."

"Let me check on this one before you ask for money, Mrs. Wheeling. You know Mr. Pilot's strict rules against requiring students to pay for things, although he usually doesn't worry about anything less than a dollar. And, for that matter, I'm always amazed at how these kids do seem to have money for such items."

"Yes, I've noticed that, too. It ties in with what surprised me when I first taught here in the inner city. I really expected kids to look ragged or shabby, I guess, and instead, they're almost overdressed, if anything. I suppose it's because they work and buy their own clothes, so they get a few things, but they get what they want, and they keep their clothing nice. I suppose the money they bring in for class pictures and that sort of thing is their own money, too, so they don't have to wait for an allowance or something at home. Well, anyway, you'll check on my asking for quarters? I don't especially like doing it, but it seems worthwhile, and the idea of reading this material in something like a newspaper should make them feel at least more aware of newspapers. So I will check back with you later to get the word from Mr. Pilot on collecting. O.K.? And now, I do have to run. Thank you again."

For the next few days, Mrs. Wheeling came to school early and stayed late. She felt frustrated by the tight security which closed the building half an hour after the last class of the day, and which permitted no one inside more than one hour before class in the morning. For her own convenience, she would have preferred the longer time at night, but she made the best of it. Her first mentions of the "Friday Freak-Outs" in her classes led to a few curious questions from some students, whom she recruited to preview some films which she thought might be useful, and to help her select some of the materials she wanted to use. She had made note of some magazine articles that sounded appropriate, but she wanted to read as many as possible before recommending them. She wanted to choose some to photoduplicate, and she also made a transparency of some of the most eye-catching titles, which she intended to use when she introduced the topic.

Mrs. Anderson, who was always one of the first faculty members to enter the building in the morning, chatted with her as the two of them worked in the library before classes began. In a pleasant way, she kept in close touch with what Mrs. Wheeling was planning. One morning, as she was snapping new magazines into the covers for current issues, she pointed out some she thought might be of interest.

"Another thing I'll be getting soon," she said, "is a new supplement that is going to come with the Sunday papers. It's directed to young people, and libraries will receive ten copies of it for the first month. It sounds exactly like what you're interested in, so I'd be glad to hold several copies for you—perhaps one for each of your three classes? There won't be enough copies to go very far among 2,500 students, anyway, so I'd be glad to share these with you."

"Thank you, Mrs. Anderson," Mrs. Wheeling said. "I know about the new supplement, and, as a matter of fact, I've ordered one copy for each student in this special program."

"One copy for each student! Why, the library could never afford that! It must have cost fifty dollars!"

"I sent a check for twenty-two dollars and fifty cents, for the eighty-nine students in my three classes, plus myself. And I've collected all but the last seventy-five cents from the students."

"Well, good for you!" Mrs. Anderson said. "Just think—when you want a quarter for something like that, which no one has even seen yet, you can just go around and collect it, while, with the little budget I get for the library—just about two dollars per student for the whole year—I have to get dozens of clearances, read lots of reviews, use all kinds of forms to get the order placed, and then wait months for the materials to arrive. Of course, ordering for the library is a much bigger operation, but—"

"But also, you don't have to hound the kids for their money—something which I certainly don't enjoy. And you probably wouldn't feel as responsible if it turned out to be a bad choice."

"Oh, maybe. But now, in the case of this new supplement, we're getting the ten copies only as a sample. After that, of course, it will just come with the subscription to the paper. But if it were something brand new and unrelated to what we have to date, it would have to be approved after several issues had come. Oh, I remember how Mr. Jekyll used to carry on about one of the Negro periodicals which we didn't get till the second year, and by that time, the first year's issues had become practically collectors' items!"

Mrs. Wheeling, remembering the issue Mr. Jekyll could make of things, smiled at Mrs. Anderson's example. The two women worked a while longer without saying anything, and then, as Mrs. Anderson passed behind Mrs. Wheeling to return some material to the vertical file, she glanced at the slips spread out before her.

"Why, you're really building up an excellent bibliography there! And it's all quite recent, too—probably better than one could get from the *Reader's Guide,* or any place else, for that matter. And so many of those are things we're always being asked for. I just never have time to sit down and prepare bibliographies, as I used to do for the teachers when I was in a smaller school. But when yours is finished, perhaps we could duplicate it and keep copies on file here?"

"Mr. Dearborn has seen most of it, and he wants it duplicated, too. He intends to distribute it to all the social studies teachers, and also send a few copies down to Warren Street, to see whether it's something that other high schools might also use."

"If he's doing that, fine," the librarian said. "But, you see, the library, as the materials center for the whole school, is the only place where teachers in all departments would have easy access to them. And a lot of those topics, like health care, relate to other departments, like the home economics unit on family care, for example. I just wouldn't want all your effort and talent to be wasted."

Somewhat to her surprise, Mrs. Wheeling was irritated rather than pleased at the librarian's complimenting her on the bibliography. The following day, the feeling she had not quite been able to identify boiled up as she sat in a faculty meeting. It was one of the six fairly formal faculty meetings that were held during the year, and it was held after school. Mr. Pilot introduced a man who looked dimly familiar to Mrs. Wheeling as someone she had seen visiting the school, and on her visits to the administration building. His title was media supervisor for the district, and he responded to Mr. Pilot's introduction by saying he was delighted to be with them, and that he hoped to get response and ideas from them about what the future of their school library as a true media center might be. He showed slides of the floor plans of several he had visited in other parts of the country, and he projected transparencies showing what the growth in numbers of librarians, library aides, sizes of collection, and many other categories had been in the last few years. He referred to national standards for media programs and the concept of all media organized for use in one central program. He suggested workshops that might be set up in individual schools or perhaps even subject departments, and then concluded by saying that hopes were high and dreams were many, but he would welcome their suggestions and their criticisms in achieving both.

Mrs. Wheeling looked around at her fellow teachers. Mr. Dearborn had brought with him the completed order for social studies materials which he was going to hand over to Mrs. Anderson, and he was idly tapping the cards. Most of the other teachers had responded politely to the supervisor's presentation, but they were looking wary now, as Mr. Pilot stood up and said, "I'm sure we'll have a few questions for our visitor." None of the teachers seemed to want to catch Mr. Pilot's eye at this point.

But Mrs. Wheeling was suddenly aware of a perspective on the use of library materials that she had not realized she had. She stood up and began: "Yes, Mr. Pilot, I have a question, or rather, a pile of questions. I'm perfectly willing to cooperate with the library, as has been suggested this afternoon, but I've just had an experience which makes me wonder whether the library will cooperate with me. It seems to me that instead of my doing bibliographies, which the library can duplicate and distribute, it ought to be the library providing them for me. I'd rather my students spent their time getting to know what materials they'll be using, and I regret their having to spend time previewing films which should have been discarded from the district film library ten years ago—not just because the content is bad, but because the prints are so scratchy and the sound so bad that they're really unusable. I wonder why it's easier for a teacher to bring in his own equipment and use it than to go through the red tape of getting the same thing from the library, then finding it really isn't available or won't work. Mrs. Anderson works hard, and no one knows or appreciates that better than I, and I think she has one or two clerks who help her, but I am sorry to see the day coming when this program will be expanded, as you describe it, when, as far as I'm concerned, it isn't even a good library program yet. When the librarian says, 'Oh, I'm sorry, but current material simply can't be supplied in the quantity you want,' how come I, as a teacher, am the one who has to do something about it? Isn't *all* material the responsibility of the library? I think I heard our speaker mention a program for a media center in every school, and he then talked about what media meant. Well, I know about that. I want to know about that program—if it means, as I think it does, service for people—and I want to know about that center—if, as I think it should, it really means some kind of central responsibility, so that I won't have to sell newspapers during class time. Here I am, spending time running the copying machine, and you're telling me I should be more aware of what's new. If I were, wouldn't I be more frustrated? And wouldn't I just have more things I'd have to scrounge for myself? Well, I guess I should give you a chance to answer."

12.
The Case
of Placing Priorities

· · · · · · · · · · · ·

Jack Hampton succeeded Sarah Conrad as librarian at Greenfield High School. Miss Conrad had been librarian at the high school from the days when it was newly consolidated, with one hundred students in each of the three grades ten through twelve, through its growth to an enrollment approaching 2,500. The years which had seen the population increase so dramatically had brought other changes. The collection of books in the high school library had been noted as strong by a visiting accreditation committee in the last spring of Miss Conrad's tenure, and she was proud of telling people that long before the American Library Association had endorsed the idea of an instructional materials center, she had developed one at Greenfield. One of the industrial arts teachers maintained such items as overhead projectors for classroom use, and a crew of student volunteers assisted him by delivering equipment to the classrooms. With departmental funds, teachers had supplemented the materials available from the library collection and used rented films as well as the school's collection of filmstrips, transparencies, and other nonprint materials extensively.

Miss Conrad's unhappiness in her last years at Greenfield apparently stemmed from the problem of adjusting to the changes in people and attitude which size and the encroachment of the city had brought. When Mr. Hampton had visited the library in the spring for an interview, Miss Conrad had been concerned to hear he did not plan to live in the immediate vicinity if he were appointed librarian. Mr. Hampton had smiled and said, "But we have a house that we like very much, and we've had it only a year. It's in Fox Point, just fifteen minutes away on the expressway. Why move?"

Miss Conrad, who knew Mr. Hampton from meetings of school librarians in the region, could not resist saying that she had never known a real librarian who was satisfied to live so far away from his library. She herself would never have been able to put in the long hours she had in the evenings and on Saturdays if she had not lived within a stone's throw.

Mr. Hampton was aware of her reputation for work. In fact, the principal of the high school, Dan Marlin, had commented in his interview with Mr. Hampton that he was anxious to find a librarian who could get the job done without being a martyr. It seemed to Mr. Marlin that more efficient organization should make it possible to run the library in forty or fifty hours a week. He found it hard to see how the job could be more time-consuming than his own, which he enjoyed, and which he thought he performed rather well. Mr. Hampton had liked his candor, and felt his offer to discuss the possibility of additional staff was given honestly.

Mr. Hampton talked with other faculty members at the time of his interview, and was impressed by their indications of interest in the library. Janice Hurley, who was slated to become chairman of the English department the following year, said to him, "I hope you won't mind being overworked. Our students read like crazy, and we encourage them to keep it up. The public library is really inadequate, and students have to depend on the school for almost everything. Of course, we keep paperbacks for them to use for most of the novels, plays and short stories which are assigned outside of the texts."

When Mr. Hampton asked to see the collection of paperbacks, Mrs. Hurley led him to a room, smaller than a classroom, which had been left when two large classrooms had been combined for a team teaching area in the humanities. The walls of the room were lined with shelves where paperbacks in quantities of ten or twenty of each title were arranged alphabetically by title. He spotted familiar authors and some collections of modern plays and poetry which he knew. When he commented on how extensive the collection was, Mrs. Hurley was obviously pleased. "It's really a lot of work to keep up, with more than twenty of us teaching English, but I think it's worth it."

"Oh? What work is involved?" Mr. Hampton asked.

"Well, as a librarian, you must know. I keep a record of the books by author and title, make out lists of them for the teachers, try to get teachers to schedule use of the paperbacks so that everyone has a fair chance at them, and keep them informed about who is using what, so they won't repeat for the students. It takes a great deal of time, and I'm not sure how I can swing it next year, when I'll have more paper work, meetings to go to, and all that, as head of the department."

"Perhaps you could work out something with the new librarian," Mr. Hampton ventured, well aware he had not yet been officially appointed to the position.

"You mean have the library run this? Well, of course, Miss Conrad has never wanted any part of it, and hasn't even cooperated with us in keeping these same titles out of the library. You see, we in the English department think these books should not be available to students on the library shelves when they are, in a sense, texts that we'll be requiring them to study." Mrs. Hurley's chin set as she finished her statement. Mr. Hampton was beginning to get a picture of the kind of steady friction that might be causing Sarah Conrad to leave Greenfield several years before mandatory retirement. He had heard her comments at some professional meetings about faculties where everybody wanted to be a librarian, but no one wanted to help the librarian, and he now guessed that some of those might have been based on Mrs. Hurley's running of this library operation in the English department.

One of Mr. Hampton's few personal friends on the Greenfield faculty was a college classmate, Jim Kimball, who was basketball coach and social studies teacher. One evening in June, Jim and his wife invited the Hamptons to dinner to celebrate Jack's appointment at Greenfield. Jim sensed this was a step up for his friend, who had been one of four assistant librarians at a large, overcrowded high school near the city. In the course of conversation, Jim said, "Say, Jack, you can do me a favor, since you're here. I have to turn in the names of three professional books I'd like to have added to the library by nine o'clock tomorrow morning, and I don't even have one. Know some I could suggest?"

Jack Hampton hesitated, then said, "Well, aren't there any on basketball you might want? Weren't there new rules set up this year? There must be lots of changes that the books will be showing now."

"Oh, sure, but anything that I want right away, I always just go ahead and buy. I can always pick them up at a bookstore in the city, and you know how coaches are always being accused of having little slush funds here and there. So what better way to use them?"

"That's a good way, I suppose, Jim, but librarians tend to think it's good to have all those things available for other faculty members in some kind of central place. And there is a professional library at Greenfield."

"Sure, there is. That's why I have to come up with three books by tomorrow, but it'll be months before they come in, get cataloged, or whatever it is you librarians do to them, and I don't want to wait for what I really need. And I play it fair. I share the books I buy with school funds —and a lot of my own, too—with the other coaches. I suppose the names I take in tomorrow should really be social studies books anyway. Surely you know some?"

Mrs. Hampton saved her husband from having to answer by reminding him they had a thirteen-year-old babysitter that evening and had agreed to be home soon after ten. A dozen questions came to Mr. Hampton's mind later: Why did Jim have to suggest three titles? Did every faculty member have this responsibility? What did the others do? Why weren't items like books on the new basketball rules ordered on a rush basis if needed? How many kinds of instructional materials were being bought throughout the school without being available through the library?

Mr. Hampton was one of the first members of the faculty to enter the building on the Monday morning when faculty reported for the new school year. In the main office, he picked up a schedule of meetings that would be held during this two-week period before students came back to school, and he went on to the library. Even in the closed, musty smell of summer, he grinned to himself as he turned on the lightswitch and looked around. It was an attractive room. Miss Conrad, as the school secretary had mentioned, had come in reguarly during the summer to water the plants, but when she had left yesterday, she had taken her watering can, her last possession left at the school. Mr. Hampton remembered Miss Chester, the most forceful library school instructor he had had, who had two favorite dicta for future school librarians: "Never, no matter how bad, change things the first year on a job. Live with them till you're sure that whatever you do is an improvement." And the other: "Get rid of potted plants! They're dust catchers and they're unhealthy. Libraries have the most attractive things in the world—books—for decoration, and they don't need foliage." What would Miss Chester say if his first move were to get rid of these well-tended plants?

Mr. Hampton had a feeling that there were more urgent decisions to make, but that he would have to learn more about the library and the school before he made them. He looked over the collection again and realized for the first time that there were no paperbacks included, except for one or two university press books of literary criticism which probably had not been available in any other format. He found dozens of neatly labeled files: circulation, query, order, desiderata, orders received, books on reserve. There were forms left from last year that asked teachers to submit the names of books they wanted to have placed on reserve for their classes. Miss Conrad had left these on a table in the workroom, along with a copy of the list of faculty members. In the left margin, beside several names, she had written "N.U." in light pencil. He recalled her telling him in the spring that she would leave him word about which teachers there was "no use" in trying to interest in the library. Jim Kimball's name was one of those marked "N.U."

As he stood in the workroom, Mr. Hampton heard someone come into the library as he walked out into the main reading room. Mr. Marlin was there, and with him, a young man who looked fresh from college.

"Jack, this is Derek Grafton, who'll be teaching industrial arts for us this year. He's had a couple of courses in educational media and when he asked to work part of his time in the instructional materials center, we decided this was a good way to give Len a break. Len's handled all the equipment and the boys who move it around for several years now, and he's taking on a new course in urban planning, so the timing seemed just right. And I've felt for some time that more could be done with all that equipment if someone could devote more time to it. I think Derek here could carry a half-time schedule in industrial arts and work with you the rest of the time. Could you use him?"

Watching young Mr. Grafton's eager face, Mr. Hampton was sure that a half-time assignment would be what he most wanted, and a sixth sense told him they could become a good team. He assured the principal that the arrangement would be fine with him, then added, "Maybe we could get together later in the morning to make some plans. But I wondered when the library clerk would be in?"

"Oh, a clerk. Didn't the office send you a memo about that? Maybe it's in the pile of magazines and other mail that's accumulated during the summer. Miss Conrad always liked to keep a clerk just for a year or so, so she usually hired one of our graduates who wanted to earn money for a year before going to college, or she sometimes caught one of the women in the neighborhood after her children were in school but before she wanted to start commuting farther to work. But the clerk last year was one of the best, and since we hated to lose her, I've hired her for the main office. Her name's Betty Jane Omak. I'll send her down about 10:30 to show you any things you may not be able to lay hands on right away. And you can let her know when you'd like to interview some of the people on our list. We always have applicants for the jobs in the cafeteria, and one of them may be the kind of person you could use. Okay?"

"Sure, that's fine, Mr. Marlin," Mr. Hampton answered, as he wondered whether it was or not. "And it's all right to plan to use student volunteers for some of the other clerical work, once school starts?"

"Yes. That's what Miss Conrad always did. She was never interested in having any of the students we have in the self-help programs. They do part-time work around the school, cleaning, assisting in the office, that sort of thing. But because they're from poverty families, Miss Conrad thought they probably didn't have the background to work well in the library. Would you like to try some of them? I'm sure we have the funds to swing it if you're interested."

Mr. Hampton was just ready to say that of course he'd be interested when the telephone rang. It was the secretary in the office, asking Mr. Marlin to come right back to the office to greet the district's new director of curriculum, who had just dropped in.

He motioned to Mr. Hampton to walk back to the office with him. As they went down the corridor, Mr. Marlin said, "I'm sure you're not going to be another Miss Conrad, and I don't especially want you to be. It seems to me that with young Grafton there, you should be able to start fresh and perhaps make this library mean something to the school. I'll back you in whatever makes sense, but I won't go out on any limbs for you. If you want something, you may have to explain to me what it is, and give me enough information so I can talk it through the superintendent or whoever else may question it. I see this year, with lots of new faculty members, as a year of great problems or great promise. I don't mean to sound like a commencement speaker, but I hope you'll help with the problems. We'll always have to talk on the run like this, but that doesn't have to mean we can't communicate. You can push me into that." He said the last words as he reached the door of his office. The next instant, he was greeting the curriculum director. He introduced the man, Everett Gold, to Mr. Hampton, who was not impressed by his appearance or his weak handshake.

"Hampton, mm, yes, you're the new librarian, aren't you?" Mr. Gold said. "You're not in my bailiwick, but I'm always interested in libraries. They're the heart of the school, all right. Like to see your library sometime, but not today. I'm here to drop in on the meeting of the academic department heads, but I'll be back, I'm sure."

This was the first Mr. Hampton had heard of a meeting of the "academic department heads." It had not been on his schedule, and he wondered why. But as the two men went into the principal's office, an attractive young woman came over from one of the desks in the main office. She introduced herself as Miss Omak.

Miss Omak walked back to the library with him, telling him how much she was enjoying the office work, which she thought was not tedious at all, marveling at the fact that a young man like him was a librarian, assuring him she had liked Miss Conrad very much. She also seemed to like the look of Mr. Grafton, who had stayed in the library and was just looking up from an open drawer of filmstrips as they entered the room. As the three of them sat down around one of the reading tables near the door, Mr. Grafton said, "Hey, this is quite a filmstrip collection. A lot of it is old and out of date, of course. Funny thing about librarians, they always want things to be up to date, but they never like to throw out stuff that's so old it's inaccurate. Would you like me to go through these now, before any of them go out? And while I'm at it, I could rearrange them. They're filed by Dewey numbers, and that means a lot of lost space in the drawers. You agree they should be in order just by numbers as they come in, don't you?"

Mr. Hampton sensed that in those comments, Mr. Grafton had revealed himself—his enthusiasm, his biases, his background, his eagerness to please and to get agreement and approval. For the time being, Mr. Hampton felt he could only hope to encourage the eagerness and channel the energy. Right now, his own thoughts were on the meeting of academic department heads that was opening without him. Perhaps he could just walk in to it, explain later to Mr. Marlin why he thought he belonged there. But with Miss Omak and Mr. Grafton both here in the library, perhaps he should use this time to sort out the past and the future of this library. Both were looking at him expectantly. He would be seeing them often, but although he might see the principal much less frequently, he sensed Mr. Marlin's interest and hoped he could continue to keep up the communication that seemed to have the prospect of being open and direct.

• • • • •

In Mr. Hampton's place, what priorities would you set for the next hour? For the next week? For the year?

What means of communication with Mr. Marlin do you think would be most effective for Mr. Hampton to use?

How might responsibilities for various tasks be assigned by Mr. Hampton?

What might he request from Mr. Marlin first? With what priority? With what rationale?

13.
Schedule for
a Student Librarian
· · · · · · · · · · · · · ·

In the five years since she had completed a master's degree at Wilson University, Martha Drexel had kept in fairly good touch with her former teachers, classmates, and others. She had not returned to the campus, but occasionally, at a state or national library meeting, she attended some social gathering of alumni, at which the dean usually gave a short talk, intended to assure them that Wilson was maintaining its high academic standards and its interest in them, as well as its need for their contributions. She considered herself a loyal alumna, and she was, in general, proud of the education in library science which she had received there. She was accordingly pleased and interested to receive a letter at school one day, inviting her to attend a meeting on the university campus about the program of education for students who would be responsible for school media centers. The meeting was to be held on a school day, so a copy of the letter of invitation had been sent to her principal, Mr. Branson, and a carbon of the letter sent to him was included with her own letter. Both the invitation and the letter to the principal stressed the importance of the invitation, and she was sure Mr. Branson would encourage her to go.

In the faculty lunch room, when the principal seated himself next to her that day, he said, "Well, I see they're rounding up the old grads among the librarians, too. I'd forgotten you'd gone to Wilson, but I hope you're planning to go for this meeting."

"Yes, I'd like to," Martha answered, "and I take it you're encouraging me to go. So that's all it takes, I guess. I wonder what's going on there."

"Oh, I think it's probably the next step in this big change in professional education that the state's been pushing for. You know, Mr. Glens went to a meeting of counselors a few weeks ago, and I think Hal Lead had to beg off from one for physical education teachers a few weeks back, because he was going to the regionals with the track team."

"I guess I hadn't paid much attention. What was that all about?"

Other teachers at the table had gradually stopped their conversations, and were listening now to what the principal had to say. This often happened when he joined a small group during the lunch hour. Mr. Branson leaned forward to include them all in his conversation.

"Well, it's an idea I really like. You know, we've had student teachers galore at this school, and everybody with a teaching certificate has been through some kind of experience like that, or, as they're calling it more often now, a practicum. But the state feels that there's a problem since so few students in the special fields, like counseling or librarianship, for instance, really get actual experiences in their specialties. So the state is putting a little pressure on the colleges and universities to offer this. And, since you're one of Wilson's leading graduates in school libraries, I suppose they have their eye on you perhaps to offer suggestions about the kinds of experience that would be good, or maybe even to have a student come and work with you."

"Say, that's right, Martha, you never have had a student librarian!" Jerry Champaign spoke up. "Here I am, run ragged with student teachers two or three months every year, and you've never had one. I wish I'd thought of this myself!" He was teasing, and Martha Drexel smiled at him. She was thinking that the experience should be interesting, if that were, in fact, what the invitation to Wilson was all about. She had many ideas of her own about the value of working under a more experienced librarian. She had often regretted the fact that she had come straight from her own classes into this high school, where the media program had grown under her leadership so that she was now assisted by another librarian and two aides, without having had the experience, herself, of working under someone else's supervision.

"Is there a lot of red tape about this?" she asked.

"Oh, I think not. After all, we've had student teachers here for some time, and it seems to me this would just be an extension of that program. There might be a few things to iron out, but it shouldn't be too difficult." Mr. Branson was obviously pleased that the school might be selected to have a student librarian, and Martha looked forward to learning more about the program, if that was, in fact, the purpose of the meeting at Wilson.

When she arrived in the conference room on the meeting day, Miss Drexel recognized most of the dozen or so people already there. She knew some of them from her work in the state professional association, and one or two of the others were familiar from her student days at Wilson. The group was engaging in casual conversation, and Dr. Lebanon, the faculty member present, introduced himself or greeted each person to arrive. Promptly at nine, he raised his voice and said, "Good morning, all of you. There are two or three more to come, but I believe we may start. I suppose most of you have guessed why we have asked you to come."

Dr. Lebanon went on to say that Wilson was now recognizing the need, as expressed by its students, as well as the virtual demand by the state board of certification, for more practical experience in school media centers before students completed their classwork. He said that the lack of such experience was often mentioned as a handicap by alumni, but that until recently the university or, more precisely, the library science program, had not seen any possibility of offering that kind of experience. He pointed out that he, who was primarily responsible for the program for school librarians, had been dubious about setting up such a plan until there were a number of good library programs in schools in the area. In the beginning, the program would be limited to only a dozen or so students— not necessarily the best students, he said, but those who might benefit the most from such experience, and those who were able, on somewhat short notice, to allow time for a six-week practicum. It was obvious, he said, that the reason the librarians present had been invited today was that they were considered the best possibilities to serve as the "master librarians" for this first group. He made it very clear that the university and the school district would work out details of the arrangement, but said that since the plan was a new one, they wanted to have the best background on all sides, and therefore, he had thought that a meeting of those who might be "master librarians" was important. Whether or not they later had students assigned to their schools, he said, he was interested in getting their reactions to the program and their ideas about how it could best be carried out.

It was clear that the group as a whole, like Martha Drexel, had had some idea of what might be forthcoming, for they burst into spontaneous discussion when Dr. Lebanon paused. Tom Barnard, who was accustomed to being spokesman or chairman in many groups, said he was sure he was speaking for the others when he thanked Dr. Lebanon for his confidence in them. He was sure his school would wish to participate, but on the drive over, he had been talking with Georgia May, and they were wondering how much they could take for granted that these kids knew.

Before Dr. Lebanon could reply, Ada Clayton spoke up. "Well, one think I know for sure," she said, "whatever they know now, it's more than we did at the same stage of the game. You know, Dr. Lebanon, I have Sharon Perry as an assistant this year, and if she's an example of your recent graduates, she's a good one. But I have even heard her say that she'd like to have had some kind of practical experience before she started out. I think it would have helped to give her confidence, more than anything. She certainly does an excellent job without it."

"Now, that's the sort of thing we like to hear about our graduates!" Dr. Lebanon remarked appreciatively. "I wish I could promise you that all our students were of her quality. They aren't—they couldn't be. In fact, a statistic that might surprise you is that we have learned, in a recent survey, that one out of five of our graduates who earn school library certificates does not even work in school libraries. Sometimes, that's because they've had their eyes on some other area of specialization, sometimes it's because they marry and perhaps never work at all, but I'm afraid sometimes it's because they simply cannot cope with the prospect of working on their own so much, when they have not had practical experience. It's my guess that, as this program develops, we will find, as other departments have found in student teaching experiences, that students will 'wash themselves out,' in a sense, and realize, on this short-term assignment, that this is not the right place for them. When that happens, it is possible that you who will be helping us will also be helping to prevent much misery and many problems which might otherwise arise more seriously later."

Martha Drexel was interested both in the statistic he had quoted and in his attitude. She listened intently to all the discussions of the day, and she became more and more aware of the responsibility that was to be hers. It was made clear that students were not to be used for clerical routines, but that, since their work was to be as school media personnel, they were to be given experience most like what they would eventually do if they were to come to work after graduation. Inevitably, someone pointed out that much clerical or technical work was impossible to avoid, and that everyone took a share in it in most of the schools. Dr. Lebanon held up his hand as though to fend off an attack.

"I understand the problem," he said. "We realize that emergencies arise, and that all of you probably spend some time on work that doesn't demand your most professional skills. We are not asking you to spare or to spoil these students, but rather, to give them experience with the whole spectrum of your responsibilities. I suppose the best thing would be to have you assign them tasks that you wish you might have done at a time when you could have benefited from the supervision of someone else. In fact, I'd be interested to know how many of you have ever worked in school libraries under someone else's direction."

Two hands went up, somewhat tentatively. Helen Park had spent her first years as librarian at City Polytechnic, a large school in those days, which boasted two librarians long before most of the other schools in the area had such staff. And Dal Erie had been the assistant at the university's own library school until the head librarian had retired.

"There's something else to consider, and you may be going to bring it up, Dr. Lebanon," Tom Barnard said. "Most of us have picked up information about media programs in a dozen different ways, and we've really converted our school libraries into media centers, but these kids who'll be coming to us will have gotten, if I understand it correctly, a lot of background in all kinds of media already. That puts them in a pretty different position from us."

"That's true, Tom," Dr. Lebanon agreed. "In fact, one of the things we hope to learn from this is how our program for educating directors of media centers can be improved. We hope to get that kind of information not only from the students after their six weeks with you, but from you, in your comments about them."

"What kind of comments should we be prepared to make?" Dal Erie asked.

"There would be just one formal statement at the end, pretty much like a recommendation form, such as you might fill out if you were a reference for someone applying for a position. There's a copy of it in these folders we have for you. Of course, if there should be any problem, any question of your not recommending the student for certification, we would want you to alert us to that within, say, the first three weeks of the assignment. And, as I've explained, a supervisor from this campus will be visiting you during that time. With our limited staff, and with the geographic spread we will have, it will not be possible for that supervisor to be a member of our faculty in librarianship, but it will be someone who's had experience in supervising student teachers in other areas."

As she returned home from the day on the university campus, Martha

Drexel found herself stimulated by the discussions and by the prospect of having a student assigned to her school. As she had expected, the arrangements were handled quickly and efficiently, and Mr. Branson gave his wholehearted support to the plan. It was agreed that a student would report to the school the second week after spring vacation. A sheet of information about the student arrived with six other sheets from Wilson for students who would be working in other departments. The librarian, Pamela Baker, was the wife of another student teacher, who was assigned to Mr. Champaign in the English department. On the Friday before the student teachers were to arrive, Martha Drexel chuckled as she and Betty Tampa, one of the aides, surveyed the library just before they closed for the afternoon.

"I feel just the way I do when I wash all the dishes in the sink before my cleaning woman comes. I guess it's silly to have made this extra effort to make everything look especially neat and cleaned up, but I do want Mrs. Baker to like it here, and I want things to be right for her." Martha looked at the suite, which was now twice the size it had been when she first came to the school. Six chairs were at each table. The drapes, half drawn, added the warmth she had longed for during the first three years. The current periodicals, for once, were straight on the shelves, and she and Betty had hastily straightened the books also. They had cleared the top of the circulation desk, and had even added a small nameplate, "Mrs. Baker," to the desk where the librarians worked while responsible for service to students. The carrels, most of them equipped with pasteboard screens for individual viewing, were in order, and that included the two where microfilm readers stood under gray dustcovers. She was proud of this library, not only of what it was, but of what it had grown from.

The following Monday, when Martha Drexel arrived at school early, there was a small sports car already in the parking lot. When she opened her car door, a young couple stepped out of the other car. She greeted them and introduced herself. They were Mr. and Mrs. Baker, all right, and they followed her into the building, where the custodian was the only other person in sight.

They proceeded to the library, with Mr. Baker doing most of the talking. She watched their faces as she switched on the lights, and they looked appraisingly at the suite.

"A lot better than you expected, isn't it, Pam?" Mr. Baker asked.

"Oh, yes, I think this will be fine."

In spite of the enthusiasm and relief in Mrs. Baker's voice, Martha

Drexel was disappointed. What had she been expecting? As though he had read her mind, Mr. Baker said, "You know, we took that future teachers' tour over the spring vacation, and the more we saw of all those great library setups, with dial-access computer hookups, media centers with closed-circuit T.V., and all that stuff, the more depressed Pam became because we knew there wasn't anything like that here."

"Well, I guess we're no showplace, but we are proud of what we have," Miss Drexel said, wondering whether she sounded defensive.

"Oh, and you should be," Pam Baker said. "I've heard some good things about your program here."

"Well, that's nice to know. Was that how you happened to choose us? Or did you have a choice?"

"Yes, we could indicate our top three, at least. And when Bill decided he wanted to teach under Mr. Champaign here, I put this down as my first choice. It's obviously cheaper and easier if we can do our student teaching together. I'm just glad this worked out for us."

Martha Drexel showed them around, then directed them to the conference room near the main office, where student teachers were to have a brief orientation. She felt her own enthusiasm ebbing, although the Bakers were pleasant and interested in all she pointed out.

Through the first week, Miss Drexel continued with the general plan she had had in mind. She suggested that Mrs. Baker follow her through an entire day, thinking she would get a feeling, in that way, of the variety of tasks she performed. As she pointed out, even the interruptions were a part of the job, and one simply had to cope with them. Since the first day was cut short by the orientation session for the student teachers, she had extended this "shadowing," as she called it, to a second day. On the third day, Mrs. Baker followed the same plan with the assistant librarian, and on the next two days, with the two aides. Miss Drexel realized by the end of the week that "shadowing" someone who was typing or checking out books at a desk or even putting up a bulletin board could give one the feeling of being a fifth wheel, so she set up a schedule for the following week that would have Mrs. Baker alone on the desk much of the time, working with student requests. As the week began, Mrs. Baker accepted the assignment with little reaction, and she helped when students approached her. The problem was that students tended to seek out Miss Drexel, the assistant librarian, or even the aides, whom they recognized. When they did so, Mrs. Baker went on with her reading of professional journals. Miss Drexel had told her that when on the desk, in order to look available to students, she and the assistant usually read, rather than try to work on something which would have to be interrupted frequently. She felt that students felt freer to approach someone reading than someone working with cards, order slips, and that sort of thing. Mrs. Baker had responded enthusiastically, saying that when she returned to the university, she would have her final exams to face, and much of the material in recent journals would probably be related to what she should know. The difficulty was that she appeared to be so absorbed that students did not tend to approach her, and also that they, of course, knew the rest of the staff.

Once again, Miss Drexel felt the need for a change of tactics. She suggested that Mrs. Baker visit a few classrooms where she could observe the kinds of use being made of materials or perhaps see teachers assigning work to groups who would later come to the media center to get the supplies they needed. What Miss Drexel hoped was that Mrs. Baker would have the opportunity she often wished for herself, of seeing how classroom instruction related to what was needed in the library, and also that she would become known to both teachers and students so that she could work more effectively with them.

On Friday of that week, when Miss Drexel flipped her desk calendar to the following Monday, she was appalled to realize the supervisor from the university would be in the library that Monday afternoon. The supervisor was an instructor in English education, one whom she did not know, but she looked forward to the opportunity of sharing with him some of her concerns. She had had in mind that the third week of Mrs. Baker's stay should be devoted more to the library responsibilities, such as planning for the budget, setting up dates for film loans from the university and other sources, and rechecking on some dates she had made with teachers for introduction of reference materials to their students. She wanted to turn one of those dates over to Mrs. Baker, but as the time drew near, she realized she was quite unsure whether the student librarian, who was placid and pleasant, would really be capable of the initiative and effort that would have to go into this kind of planning.

When Monday afternoon arrived and the supervisor from the university appeared in the library, Miss Drexel herself was scarcely prepared for the turn that events took. Dr. Monmouth introduced himself, toured the library with Miss Drexel, spoke briefly to Mrs. Baker, and then asked to talk with Miss Drexel. She was grateful for this opportunity to present some of her concerns, but before she could begin, he opened the conversation by saying: "Of course, this is a new program in librarianship, Miss Drexel, but I want you to know that I'm deeply interested in it, and I've discussed it fairly thoroughly with Dr. Lebanon. I'd hoped to find it would bring out the students' initiative, and be personally rewarding to them, as student teaching typically is in other areas, but I'm distressed to learn that you've been using Mrs. Baker more as an assistant with no specific responsibilities, and, last week, as a visitor to classrooms. I'm sure we can work this out, but—"

"I suppose this is something you must have heard since coming here. From Mr. Baker, I suppose?"

"Frankly, yes. I observed him this morning, and a fine young teacher he is. At lunch, we talked about his wife's disappointment here, and when Jerry Champaign mentioned that you'd never had a student librarian here before, I realized there was probably a good deal we could do in the short time left to straighten things out. Mr. Baker tells me his wife has lesson plans for library skills instruction, for example, but that she's had no opportunity to use them here. Now we can—"

"I'm sorry. I've not been told about any of the things she has prepared or what she has in mind. But we can't just manufacture a class for her to teach library skills to. That would be artificial, and—"

Martha Drexel was surprised to hear her own voice shaking, either in anger or embarrassment. She began to realize that through all the days when she had so meekly followed along with the schedule of the library, Mrs. Baker evidently had been complaining to her husband about the experience she was getting. Why had she not spoken to Miss Drexel herself? She also realized that her own embarrassment came, in part, from something she had not realized thoroughly before. Whatever happened, with this new kind of assignment of student librarians, the bad as well as the good, would reflect on her as well as on the student.

• • • • •

Identify preparations or actions Miss Drexel might have utilized to avert the criticism she is receiving.

If some of the problems which are emerging here are attributable to the way the program for student librarians is set up and administered, identify them, and indicate how they might have been avoided or solved.

What is your assessment of Mrs. Baker's attitudes and actions in this situation?

14.
The Architect
Comes to School

· · · · · · · · · · ·

"Until I came to this school, I would not have believed it," Sybil Rehoboth said at lunch. "As a matter of fact, I didn't believe it when they told me about it—seven-foot shelving in an elementary school materials center! Chairs and tables enough even for your class, which is the largest, plus our listening center, and it's not too bad. Of course, kids can't get around easily when a class is there, but it works. And I wouldn't have thought it possible."

"Take some credit for yourself," Grace Waldwick said. "You've made the place mean something to the kids, so they're willing to climb around like monkeys to get what they want from those high shelves, and you've fixed it so the younger ones can get what they need on the lower shelves. It wouldn't work every place, but I'm glad it does here, because I couldn't teach now, without the kind of center you've developed."

"Well, I guess that's twisting a compliment out of you," Mrs. Rehoboth said with a chuckle. "But it now looks as though it may not be that way much longer. The architect who's going to work on the new wing is coming in today, and Mr. Bozeman has asked me to meet with him in his office after three o'clock. That's why I'm armed with all this." She held up a manila folder bulging with papers.

"What is all that?"

"I've gone back over the last several years, to see what's been written about planning materials centers or libraries. And fortunately, I've always kept sketches, sort of, of the places I've visited myself, when I've gone to conferences, for instance.

"May I see some?"

"Of course." Mrs. Rehoboth opened the folder and pulled out a few articles. They described new libraries, most of them including a floor plan, and sometimes a photograph of the room in use. Miss Waldwick picked one up. "Say, this is a honey! It looks like a book palace! Have you seen it?"

"Let me see it. Oh, yes, I have. It has some features I like, but it's on two levels. That pretty little stairway may look like a palace staircase to you, but when I look at it, I wonder who's going to shelve materials on the upper level, who's going to keep an eye on the kids up there, and even how the materials are going to get up there."

"Is the stairway the only way up?"

"Yes. Actually, when I visited, they told us a sad story. The center had been planned to have a dumbwaiter for books, but they'd measured wrong for it, and finally had to leave it out. They wound up putting only the teachers' professional materials up there, because it just didn't work with kids going up and down, and as a result, they had hardly any more really usable space than they'd had in the old library."

"I can see how that would happen. But still, I think it has features that would be great for us. Like those big wall bulletin boards."

"Oh, they were attractive, all right. You know, I love to fix bulletin boards, and I like to use them for student work, too. In the past two years, since Miss Bremerton has been teaching art, we've had some wonderful things to put up. But I keep thinking of two things—I won't be here forever, though it may seem like it, and also, the art program may not always lend itself to this. The other thing is, when you're working with a budget like ours, you have to look at that wall space and figure that there are hundreds of books and other materials that cannot be shelved because of the use of walls for displays and bulletin boards. I think we'll have to keep that sort of thing to a minimum."

"There certainly is a lot to this, isn't there? I'm glad it's your job, not mine. But you will have room to make a real media center, won't you? We won't have to go running all over the building to closets for equipment, the way we do now?"

"Oh, I think that's one thing we're all agreed on. This will be a really centralized collection. And one of the features I'm sure we're going to have, because Mr. Bozeman is, if anything, more enthusiastic than I am, is plenty of carrels for the children for studying, listening, viewing, all that."

A few minutes before three that afternoon, Mr. Bozeman entered the library with a visitor who turned out to be Norman Trenton, the architect. The two men watched the children who had come on their own to use the library during the last period of the day, when no class was scheduled. Mr. Bozeman always delighted in pointing out to visitors the number of film-strips and filmstrip projectors which circulated overnight. These were re-served up to one week in advance, and when the six projectors were taken, the next children who asked were allowed to take previewers. The smaller children, who could not have carried a projector home, also took previewers. The system had been in operation for several years, and both the principal and the librarian were proud to point out that not a filmstrip had been lost during that time, not a projector or previewer damaged. That was a better record than had been set for the same media loaned to classrooms during the school day.

The architect walked around the center by himself for a few minutes, after the school secretary had summoned Mr. Bozeman back to the office. Mrs. Rehoboth, busy talking with children, noticed that he looked care-fully over the listening center, reached up to the top of the high shelves, and watched carefully as children rolled little two-step stools back and forth to get what they wanted from top shelves. When Mr. Trenton chatted with Mrs. Longmeadow at the charging desk, he was looking carefully at the card files, drawers, pencils, and other things she was using as she worked. Mrs. Rehoboth was pleased to see how interested the architect appeared to be in the present pattern of use of the center.

When the three of them met a few minutes later in Mr. Bozeman's office, the principal began by saying that Stan De Kalb, the director for media in the school district, would probably come, but had suggested that they not wait for him. Mr. Bozeman spoke with his usual enthusiasm as he leaned forward on his desk and looked at the architect.

"Well, what do you think of our materials center? We're proud of it, but we know we have a long way to go, and we're glad to have you to help us."

"Yes, and I'm glad to be working here, too. It does seem that any-thing we come up with, would be an improvement over what you have now. It's a far cry from the school where my kids go. Your center is very active by comparison, but you don't have half the space or many of the features I'd have thought necessary."

"Well, there'll be no holding us when we get into that new wing, I can tell you," the principal said expansively.

"Okay, let's start with that. There's one thing we don't need to settle today, but I think we have to consider. That is, one option in the planning would be for the center not to be moved into the new wing. With the space that will be released by moving classrooms into the new wing, and even allowing for the growth factor, we could enlarge the present center and, I think, make it extremely attractive."

"But I thought that after all these years in that crowded little room, we'd be sure to get into the new wing!" Mrs. Rehoboth's distress sounded in her voice.

"You understand I'm talking about a greatly enlarged library, but with the same location in the building you have now. And it seems to me that's a choice location. When they built school buildings in the late 1920s, when this one was built, they did some wild things. The thing of having the media center on the second floor, just above the front door, has meant that it is really one of the most accessible locations in the school. It wouldn't be the same in the new wing. Since we can only build to the west and on one level, the library would be a long way, for instance, from the classrooms down the east side of the building on the second floor."

"Yes, of course, but if it stays where it is, it will be a long way from the classrooms in the new wing."

"Ah! But with those, we'll be building more closets, more built-in shelves in every classroom. They can keep materials there overnight or on whatever terms are convenient for you and for the classes and teachers there. They'll be geared to the problems in distance. There's no way that the present classrooms could be changed to that—at least, not in line with the present budget. Actually, I like the idea of keeping the center in the old part of the building. Even as crowded as it is, it has a certain charm, and I rather doubt that the new classrooms will have that same charm. But anyway, this is not something we have to decide today. The educational specifications would probably be the same whatever the location. Do you have yours?"

"Oh, yes." Mrs. Rehoboth pulled out a typed sheet from her folder and handed it to the architect. "This is what we need. You'll see that the first column is the space as it's used now, and the second column shows what we really need and could use." She looked at the principal. "You have a copy of this somewhere," she said. "It's what I gave you when we first began to discuss this."

The architect seemed puzzled. "Now let me see," he said thoughtfully. "This list is all in square feet, and it looks as though you've multiplied everything about two and a half times and put that figure down in the second column."

"Yes, that's about right," said Mrs. Rehoboth. "Everything except the work room. Now that most of our materials come processed, I don't see a need for as much space as that, so we're combining it with production space, where teachers can bring materials and, depending on what the traffic will bear, have us reproduce them or reproduce them themselves."

"I'm sorry, Mrs. Rehoboth, but I find this a very difficult way to work. It seems to me it is the educational specifications that should determine the size of various areas, and if you've developed those, you've left them out of this sheet you've prepared." Noticing her crestfallen look, Mr. Trenton went on. "There's no reason why we can't prepare such a sheet now. This is the sort of thing I have in mind." From his briefcase, he pulled out a sheet with several large circles, smaller ones within or touching the circles, and neatly labeled areas marked off for various activities. "This happens to be for the Home Economics suite at the county high school," he said. "You see, this tells us the relationship between the dining area and the kitchen, the different components of the dressmaking and tailoring area, and where the conventional classroom should be in relation to the rest of it. This is what we need here."

Mr. Trenton drew a large circle on the oversize pad of paper he had taken from his briefcase. "Now, let's say this is the center as a whole," he said. "What are the most important activities we should identify first?"

"Well, the listening center," Mrs. Rehoboth began.

"We can put that down," Mr. Trenton said without looking up. He drew a rather small circle near the edge of the large one. "But you may want to keep in mind the possibility of discarding that listening center in favor of a general area for individual viewing and listening. For that matter, since Mr. Bozeman here has already been talking to me about having carrels, it seems to me that a listening center of the kind you presently have, with jacks and two sections, one for tape and one for disc recordings, will just simply be outmoded."

"How about that?" Mr. Bozeman exclaimed. "Here, it's the newest thing we have, what we're proudest of, and you sit there and tell us we may not have it in the new center, whether we move to the new wing or not. I think I see what you're driving at, but I'm going to need to think this over."

Embarrassed at having seemed so unknowing about the kinds of specifications that would have been helpful to the architect, Mrs. Rehoboth opened the folder and spread some of the articles out on the desk.

"You can see we've been hoping and dreaming for a long time, and I've been saving things of interest. These are the articles. Some of the other things are sketches I made of places, with notes about what seemed good, and what didn't. I also found that most of the librarians who showed me their centers were anxious to point out what the problems were with the design, and I've made note of them. This one, for instance, is a so-called open library. It's in a second-floor corridor of a building, and it really takes up the whole center of the building, extending across the corridors. It was entirely carpeted; for that matter, the whole school was. It was a small school, of course, but it had its problems."

"Such as?" the architect prompted.

"Such as no ventilation. I can still remember how stuffy the place was. You see, it was planned that the building would have air conditioning, but they ran out of money, and couldn't put it in, so there's this library with two narrow slit windows on either side, some kind of a ventilator up near the ceiling, and all the classrooms shutting it off from the outside. I don't know how the librarian stood it."

"Yes, I can imagine," Mr. Trenton said. "I guess I should tell you before you find out on your own, that's one of my designs. It's the Millersville School, isn't it?"

"Yes," said Mrs. Rehoboth. "Oh, I am sorry. I didn't mean to pick at one of your schools right off like that. I never even thought to ask who the architect was."

"You can't hurt my feelings. I'm just glad they don't advertise that I did it. The plan is really a very promising one, and I think we'll try the idea again somewhere, in another small school like that, but I think I'll make the district sign a bond that they will install air conditioning. When I think of the problems of light control, for example, that we had to lick with that arrangement, so that kids could be viewing films while classes were going back and forth in the corridors, and then to have the whole thing blown by running out of money for air conditioning, it really makes me sick." He turned the plan so Mr. Bozeman could see it. "There you are— a room cut in three pieces, with the corridors leaving about one fourth on each side between corridor and outside wall, and the central core being the half in the middle."

"There's something else," Mrs. Rehoboth spoke up. "I think I run a fairly relaxed kind of library, but there's absolutely no control in a center like that one! Kids and teachers could haul off books by the dozens, it seems to me, and no one would be the wiser. I'll have to admit, the librarian said it was no great problem."

Mr. Trenton answered, "I'm glad to hear that. They had their qualms at the school, I know, but they decided to try it. If necessary they could have put a partition down the center, so that the inner core could be locked up. But I'm glad it's working out so well. That's one problem we architects have—we seldom have the opportunity of seeing what really happens in operation. And a lot of this is a gamble."

"Here I am, fifteen minutes late, and you're already gambling!" Mr. De Kalb spoke from the doorway. He greeted everyone and sat down. "Now, what have I missed?"

"Oh, I was just saying that a lot of planning is gambling, in a sense," Mr. Trenton repeated.

"True," said De Kalb, "and it's especially appropriate to discuss that here. You've heard, haven't you, that we're now thinking about enlarging the present center instead of moving you into the new wing?" He had directed his question toward Mr. Bozeman and Mrs. Rehoboth. The two of them nodded. "There'd be some disadvantages, but I think it may be hard for you to envision just how great your present location could be, if it were adequate in terms of space. We could knock out—let's see, is it all but one of the walls, Norman?"

"Yes. The one on the east would have to stay. It's a load-bearing wall. We could cut a door through it, of course. But all told, the library could be expanded to three times its present size. And, of course, it would be a great financial saving."

"But if you're doing this at least partly because of budget, isn't it possible that we could be like the people who didn't get their air-conditioning, and end up without any enlargement at all?"

"Oh, that's unlikely, Sybil," said Stan De Kalb. "It's obvious you need space, and you're high priority. In any case, you know the old story —classrooms always come first. But if there were any problems about money, enlarged enrollments, or anything else in the new wing, the center would have to be the first part to be eliminated. So whatever happens, you'll be far ahead of where you are now."

"That's a big help," Mrs. Rehoboth said tartly.

"As I see it, our work at this stage of planning should be to identify the kinds of activities or services we'll want to provide in the new center. You've provided a lot of them already, of course, under very difficult conditions, but now we should establish priorities, I think. And I'd suggest doing it by type of audience first. That is, will we want space for whole classes to be able to sit together in the center, will we want more individual space like carrels—and I know they're dear to your heart, Mr. Bozeman—and how much of it will we wish to keep adaptable, with the idea that we can't outguess kids, or for that matter, developments in media? We should keep reminding ourselves of that. For instance, I can recall not very long ago when every elementary librarian in this county would have screamed if teachers did not accompany their classes to the library, at least with some regularity. Now, with schedules like yours, Sybil, it's rare for a teacher to bring a whole class. And this has its effect on the facility, too."

"I think I see what you mean, Mr. De Kalb," Mrs. Rehoboth said. "You're talking about kinds of users, and Mr. Trenton is talking about kinds of use. I'm not sure I see how to plan for both of them, or to prepare those circles with them in mind."

Mr. Trenton chuckled. "You don't have to do it graphically, Mrs. Rehoboth. If you'd be more comfortable, tell us in a few paragraphs what you want to have happen in the new center, regardless of its location. But I think we all need to stand back from what is presently going on in this center, and decide which of those things we want to go on in the new one, and which things that may never have been tried we want included, and what we may want left out altogether. For example, I assume you don't think it's essential for kids to have to climb up to get the books they want?"

"Heavens, no!" Mrs. Rehoboth exclaimed.

"But on the other hand," Mr. De Kalb broke in, "the days when we could build elementary libraries with all low shelving, say forty-eight inch, are gone. We just cannot afford that kind of floor space. And I've just about decided that one depth of shelf should be standard."

"But they're all adjustable—or at least, would be in a new center, wouldn't they?" Mrs. Rehoboth asked.

"Oh, I don't mean the height. Of course, that will be adjustable. I mean the depth. You know, the centers built like this one have about three different depths, and it can mean you can't move your reference section or, for that matter, some of the sections like art, where there are quite a few large books, without having to shift shelves."

"Yes, I see that. Goodness, there is a lot I hadn't thought of!"

Mr. Bozeman looked at his watch and spoke. "I think we don't have much longer for this, and, frankly, I'm sorry we seem to have accomplished so little today. I realize that not all architects are as interested as you, Mr. Trenton, in getting insights from the people in the school, but does it always go so slowly?"

"I think our next session will go much more quickly. And I'm not planning on a series of meetings. Perhaps two or three half-hour sessions altogether. After all, there are other areas to go in the new wing, and, for that matter, other jobs. But I'd suggest that you two, who are here in the school, take this sheet to use in preparing some kind of specifications for our next meeting. You'll only need to refer to the top few items, I think. It's a projection of what will be in the new building with the new wing, compared with what's here now."

Mrs. Rehoboth felt as though she were receiving a homework assignment. The information was typed on the architect's letterhead stationery, and she read:

"This elementary school, completed in 1928, currently enrolls 400 children. In addition to eighteen classrooms on two floors, there are a principal's office, nurse's office, materials center, auditorium used for community activities as well as school programs, and space in the basement for indoor play, lunch room, and some temporary partitions for remedial classrooms.

"The materials center, on the second floor of present building, includes 1,000 square feet, with two areas partitioned at the side, one for work area for the librarian, the other for a small conference room. Wall shelving is seven feet high, and there are two counter-height shelving islands. Usual furnishings and equipment: thirty-four student chairs, including four at listening center.

"New wing is to house minimum of nine classrooms, since new housing in area indicates growth rate is increasing, and in next academic year, students will also be bussed in from western section of city. Enrollment expected to level at 600 in three years."

There was more to the report, but Mrs. Rehoboth was to work with this portion of it in preparing for the meeting the following week.

15.
The Case
of Ogden's Opportunity

· · · · · · · · · · · · · · · · · ·

Neil Ogden came to the Sloatsburg High School to develop the fairly adequate library, administered by Hedy Lewis, into a strong center for all media used in the school. Miss Lewis had often said that she was convinced of the value of a media center but unsure of her abilities as a leader in developing it, so she was delighted with his appointment as media coordinator. Mr. Ogden consulted with her frequently as the time for planning a new physical facility approached. He also discussed some of the possible program changes with Dolly Malone, whose experience in communications as a Wave had made her the logical choice from the faculty for a teacher to administer the slowly growing collection of equipment and materials such as films and recordings. Mrs. Malone had made it clear that when a new facility was planned, she looked forward to a full-time position in the center, where there would be more opportunity for local production of videotapes, graphic materials, and slides. In the three years she had been at the high school, she had done some of this sort of work for teachers in her own home in the evenings, and the group of teachers working with her and contributing ideas for transparencies they would like to make or to have made had become what Mr. Ogden considered the best nucleus for further development of an alert faculty making the most effective use of media.

The prospect of funding from a foundation spurred new interest in plans for the new center. Charles Malverne, a longtime Sloatsburg resident, had recently been named to the board of the foundation, and he approached the high school principal at a meeting to suggest that the high school develop some kind of proposal. "I've told those Wall Street lawyers on the board that it's high time they passed some money out to us here in the midwest. They say they're willing, but it's hard to get a good proposal from an area like ours. Your school, maybe, doesn't have the staff to come up with any way-out ideas, or the money to go running back to New York to try them out on the board. But I can help out there, too. I'll put up, say, 1,000 dollars to get you started. That ought to pay to bring in somebody who can tell you what to do, or let you and some of the staff go see them, and it should be enough for some kind of preliminary drawings or sketches from an architect, for example, if your plan relates to building—just enough, of course, to give the general plan to the foundation. They're ready, willing, and able, as far as I can tell, but the first push has to come from here. You give me a statement of how you expect to use the thousand dollars, and I can get that piece of it going right away."

John Dobbs, the principal, was determined to make the most of Malverne's interest. This was the first gesture of this kind Mr. Malverne had ever made toward the high school, and it was possible it could lead to others.

The next morning, Mr. Dobbs sent a memorandum to all department chairmen, briefly outlining the possibility for extensive funding, but asking for immediate suggestions for use of the thousand dollars from Mr. Malverne. He did not mention Malverne's name, but he stressed the need for emphasis on innovative programs and use of the thousand dollars as a kind of bait for a more extensive proposal. Although he was accustomed to arranging for expenditures and requests for state and federal funds, he had not had the opportunity before to encourage such free-wheeling planning and suggestions. The superintendent, with whom he had discussed the matter that morning, had shared his enthusiasm.

"I'm glad this has come up, John," Superintendent Orchard had said. "That thousand dollars could start a lot of things, and I don't just mean the larger grant from the foundation. How we spend it will tell Charles Malverne what we think is important, and may do us a world of good in this town for that reason alone. And it gives you a chance to find out who on your staff has ideas and who is willing to take the time to lay them out for you. Keep me informed."

Aware of this prospect for staff development, Mr. Dobbs waited for the replies from department heads with considerable interest. Several were predictable: the head of the social studies department responded that his heavy class load did not permit him to engage in unrealistic games on the chance of getting more money; the science department head stapled a rejected request for laboratory equipment to Mr. Dobbs' memo and returned it, noting that the needed equipment could be the start for a more extensive program in the sciences which would require a large foundation grant for real development; a third department head asked for funds for three teachers to attend their national professional meeting on the west coast, where they might get ideas for use of more funds. As he looked over these and other replies, Mr. Dobbs felt there was really no contest. Neil Ogden seemed to have been waiting for just such an opportunity. His memorandum read:

When the projected bond issue passes, the school district will be ready to proceed with plans for the addition to the high school. The fact that classrooms and laboratories were added in the last addition with no increase in the library facility gives some idea of the desperate need for that facility's expansion. However, enlargement of space is not enough. This is the time to plan for a full program of media services for this high school. The enrollment projection in three years' time is 2,000 students. We should be thinking in terms of a facility providing for storage and access to all instructional materials. The absolute minimum for which we should plan is 40,000 square feet. Even this is a conservative figure, according to the 1969 *Standards for School Media Programs.*

But in my experience I have seen enough poorly-used facilities to be wary of planning in these early stages without adequate staff information and support. The prospect of this thousand dollars means we might invite to a faculty meeting a name speaker who could impress on the faculty what the prospects are for improvement of instruction by good use of materials. If we can tie in a date with the speaker's attendance at some other conference, we could probably provide expenses and honorarium for 300 dollars, and also get the benefit of the speaker's visit to evaluate and comment on our present program.

As a follow-up to this, Mrs. Malone, Miss Lewis and I could travel to several high schools that have good new facilities. These may not all have good or innovative programs, but they are accessible for us, and each of us could travel with perhaps two other faculty members, so we would really use the time of driving back and forth to think out and plan what we want for ourselves. We could learn as much from these schools' mistakes in planning as from their successes. I am listing below eight or nine of these in three different areas. Since each area is within 200 miles of Sloatsburg, overnight trips should be sufficient and, based on three persons for each trip, and keeping expenses down, we should be able to make these group trips for one hundred dollars each.

It seems to me unwise to bring in an architect too early in the game, but it would be helpful to have someone sit down with Mrs. Malone, Miss Lewis and myself to comment on specific plans we might draft after these visits. With this in mind, I would like to reserve the remainder of the thousand dollars, with the idea that we might use it for two consultants, at two different times, at 200 dollars each, to meet with us here and give us a critique on our thinking as of that time.

Obviously, I have not worked out all the details on this, nor have I discussed this with either Mrs. Malone or Miss Lewis. That would be my first step, but for now, the budget I would offer is this:

Honorarium and expenses for speaker at faculty in-service day	$ 300.00
Three trips for three faculty members each, budgeted at 400 miles round trip @ ten cents per mile, per diem allotments of twenty dollars per person for lodging, meals, etc.	$ 300.00
(Possible destinations: East Panama and West Panama High Schools near Milford; Ivywild High School, Salina; R. L. Fish High School, Live Oak; Wetumpka High School; Oneonta High School and the site of the new high school in Oneonta; and Winslow High School, Leeds.)	
Honorarium and expenses for two consultants for one day each	$ 400.00
	$1000.00

Mr. Dobbs smiled to himself to see how neatly the budget came out to the 1,000 dollar limit. Mr. Ogden had not concerned himself with costs for substitutes, the long-distance calls that would be a part of getting a speaker or consultant or planning the trips, or other incidental items.

But it was a workable plan, and the feature that especially struck Mr. Dobbs was that it would involve more of the faculty in planning for the new media center. It should appeal to both the superintendent and to Mr. Malverne because it hinted at the need for outside financial assistance for the forthcoming building program but, whether or not that happened, it would be a means of making the entire faculty better prepared for the building the school district could provide. With the freedom he felt Mr. Malverne wanted him to practice, Mr. Dobbs gave Mr. Ogden the go-ahead to start planning, even as he photocopied the memorandum and budget to forward them with his cover memorandum to Mr. Malverne.

It was unusual for Mr. Ogden to ask Miss Lewis or Mrs. Malone to meet with him formally, but they both agreed to be in the library work-room the last period of the following day. Briefly, he outlined the possibilities of the foundation grant and, more specifically, the use of the 1,000 dollars. He gave them copies of his memorandum and budget, and of Mr. Dobbs' reply. He explained his need for haste as the reason for not talking with either of them before drafting his memorandum and budget for Mr. Dobbs, but he reported that the plan had gone through and that Mr. Dobbs had been assured the thousand dollars would be forthcoming for this plan as presented.

"Mr. Ogden, you're just like the teachers who give kids something to read and then talk all the time they're supposed to be doing it," Miss Lewis said. "I can't take all this in. Let me read this material first, will you?"

"Oh, sorry. Sure, take your time."

He watched the two women reading slowly. As they reviewed the budget, they glanced back to the preceding page as though to get a fact clear or to review the plan. When they finished, they both looked at him, but neither one spoke.

"Well, what do you think?" he asked.

Miss Lewis spoke first. "I think it's just fine that somebody is going to give you a thousand dollars, but this seems like a strange way to spend it. I've known for years what we need in the new library and I even have plans that I've spent hours drawing. I'm not expecting any credit for that, of course, but you're welcome to them, and it seems to me you could invest some of your time the same way, then talk with the architects or the powers that be or whoever, and get the new plan going. Why all this fuss?"

Before he could answer, Mrs. Malone spoke up. "Oh, I'm all for getting the faculty stirred up about the new building. They should know what we have in mind. But what worries me is whether we won't end up with lots of dissatisfied people as we get more of them involved. Do you remember last year when Gabby Safford was killed on his way to the football game, and the school got all that money for a memorial? There were so many committees and memoranda about what to do with it that everybody was mad before the whole thing was over, while nobody would have batted an eye if Mr. Dobbs had just gone out and bought a fountain or something in the first place. Everybody likes to have his opinion asked, but only when it's going to count for something. I say we would spend this time and effort better by getting informed among the three of us and then just laying it on the line to the faculty."

Mr. Ogden felt his enthusiasm evaporating. If these two took such a dim view of the plan he had outlined, what would be the effect on others? Yet he was sure there were answers to their concerns. He had come to this meeting with a handful of books and articles to stimulate thought about a facility with the most innovative concepts. Now he wished he had better ways of working with the faculty to suggest, but there was no other place or time to start but here and now.

· · · · ·

Are you in agreement with the approach that Mr. Ogden and Mr. Dobbs have made so far? What might have been done differently?

Prepare an annotated listing of the "handful of books and articles" which would have been good ones for Mr. Ogden to bring to this meeting.

Suggest points which Mr. Ogden might make in answer to Miss Lewis' and Mrs. Malone's opinions at this time.

Assuming that the plan is implemented as Mr. Ogden has outlined it, draft a letter and any necessary enclosures which he might use to invite an expert to speak to the faculty. Include any facts about the school which you think are essential. You may add ones not given in the case, without changing the facts which are presented.

Prepare an outline or checklist which could be used by the faculty members selected to visit high schools. This checklist should make their report to the rest of the faculty easy to compare with reports from other visitors.

16.
Introduction to New Worlds
. . . .

As a new elementary school librarian in the Anoka County school district, Marilyn Becker looked forward to working in a district large enough to have a school library supervisor, centralized processing, and the give-and-take offered by the fifteen elementary school librarians serving the district's fifty elementary schools. Her first two years' experience after college graduation had been as teacher-librarian in an elementary school in an eight-school district, and, as her interest and ability in handling the library had increased, she had realized this was the part of her job she wanted to keep. She had read with interest the report of a citizens' survey of the Anoka schools, especially the recommendation that every elementary school should have a librarian assigned to it, at least on a part-time basis. Her own assignment, she found when she reported for work one week before the school year began, was to two elementary schools, Evangeline and Franklin.

Miss Becker's first week of work was devoted to an orientation to the larger school district. She learned that another recommendation of the citizens' committee's had been that administration be decentralized to the extent of having one associate superintendent responsible for each of the four high schools and for the elementary and middle schools which were their "feeder schools." The term, feeder school, was new to Miss Becker, and she was amused to find this agricultural term used in a fairly sophisticated suburban district when she had never encountered it in the rural community where she had taught before. At the meeting of elementary school librarians, Dwight Benton, the school library supervisor, explained that his own background was in secondary schools and that the plans for a fifth high school to be opened as a model school the following year and the overall responsibility for centralized processing kept him fairly fully occupied. He relied, he said, on the more experienced elementary and middle school librarians to serve as "buddies" to the newcomers. During the coffee break, he suggested, they might get better acquainted and the new librarians might select a more experienced colleague, preferably at a neighboring school, to keep in touch with during the year as minor questions of procedure might arise. Miss Becker looked around at the group as she consulted her list of librarians and schools. Those whose names were not starred on the list were librarians who had been in the district before, but she was not sure which schools were nearest Franklin or Evangeline. Meanwhile, Mr. Benton continued by saying that he did not wish to shrug off any of his own responsibilities, and that he hoped they would realize he was available to talk with them. The best way to arrange this was to call the receptionist who was also the bookkeeper for the processing center. She would make after-school appointments for them.

As Miss Becker was standing in line for coffee, another of the librarians, coffee cup in hand, looked at her name badge and said, "So you're the new gal at Evangeline! That's my all-time favorite school, and I've taught in three different ones, so I know. I'm Carolyn Garrard and I've just come into library work full-time. I'm going to be at Wright, the new middle school. Have you seen it? I think Frank Lloyd himself would be proud of his namesake. Come over some day when we're in action and I'll show it to you. We're in the same subdistrict, so we'll just have to be buddies."

Miss Becker, who had rather dreaded having to search out an experienced librarian to ask for help, accepted Mrs. Garrard's offer with pleasure. They chatted during the coffee break and Mrs. Garrard introduced her to a number of the other librarians. Several expressed surprise at Mrs. Garrard's leaving Evangeline School, after teaching there for three years. But, as she explained to Miss Becker, when Bob Elliott, the principal, had announced that he was going to Wright as principal, she, along with a number of other teachers from Evangeline, had signed up to transfer with him.

"That means you'll have a lot of the dregs left at Evangeline and a horde of new people," Mrs. Garrard explained cheerfully. "I don't envy you, but we all have to begin somewhere, I guess. At least, since I ran the library on the side, with a lot of help from Bob who scheduled us in a kind of team teaching setup where I could get extra time for the library, you won't have a volunteer mother breathing down your neck and telling you how to run the library. I'm afraid that's what's likely to happen at Franklin. I know Frieda Dukes, the library chairman there, and she's one of those wonderfully well-organized people whose husband won't let her work because he wants her on hand when he runs for county council, but she's so capable she has to do something, and the school library has been her thing for several years. She slowed down on the library a little last year, while she was on that citizens' committee. But she was telling me just the other day that they'd assured her when she'd moved into that new neighborhood that it would be years before a librarian was assigned to Franklin, and now, there you are. Don't be surprised if she doesn't take to you right away."

Mrs. Garrard continued to pour out information that left Miss Becker almost breathless and more and more concerned, as the day went on, about what she could do in either of the two schools. In the day she had spent at each, she had felt welcomed by the teachers and she had enjoyed simply getting acquainted with each library. Carolyn Garrard, however, was providing her with a perspective which made her almost reluctant to return to either school.

It had been decided that the librarians with two schools would work alternating weeks in each, although Mr. Benton pointed out that it might be necessary, occasionally, to go to one school for an after-school faculty meeting or conference of some kind, after working at the other school. He also gave a brief report of actions taken since the citizens' committee's report, mentioned that the associate superintendents in each subdistrict might be calling meetings of librarians, teachers, principals, or other groups from time to time, and pointed out that librarians with two schools had been assigned so that their two schools were in the same subdistrict. More authority was being delegated to these associate superintendents, he said, and there might be some variations from one subdistrict to another.

By the end of the week, perhaps alerted by Carolyn Garrard's opinions, Miss Becker began to sense great differences within the two schools where she worked. Mrs. Dukes appeared one day at Franklin, escorted to the library by Miss Norco, the principal. Mrs. Dukes apologized for the fact that some of the library supplies, including all the plastic jackets, were still at her home, but she said she would bring them over soon.

"But I thought the books came from the processing center with plastic jackets on them," Miss Becker said innocently.

"Oh, they do," Mrs. Dukes said, "but I jacket the books the P.T.A.

buys. They keep talking about making us purchase them through the processing center, too, but as long as they're overwhelmed down there, they're not likely to catch up with us. Meanwhile, a lot of our measly little library budget goes for processing charges, and the P.T.A. would have to pay for processing of the books they buy, if we went that route. As it is, thanks to my husband, we get a much better discount and probably end up with half as many more books as we'd get if we bought them that way. Why, right this minute, I have fifty books—two big boxes, anyway—at home. I'll bring them in as soon as I've cataloged them."

It was on the tip of Miss Becker's tongue to ask how long that might be. She wondered whether the time lag in processing of which some of the librarians had warned her was better or worse in the Dukes' home than it was in the district processing center, but Miss Norco's next comment stopped her. "In a big, impersonal district like this one," Miss Norco said, "it is a joy to be in a school where people like you put so much heart into things, Mrs. Dukes. I don't know what we'd do here at Franklin without our volunteers. One reason I'm looking forward to the new district organization is that it may give us some of the closeness of a small system. And I'm for that."

Seeing the close rapport between Mrs. Dukes and Miss Norco, and watching them walk down the corridor toward the office, Miss Becker wondered whether Miss Norco saw her as Mrs. Dukes' new professional assistant in the library or as the new librarian. The schedule which Mrs. Dukes had made for the numerous "library mothers" to be on hand in the library when classes came went on whether Miss Becker was present or not. Mrs. Dukes had pointed this out, and simply suggested that during the weeks when Miss Becker was there, she would be in charge of the mothers and their assignments. When Miss Becker was not there—and that was half the time, Mrs. Dukes noted—the mothers would carry on as they had in the past.

At Evangeline, the situation seemed very different. John Gooding, the new principal, had made it clear at the first meeting with the teachers that he respected and admired the former principal, but he was going to be his own man. He had looked forward to this first opportunity as an administrator, he said, and he was eager to help everyone do a better job. He believed in a tight ship and he liked the fact that there was no pattern for using parent volunteers in any of the school's programs. He intended to maintain this.

Miss Becker sensed that the teachers who had been at Evangeline before were accustomed to Mrs. Garrard's good organization of the library program and willing to defer to her judgment concerning the schedule for class visits and anything else relating to the library. Some of the teachers seemed restrained, but Miss Becker attributed it to the fact that many of them were also new to the school and others wanted to see how she would compare with Carolyn Garrard as a librarian.

During the first weeks of school, Miss Becker found herself overwhelmed by being constantly "on-stage," as she felt during class visits to the library. At the end of the day, when her voice became hoarse, she realized she was talking more than she ever had as a classroom teacher. There were no periods of quiet while children were reading or writing, as they did in a classroom. Classes came every twenty-five minutes at each school. During that time, she welcomed them, read a story, gave some library instruction, discussed with them books they had liked, or moved among them as they selected books to take home. She had asked teachers to alert her to forthcoming assignments, and she tried to plan to introduce materials that fitted them. She pored over the district's catalog of filmstrips and films, to augment the meager collection at each school, and she sent in requests for the whole year. Both libraries could be darkened, and she used the films and filmstrips as classes visited. Recordings also provided some relief for her voice, and she knew that storytellers like Boris Karloff and Gudrun Thorne-Thomsen provided a dimension and a quality that was different from her own storytelling or reading.

At Franklin, Miss Becker still sometimes felt like a fifth wheel. She was conscious of the "library mothers" watching her as she worked with the children or talked with teachers. They were busy checking books in and out to the children—a task that was done by children at Evangeline—with mending materials, and with checking in materials from the processing center. Yet they kept an eye and an ear on her presentations to the classes. Occasionally, one of them handed her a book which she had just told a child was out, or another pointed out one of the new books that would help answer a child's question. They kept in the background, but Miss Becker sometimes felt they were judging her inadequate because she really knew less about this library and its collection than they did. Frieda Dukes dropped in almost every day, "to wave at the troops," as she put it, and the volunteers followed her directions. Miss Becker, by not interfering with their work, sometimes wondered whether she was giving up some of her responsibility, but everyone seemed pleased, and Miss Norco stopped her on the parking lot one day to comment that Mrs. Dukes reported she was doing good work with the children and teachers. Miss Becker found it just a bit ironic that Miss Norco accepted Mrs. Dukes' judgment and seldom appeared in the library or talked with her, herself.

Miss Becker once ruefully recalled a talk she had heard at a library meeting when the speaker said librarians were like the man taking eggs off a belt at a hatchery. He had to pick up two every ten seconds and place them in cartons, and although he was sure there must be a better way to pack them, he could never stop picking them up long enough to discover what it was. She had fitted into a schedule rather than devising one of her own, and she kept her head above water by repeating the same program at the two schools as often as she could. The audiovisual materials were a godsend, and she used them extensively. This would be a year of adjustment, of finding her way. After a few months, she would venture to exert more leadership.

Carolyn Garrard encouraged this kind of thinking. "It takes time to get a library program off the ground," she said one evening as they talked on the phone. "Rome wasn't built in a day, to coin a phrase. You'll get around to doing your own thing, don't worry. Even at Wright, with the best principal and bunch of teachers imaginable, I'm feeling my way this year. Next year, we'll be off and running."

Miss Becker felt reassured by that, but it was only a day or two later that the schedule she had worked out was threatened. Miss Norco asked her to come to the office after lunch. The principal was just back from a meeting of principals in the subdistrict, and she wanted to mention to Miss Becker something that Dr. Salisbury, the associate superintendent, had brought up. He had mentioned he wanted to get the librarians together for a meeting before too long. But for the time being, he simply wanted to alert the principals to the fact that, in his first informal visits to schools, he had been distressed to find librarians simply showing films or telling stories. He thought the libraries should be active reference centers and that in no case should the librarian spend time doing what the classroom teacher could do in a classroom as well as, or better than, the librarian. Miss Norco added, "I have to admit, Miss Becker, that I don't know exactly how you've been spending your time here, but several teachers have mentioned that you have shown films and so forth. My interpretation of Dr. Salisbury's statement is that that should stop. Let's get together some time next week and talk this over. If this means a change in your pattern of work, the week will give you time to work out something else to show me. I may ask Mrs. Dukes to sit in on this, too, since she knows the school and the library so well."

"I see. Next week, I'm at Evangeline, but I suppose you mean the next week I'm here."

"Yes, of course," Miss Norco said briskly. "Let's say two o'clock Monday afternoon, November fifteenth. I'll clear the date with Mrs. Dukes, but if you don't hear from me, you'll know it's okay."

Later, when a dozen questions and ideas poured into Miss Becker's mind, she regretted that the conference with Miss Norco had been concluded at that point by an incoming phone call. It seemed all backwards to her that a comment made by Dr. Salisbury, apparently almost in passing, should precipitate major changes, but she also realized it might be the means of achieving more rapidly what she had hoped to accomplish in the library. She looked forward to discussing it with Mr. Gooding at Evangeline, because he often dropped by the library after school to chat with her. When she brought the matter up, the following Monday, he seemed to have forgotten all about Dr. Salisbury's comments. Then he said, "Oh, sure, I remember now. Dr. Salisbury even went so far as to say that he was going to make it a point to visit libraries every time he came to a school, and that he wanted to see no more librarians reading to children or using visuals and such. I took all that with a grain of salt. He has a new doctorate, you know, and this is his first year as a bigshot administrator. I think he's just laying it on. Don't you worry. I like what you're doing in the library, and I'll back you up if he says anything."

This was scarcely reassuring to Miss Becker, who began to feel that she was in some kind of two-part wonderland. If and when Dr. Salisbury ever visited one of her libraries, she could scarcely act as though she was ignorant of his new point of view, and the prospect of conducting one kind of library program at Evangeline and another at Franklin confused her still more. All of this seemed to justify an emergency call to Carolyn Garrard.

Mrs. Garrard was immediately sympathetic. "Oh, sure," she said. "Bob Elliott was at that meeting, and he mentioned something about this to me, but Bob sees eye to eye with me and we agreed we'd just go along as we have been. After all, if teachers were already doing such good storytelling or even reading aloud, they wouldn't have wanted librarians in the first place. And none of them would want to go back to that. My first inclination would be to ignore the whole thing, but I'll talk it over with Bob again and see what he says."

The next evening, Mrs. Garrard called Miss Becker. "Bob thought this over while I was in his office today, and he just picked up the phone and called Dr. Salisbury. There's a lot more to it, but the upshot of it was that Dr. Salisbury said he'd call a meeting of all the librarians in the subdistrict next Wednesday morning. I guess that means that he means business, but at least we'll know where we stand."

"In the meantime, of course, I have my conference with Miss Norco and Mrs. Dukes."

"Oh, if I were you, I'd just ask Miss Norco to postpone that, till you get the word from Dr. Salisbury. I'm sure he'll have some second thoughts himself about this strong statement." Carolyn Garrard was as sure of herself as ever.

Miss Becker called Miss Norco the next day to ask to have the conference postponed. Miss Becker told Miss Norco about her conversations with Mr. Gooding and Mrs. Garrard, which evidently resulted in Dr. Salisbury's calling the meeting.

Miss Norco's voice was cool when she answered. "I—see, Miss Becker. You have chosen to make this into some kind of major issue rather than something we can resolve at our school. It may be that you have already discussed this with Dwight Benton, but I intend to call him now. We are now talking about district policy and it concerns him directly. I'm sure he will be in touch with you."

Miss Becker was somewhat shaken by this response, and she was not surprised when she was called from the library to the office during the next class visit. It was Mr. Benton on the phone, and he said he would like to drop by after school to talk with her about a complaint from Miss Norco.

"I don't have all the facts yet, Miss Becker," he said, "and I hope to get them from you, but I don't mind telling you I'm distressed and concerned. It seems you have made a federal case about a comment made in passing, and you have chosen to discuss it with a number of people in this district, but not with me. I am somewhat disappointed in you, because I have been hearing good reports of you, and I assumed that all was going well because you are about the only new librarian who has not been in to see me. Now, I realize that may be because you were confiding in everyone but me. At any rate, I shall see you this afternoon. Goodbye."

Miss Becker was close to tears as she returned to the library. Had

Mr. Benton not meant what he said about the buddy system? Perhaps Carolyn Garrard was too forceful, but it had seemed wise to get the matter settled, and soon. She was sorry that she would scarcely have opportunity to sort out her own reactions and opinions before Mr. Benton would arrive that afternoon.

17.
When the Elite Meet

· · · · · · · · · · · · · ·

One of the things which Esther Menard had promised herself to initiate, if the staff of the Tasewell Junior High School media center were ever sufficient to allow time for it, was a discussion group for the students. She had seen many films which did not fit neatly into an instructional unit, but which were wonderful beginnings for discussions. In the black community where Tasewell was located, she felt that one of the things most disastrously missing was the opportunity for students to discuss what they read and saw and heard with their teachers or even among themselves. She was sure that many of them lacked this same opportunity in their homes, and she had determined to provide it as soon as possible.

In addition to her constant nagging concern for the students whose scores were high or normal on intelligence tests, but whose school work was far below their expected potential, Mrs. Menard's interest was caught by the students in the second layer of ability—those who were not the honor students or the leaders. Very often teachers and others were prepared to make special efforts to see that top students worked up to and even beyond their best, because they saw in them the hope for futures that would include college and security. But it was the students in the second layer who were, she felt, in danger of being ignored completely in all of the school's programs. In any other kind of community, they might have been likely college material themselves, but here, infected by a kind of hopelessness which Mrs. Menard felt the community had, but to which she could never become reconciled, they were all too likely to be dropouts, either in fact or in feeling, as they went on in school. These were the students whom a teacher might neglect as he devoted himself to coaching the brighter ones for achievement tests or felt himself mired down in the ceaseless drill of working with the slower students. It was this group—the second layer, as she called it herself—that Esther Menard wanted to reach.

In her mind's eye, Mrs. Menard had always seen herself as the moderator of a discussion group which might gather after school in one of the three conference rooms which had been improvised along one wall of the media center. Each room measured about 200 square feet and was equipped with a record player with jacks, and it was possible to wheel in one of the rear-screen projection units for the showing of a film to a small group. The size of the room was an important factor in her plans, because it was the reason she could offer for limiting the number of students who might attend. She felt that an important part of the plan was to stress the idea of the students being an elite group. That should not only be stimulus and reward for them, but recognition of them by the rest of the school.

Mrs. Menard first began to change that image of herself when she was introduced to a young black man in the faculty lunch room one day. He was seated with Jack Daviess, the vice-principal, and Jack called her over as she came in.

"Esther! Here's someone for you to meet. Mrs. Menard, who runs our media center like nobody else could, this is Nate Payette, a volunteer community worker who has come to us on one of the new federal programs. We haven't been down to see you yet, Esther, but we will be, sometime this afternoon. Okay if we come about 1:30 or so? I might even leave Mr. Payette with you, while I catch up with some of the phone calls and paper work, but I'd pick him up about two or a little after. That all right?"

"Of course," said Mrs. Menard, recognizing a familiar ploy of the vice-principal's, to leave a guest with her while he accomplished things he had had to neglect while escorting the visitor around the school. "Is there anything special you'd like to see or do in our center, Mr. Payette?"

"Well, not that I know of," the young man began somewhat shyly. "I'm really here today just to case the joint, find out what goes on. It's been a long time since I was in a junior high, I can tell you, and I'd just like to get the feel of it. I will be working here in Twin Falls for the next six months or so, and I'm spending these first two weeks getting acquainted. This is the only day I'll spend at Tasewell, but it's just possible I'll be back later on to do some work."

"It's really quite an interesting program, Esther. Mr. Payette here may think you know all about it, or else not realize how interested you'd be, but the fact is, we just might get him to spend all, or most of his time, right here at Tasewell. He's done some work with a youth club, he's a camera buff, he's done some reporting on a newspaper, and quite a variety of things. But the idea of this program—which really makes some sense to me, for a change—is that he should get the feel of a community, and then present a plan for how he might spend his own time for the length of his commitment to this project. I'd like to have him up in the main office, to be a kind of administrative assistant, if nothing else. Don't you think he'd charm some of those irate mothers we get, maybe even ride herd on some of the boys who get sent down for discipline? But I'm afraid that's out."

"Maybe we could use you in the media center," Mrs. Menard said.

"Maybe you could. I might like that. I'll be along to see it," Mr. Payette answered. His words and tone were polite rather than interested.

Mrs. Menard found herself wondering whether the idea of having Mr. Payette assigned to the center was workable or not. When he came to visit it later, and she talked with him about the center's services and activities, she was delighted with the range and depth of his reading. He watched quietly while a small group in one of the conference rooms was viewing a filmstrip on presidential elections, and he listened to the questions the teachers had students write in their notebooks for later discussion at the end of the filmstrip.

"Does that happen a lot?" he asked Mrs. Menard.

"What? Viewing in the conference rooms? Oh, yes!"

"No. That a teacher lets the best time of all for discussion go by so that he can drag up the whole thing later, when the kids will have forgotten what they saw or become bored with it."

"Teachers differ, of course," Mrs. Menard answered him, feeling that her answer might be curt, but not wanting to encourage his criticism of a teacher. To herself, she noted his perceptiveness.

Mr. Payette evidently sensed the rebuff, because he went on. "I used to do the same thing in a kind of poor man's Great Books group we had going at the youth club in Kaysville where I worked. We'd read or listen to something right up to our time limit, then I'd turn them loose and try to stir them up to get going at the next session. It just didn't work. I've been there; I know."

Mrs. Menard asked him more about his work, and confided in him some of her hopes for a discussion group at Tasewell. There never seemed to be enough time, she said, but someday. . . .

The following day, Mr. Daviess dropped by the center to say that Mr. Payette had asked to come back to talk with her after his appointments for the day, and she wondered whether the idea she had had might have communicated itself to him. When he came in late in the afternoon, smiling broadly, and holding out his clipboard to her, she realized they had been thinking along the same lines.

"Mrs. Menard," he began, "I've still got about ten more days of visiting here and there to do, but I think I know already what I want to do for my project. Would you consider letting me try one, maybe even two, of those discussion groups? I've written down here some ideas I'd like to try out, and some of the stuff I'd like to use, but I know I'd have to read like crazy, maybe even come in some afternoons and look at films and stuff, before I get started. I don't want this to be an exercise in reading or anything like that, but more of an exploring thing. 'Exploring with Ideas' is what I'd like to call it. And we could take one idea a week, like Exploring You, Exploring Politics, Exploring the Past, and really focus on something that the kids would want to read and think and talk about. How does that grab you?"

His enthusiasm now was clear. Mrs. Menard wanted to encourage him, while playing down what she considered his rather hackneyed idea of using the theme of exploring. Time enough later, she thought, to stress the need to refine the subjects, to make sure that students would be working within a small enough framework to get the best discussion from them. But here, like an answer to a prayer, was someone eager to start the program she had envisioned for so long. She smothered her own small disappointment at realizing she would not be doing it herself. It would be done; that was what counted.

Their planning went on. Mr. Daviess and Mr. Stark, the principal, were pleased that one of the three volunteers who would be working in Twin Falls had volunteered to serve at Tasewell, and Mr. Daviess suggested that Mr. Payette use one of the desks in the main office as his working area. Mrs. Menard was sure that Mr. Payette felt as keenly as she did that this was making him part of the "window dressing" for the black community, but it was good for him to have work space of his own, and there was no reason why it had to be in the center. In his eagerness to get familiar with more media, Mr. Payette took armloads of books home to his furnished room, carried one of the filmstrip viewers and a number of filmstrips in his briefcase to view at home, and spent much time observing Mrs. Menard working with students. His own time during the school day was to be relatively free, but Mrs. Menard encouraged him to feel free to talk with students in the center and to visit classrooms as he was invited by teachers. His personality and intense interest were good reasons for the popularity which he quickly enjoyed.

It took almost three weeks to recruit students to The Elite, the name they had chosen for the discussion group. Mr. Payette had announced the opening of the club in a number of the eighth and ninth-grade English classes, and had followed up by talking with individual students who had been recommended by their teachers. If the enthusiasm was not reflected in great numbers, it was nevertheless strong in the students who decided they wanted to "go out" for the club, and they pledged themselves to keep up with the discussions, the readings, and whatever other activities there might be, without neglecting their school work.

Beginning with the first meeting of the group, Mrs. Menard heard the students' reactions in many informal ways. There was a special shelf in the center, including mostly paperbacks, of books to be read for the discussion sessions. Often, as students asked for one or another title from the list Mr. Payette and she had worked on together, they would comment on other readings.

"Man, I never knew before that anybody could write real poetry that wasn't, you know, like fancy English, and get it in books!" one boy commented, as he returned an anthology. Mr. Payette had read Langston Hughes' "The Landlord's Lament" at the beginning of one of the discussion sessions, and it had made a great impression on the students. Mrs. Menard, who had recalled a case where an urban school system had been publicized and a teacher eventually fired for using that poem and seeming to criticize the system of absentee landlords, had discussed with him the choice. They had also mentioned it to Mr. Daviess, but he had been warmly supportive.

"Oh, I wouldn't worry about that," he said. "I just don't think that can happen here. I read the poem when you left it on my desk, and I'd say it would be great to kick it around in a discussion. I'd just like to sit in on some of those discussions myself." The day after the meeting in which the poem had been read, he had come in, with some amusement, to tell Mrs. Menard that Georgia Wilson's mother had come to school with the anthology in her hand to complain that her daughter was not being sent to school to read "dialect jokes," as she called the Negro dialect poems that were included. Mr. Daviess was sure he had placated her effectively, and the incident had simply amused him.

Another time, Mrs. Menard had asked a student what he thought of The Elite. The boy, Ben Foley, had answered, "Oh, that Nate's the greatest! He's no sissy, but he's read about everything, and he tells it like it is. You know what, Mrs. Menard, he carries sometimes almost a hundred dollars in his pocket? That's a big man, and he says he's just working here to help out. He's so rich, I guess, he can afford to do that. Oh, Nate is something else, all right!"

That answer made Mrs. Menard curious enough to ask Mr. Payette about the money. She herself carried only a few dollars, always less than ten, in her purse on school days. She did not wish to tempt any student who might be inclined to take the money.

"Oh, the roll?" Mr. Payette asked. "Yes, I showed it to them one day when we were talking about careers, education, and all that. I want them to know you don't have to be a pimp or a pusher to have big money. It just happened I'd cashed a check from home that day, and I showed it to them. That's a trick I learned in the club work I used to do. Those boys were so overwhelmed at seeing that much cash that it really impressed them that a good guy could have it. And besides, it shows you trust them. They go for that."

"They go for you, all right," Mrs. Menard said. "Do they all call you Nate?"

"Oh, mostly the boys, I think. The girls are a little bit slower, but I like it. I want them to have the feeling that I'm in this like one of them, and that we're talking things over together. Why? Do you mind? I suppose I wouldn't do it if I were a regular teacher here, or likely to be around for long, but as it is, it helps stress the fact I'm their buddy. I think they appreciate it."

Mrs. Menard was not sure she was satisfied with that explanation, but she could not express all the complications she felt about it. It was simpler to let things ride. Mr. Payette was certainly open with her, and, in fact, in the course of that same conversation, he described some of his problems with the discussion group.

"You know, as we said before this even began, the thing on which I'm really weak is good books for girls that will be generally enough interesting so that the boys who read them won't be bored. The thing we're going to be talking about week after next is Exploring You, and I've found —or already knew—lots of boys' books about finding one's self as an adolescent, or developing a personality, but I'd like to have some girls' stuff, too. And fiction is my hang-up. We're going to use a filmclip from the story of Helen Keller, and I'm sort of anxious to see what they make of how this girl, with half a dozen strikes against her, makes herself into a person."

Mrs. Menard realized that her best opportunity to participate, although vicariously, in the discussion sessions came as she and Mr. Payette worked together on books. She was impressed with his eagerness to read everything himself, and she knew he spent hours at home getting ready for the discussions. Among the girls' books she recommended to him was *Harriet the Spy*, and he brought it back the next morning, announcing gleefully, "Oh, this is a natural for us! It's got everything. The gal's a character—sneaky, dishonest, but likeable—and she really changes during the book. I want to see what these kids get out of it. Thanks for the suggestion!"

Harriet the Spy had been popular among the students ever since it had come out, and while it was difficult reading for some, the library's two copies were dog-eared and worn. Mrs. Menard was sure that some of the girls would know the book from earlier reading. That proved to be true.

Charlotte Orton was the mother who headed up the delegation of three who came to talk with Mr. Daviess after making an appointment by telephone the day after The Elite had discussed Exploring You. She was obviously embarrassed but determined about her mission.

"Mr. Daviess, that new man that's been rapping with our kids about books has gone too far this time. He's telling them about adolescence!"

"Telling them about adolescence? How do you mean, Mrs. Orton?"

"Well, I mean this—he was telling them about the difference between boys and girls, and he was doing it right there in that little room off the library. We want you to stop this club or whatever it is he calls it. We could just tell our kids to get out of it, but there are probably lots of parents who don't hear or don't care what's going on, and we want to protect their kids, too. He's not a real teacher, my Harry says, so I guess you can just get rid of him."

Mr. Daviess realized, as he attempted to continue the interview, that he was not likely to get further details of the subjects discussed the day before. Mrs. Orton insisted that her concern was in Mr. Payette's telling the group "the difference between boys and girls," and Mrs. Wilson, who was one of the other two, had been tight-lipped and in an "I-told-you-so" frame of mind as she pointed out, "Any man that holds up for ridicule the way people used to naturally talk shouldn't be allowed in this school. All this that happened yesterday just proves it."

Saying that he would like to hear from Mr. Payette and Mrs. Menard about what had happened the day before, Mr. Daviess pleaded for time and agreed to talk with the women within the week. They repeated that their children would not return to the club, but they also said they would fight all the way to whoever was in charge downtown to see that this man was gotten rid of.

Mr. Payette appeared to be as puzzled as Mrs. Menard when Mr. Daviess described the visit to the two of them. Mr. Payette was intense and concerned, but he was obviously struggling to figure out what had bothered the mothers so much. Suddenly, he snapped his fingers.

"Why, I should have thought of that! It was such a little thing, and we just mentioned it in passing; it wasn't even anything in the books we were talking about. For one thing, sir, you must know as well as I do that most of these kids know darned well what the difference is between boys and girls. Come to think of it, that's a funny way to describe what was really mentioned!" And, having overcome his confusion, he chuckled at the thought.

"And what was that?" Mr. Daviess asked.

"Well, you see, we were talking about this one book that Mrs. Menard and I had picked out—*Harriet the Spy*, and it turned out that nearly every one of the girls had read it some time ago. They knew it and liked it, and the boys, to whom it was new, were just as interested. That made one of the girls mention the sequel to it, which I didn't even know existed. It's called *The Long Mystery*, or something like that."

"*The Long Secret*," Mrs. Menard put in, sure now what was coming.

"That's right. Well, the kids were so interested, and this was a little gal who'd barely said 'boo' up till then, so when she started telling the story, I just let her go. She told it pretty well, too, but she mentioned one part where two or three of the girls in it—this Harriet among them—are talking about menstruation. One of them says somebody had told her there were rocks that dropped down and caused bleeding, and another knows some other old wives' tale—but the thing that got me, as she told it and as

I watched the kids listening, was that they really don't know or understand what happens."

"So what did you do?" Mr. Daviess asked.

"I might not have said anything, even then, but one of the boys turned to me, and he said, 'You'll level with us. What *does* happen?' So I just told them."

"Mr. Payette, do you realize this is a community which has bitterly fought every effort to have sex taught in the schools, and that answers back that these are matters for the home, every time the school board—downtown, as they put it—tries to force the issue? It may seem crazy, but it's one issue that unifies this community whenever it comes up. So you, in a sweet little book discussion group of some bright kids, just tell them all about menstruation! Well, I must say, of all the subjects, that's the one likeliest to set off the parents. They'd rather have you show a film on intercourse, I think. But the idea of discussing menstruation, in a mixed group of this kind—oh, Mr. Payette, this is something I'll have to handle with kid gloves."

"But, Mr. Daviess, I think maybe you should know that the kids loved it. I don't believe they were opposed to my telling them, and I'll bet every one of them had some goofy idea that I was able to dispel for them. They trust me; I'm their friend. Don't you think that's important?"

· · · · ·

In the events and decisions leading up to this point, what action might Mrs. Menard have taken to avert this incident? What is her responsibility to Mr. Payette in his work as a volunteer?

Does Mr. Payette's status as a volunteer not in the employ of the school system make a difference in how this matter should be handled?

Assess Mr. Daviess' response to the delegation of mothers and his action in calling in Mrs. Menard and Mr. Payette. What action should he take now?

Maxine Grove had completed her student teaching at Donora Elementary School, and had been pleased when Mr. Picher, the principal, suggested that she consider an appointment in the school district. Donora was near the farm which had been her home all her life, and she figured that a year or two of teaching in her own community and living at home could make possible the graduate work she hoped to take. She had experienced no particular problems caused by doing her student teaching in the same school she had attended as a child, although two of the teachers had been there since her own school days. One, Effie Glass, was the librarian who had been her eighth-grade teacher. Mrs. Glass had supervised her work in the library for the half of her student-teaching time that was allotted to the library. The other, Lee Gallitzin, seemed scarcely to remember her and had never been her teacher.

Miss Grove's first letter of appointment specified that she would teach fourth grade, with some responsibilities in the library. That was an assignment frequently given to first-year teachers, but in her own case, with her minor in library science and her interest in doing graduate work in that field, it was good news. She knew from her own experience that the assistant librarian often did little more than keep order during the two browsing periods in which the library was open for children from all classes, and which coincided with the two periods when Mrs. Glass taught mathematics to the seventh and eighth graders. But Miss Grove hoped to do something more than maintain the rigid discipline which Catherine Fox, the teacher she was replacing, had done.

Mrs. Glass's sudden death two weeks before the opening of school changed things. Mr. Picher stopped by Miss Grove's home the day after Mrs. Glass's funeral and asked her whether she would be willing to run the library for the coming year. He minced no words.

"Effie Glass was one in a million. I'm not asking you to take her place. No one can. But I'm asking you to help out, in the way that you'll have to get used to doing in a small school like ours. I've thought this over, and I just don't see any other way to keep the library going. You've got more credits in—what do you call it—library science, than any of my other teachers, and you worked under Mrs. Glass last spring, so I want you to pitch right in. I can get Linda Haddon to take that fourth grade you were going to have. She's always willing to substitute for a while, and she's been around long enough, between babies, to be able to take hold. By the semester, I may be able to get somebody who's just getting out of school, but I'd still want to count on you to run the library. I know it's a lot to ask, but will you give it a try?"

"Oh, Mr. Picher, I'd love to try! If there hadn't been so many advantages to staying here in Donora, I'd have tried to get a job in a school library somewhere else, but now—well, it's sad to say it because I'll miss Mrs. Glass, too—but it's just what I'll love. Thank you. When may I come in to get better acquainted in the library? Oh, and will there be someone else to help me?"

"Nobody but the secretary in the office, who should be able to do your typing and that sort of thing. When Mrs. Haddon substitutes, she always does it on condition she can be home with her children, so we'll be short a little time there. It's just in the last two or three years that we've had this fancy library schedule with browsing periods and all anyway. I think you'll just have to cut it back to the way it used to be. Come to think of it, you'll be coming out just about even on time anyway, because you won't have to teach the math classes the way Effie did. We can take up that slack somehow."

Miss Grove's enthusiasm carried her through the first week of school. It was a short week, with two days for the teachers to work in their rooms and two days with the children present. Only the first grades, on their tour of the building, came slowly in one door of the library and out the other. Miss Grove came from behind the desk to greet them and to say she looked forward to having them come visit the library. They smiled shyly, one or two said, "Goodbye," and others waved as they walked past.

Mr. Picher introduced her at the faculty meeting that Thursday by saying that they had been fortunate to find someone so well qualified to take Mrs. Glass' place on such short notice. Since she had been with them in the building last year, she scarcely needed an introduction to most of them, but he knew they would be interested to arrange with her times when their classes could visit the library.

Lee Gallitzin, now the senior teacher in the school, spoke before Miss Grove could begin. "Since we've had this tragedy," she said, "I know we'll have to do our part to help Miss Grove. But I think this might be a good time to discuss what the library is or can be. You know that, good friends though we were, Effie and I did not see eye to eye about many things, and discipline was one of them. I'd like to be sure that when my class is in the library, they won't turn into hellions who have to be corralled and fought the whole rest of the day. What's your view, Miss Grove?"

"Well, I wouldn't want to see them turn into hellions, Miss Gallitzin." Then, in loyalty, she added, "but then, I never thought Mrs. Glass let them misbehave, either. I hope to have the same kind of atmosphere she did."

"One of the problems, I think," said Fergus Amboy, an eighth-grade teacher, "is that, if we're honest, we'd have to admit that each one of us runs a different kind of classroom. And we want the library to keep that same kind of discipline. That's not an easy job, and anyway, it seems to me the library should have an atmosphere that is its own—not just an extension of the classroom."

"Now, that's where you're wrong," Miss Gallitzin said firmly. "Everything I've ever read about the library says it should be just that—an extension of the classroom. When our classes visit the library, they should do it in the same kind of order that they have their reading classes or science or any other subject."

"Oh, Lee, we've been over this ground before," Pat Nutley spoke up. "The library isn't just another class; it's another place, and I think the fact that it's bigger than our classrooms and has some comfortable chairs, for example, should mean that children should have more freedom there, just as long as Maxine can handle them. I don't envy her her job, but let's not start her off by trying to remake the library. Let's hear what she has to say."

Maxine smiled gratefully at Mrs. Nutley as she began. "Of course, I don't want to change things unnecessarily or anything, but Mr. Picher has suggested we might do away with the browsing periods. I remember that Mrs. Glass told me you had had these for only two or three years, and she was not sure how successful they were. The idea of having children be able to come to the library just to exchange books at a time other than their regular class visit was one she had been wanting to try, but she did say she wasn't sure it was entirely satisfactory."

"What two periods were those?" Linda Haddon asked.

"Let's see—last year it was the forty minutes before the library closed for lunch and that last forty minutes in the afternoon—from 11:20 to noon, and from 2:20 to 3."

"I always liked being able to let kids go to the library in smaller groups," Mr. Amboy said. "And those were periods when the kids were apt to get restless, anyway. I do remember, though, that when I came in at those times myself, there usually weren't many kids from other classes there. Maybe I was the only one who took advantage of it."

Mrs. Nutley said, "I think it's something we should try another year before we give it up. Just speaking for myself, I'm sure I didn't use it too well, but I do tend to get all wrapped up in what's going on right in my classroom, and I forget about suggesting that the children can go. I'd like to try it again. If we keep those periods, is there something else we could cut?"

By this time, the faculty had copies of Miss Grove's tentative schedule in their hands, and Jill Paramus, one of the first-grade teachers, spoke up. "Since you weren't here until second semester last year, Maxine, you probably didn't realize that the first graders don't visit the library until after Christmas. It really takes us all that time to get them organized enough to go to and from the bathroom or out to recess, so you could use the times you've reserved for us for these browsing periods."

Miss Grove had not thought of this, and she said, "But it seems a shame to limit their use of the library. Perhaps I could come to the first-grade classrooms during those periods instead? I could bring books and tell a story or something, so that by the time they came to the library, at least I wouldn't be strange to them. How about that?"

"I'd never thought of it. We might try it. But that leaves you right back where you started with juggling this schedule."

"And I think we shouldn't take more of this group's time to do that," Mr. Picher said. "Miss Grove will work out and post a schedule for your classes, and we'll work it out just as it is for these first few weeks. There are twenty classrooms, and just figuring the day from nine to three to allow time for classes to get going first thing in the morning, there would still be five and one half hours every day, five days a week, to fit them all in. You ought to be able to do that and still keep the free hours you may want for the other necessary jobs. Now, let's go on. Did all of you bring your forms for requesting supplies?"

Miss Grove was grateful to have had this much opportunity to get reactions, and she worked on the schedule some more that evening. It was fitting the library schedule around recess periods, physical education, art, and music that made it complicated. Then, too, the seventh and eighth-grade teachers were accustomed to having longer periods twice a week in the library, and several of the teachers had indicated their preference for a "switch-period," when they could bring a class at a time not formally set aside for anyone, but which would be available on call. That meant leaving one or two periods unscheduled, but open for that kind of request. Although it did not entirely satisfy her, Miss Grove did have a schedule ready to post by Friday afternoon, and copies of it were in every teacher's mailbox by Monday morning. She also took the precaution of mentioning to the four teachers whose classes were scheduled for the first morning that she would be expecting them.

As she thought back on it later, Miss Grove realized that her first interest in the library had been based on her own interests in reading and in people, and that one of the appeals had been the opportunity to work with all ages of children. Then, in those first few days, when the schedule and checking with various teachers and making herself familiar with the collection had absorbed so much of her time, she had almost forgotten that the library would come to life for the year only when the children came. She discovered that during the first class period. Linda Haddon's fourth grade, the class she might have been teaching herself, came in, and Mrs. Haddon stayed until they were seated. They had the fresh, clean look appropriate for the new school year. Miss Grove welcomed them and asked them what they knew about the library and about their favorite books. Then she suggested they search for books they would like to borrow. There was a stir of movement as they went toward the shelves. They grouped themselves around different sections of books. Miss Grove noticed none came near her, and she moved among them, picking up snatches of conversation and chatting with them about books. They still seemed restrained and shy, and she found herself ill at ease. They seemed to have no special interests to look for in the books, and four or five of them had not even bothered to go to the shelves. After all she had read about motivation and sharing enthusiasm, she realized she still had a lot to learn in communicating with a class like this one. Then, one boy leaned back on his heels and held up a book about raising puppies, calling to his friend, "Hey, Jimmy! I found it! That book about bitches!" Several of the boys chortled, and some of the girls put their heads together and giggled. Miss Grove felt many eyes on her, as the children waited for her reaction. And at that moment, Lee Gallitzin walked in the door of the library.

"Miss Grove," she said, as she walked over to the librarian, "I'll be late coming with my class because we're going to be responsible for the first all-school assembly, and we're planning it right now. We should be along about 10:30." She lowered her voice and added, "And while my class is here, I hope there'll be none of this kind of noise and confusion. In case it wasn't clear last week, it's this sort of behavior that Mrs. Glass used to tolerate that I just will not have. Of course, we can all make exceptions for the first day a class comes, but I hope you won't get off on the wrong foot."

After Miss Gallitzin had left, Miss Grove asked two of the children who had been library helpers the year before to help check books out for the day. One child called out, "But you chose C.L.! He's not supposed to get to do anything!"

Miss Grove said, "C.L. is one of the helpers for today. There will be others another time. Now, this is the way you write on the card. Remember?" She held up a book card for them to see.

With the inimitable officiousness of fourth graders, the two helpers carefully stamped books as the children prepared to leave. Mrs. Haddon appeared in the doorway. She looked over at the charging desk and said, "C.L. Caldwell! What are you doing there?"

The boy helper grinned engagingly. "I'm just being the library helper," he said.

"Well! I'll see you in the room," Mrs. Haddon replied. She turned to Miss Grove and said, "I guess you couldn't have known this, but he's really incorrigible. He bit another boy while they were on the playground today, and I told him he'd be penalized. Then, here you go and reward him! Of course, it's not your fault, but I'm sorry it happened."

Miss Grove realized why Mrs. Haddon might be discomfited at this kind of thing on one of the first days of school. The children could quickly learn to play the teacher against the librarian, and her hopes of maintaining a firm, fair discipline could come to naught. This, of course, was what the other child had been trying to tell her. And C.L., as he strutted out of the library, gave every indication of having emerged as the winner.

In the days that followed, Miss Grove often thought of the winner-loser analogy. She earnestly tried to allow an atmosphere of purposeful busyness in the library, but some of the teachers commented, among themselves if not to her, that it was chaos, while others seemed to resent any correction she gave to a child. One day, when an eighth-grade boy had answered her query, "May I help you find something?" with "No, I'm okay, sweetheart," she had felt her patience snap. She had had to interrupt her book talk to the class several times because of his very evident boredom and restlessness, and now she took him by the arm and escorted him down the hall to Mr. Picher's office. The boy's swagger had left him, and when they were well away from the library, he turned to her and said, "Please, don't take me down there!"

"If you didn't want to get a scolding by Mr. Picher, you should have thought of that before. You have distracted the rest of the class, and now, Mr. Picher will have to know about it." This was the first time Miss Grove had taken a student to the principal, but she knew it was not uncommon among the teachers, and she felt she was at her wit's end. She hoped the principal would give the boy a good talk on behavior, both in the classroom and in the library. But when they entered the office, the secretary raised her eyebrows at sight of them and went to the door of Mr. Picher's office to announce: "It's Lon Pitman, Mr. Picher. He must've been at it again."

The principal was standing when they came in. "Oh, it's you, Miss Grove. Well, what's our perennial villain done this time?"

"He—he called me sweetheart," Miss Grove said. "And he was restless and disruptive during the class's time in the library."

"Mm, I see. Well, I hate to have to call your father over something as minor as this, Lon, but that was our agreement, wasn't it?"

"Oh, please, Mr. Picher, give me another chance! This librarian didn't know what it was all about!" The boy was more disturbed than Miss Grove had imagined he would be, and she realized that there was evidently a record of misbehavior which meant he would be heavily penalized for this rather small matter. She began to feel guilty, but as Mr. Picher waved her aside, she left the office.

As she approached the library, it did sound like bedlam. She could hear voices from far down the hall, and Lee Gallitzin was just coming out of her classroom. When she saw Miss Grove, she stopped. "Oh, you were called away. Well, I hope you can quiet those raving animals in there." Miss Grove said nothing, but hurried on.

At the sound of her step, the class quieted down somewhat, but there were still giggles and much shuffling of feet, and several drawers were hastily banged back into the card catalog. One of the girls, clumsy and overweight, who was often the butt of the others' jokes, had her head down in her book, and her face was puffy from crying. Embarrassed as she was at her first mission to the office, Miss Grove did not want to inquire into more problems. Instead, she let things go on quietly until the period came to an end. Mr. Amboy came to the door to meet his class, and they filed past him out the door. Miss Grove asked him to step over to the desk where she told him about taking Lon Pitman to Mr. Picher. He looked genuinely concerned.

"Oh, that poor kid! I've seen his father. He'll beat him to a pulp. I was right there when he threatened to do that, the last time we had a problem with him. Lon's been on his good behavior for weeks now, and I know he's scared of what his father will do to him. But I guess Mr. Picher figured he had to call him, since he said he would the next time there was trouble. Who'd have guessed it would have happened in the library? Well, I'm sorry for your sake, too. I guess I should have warned you."

Miss Grove was really dismayed at this. She had the feeling that library discipline was expected to be fair and similar to that of the classroom, and yet she was expected to administer it in a kind of vacuum, with none of the background that classroom teachers had as a matter of course. Her first thought was that all this showed some weakness in her, some lack because of her inexperience. The fact that she could not identify a way to resolve some of the problems now distressed her still more. She felt really lost, isolated from the classroom teachers who seemed free to develop discipline styles of their own. At this stage, she was not even sure of what she wanted.

· · · · ·

Analyze the positions, in terms of discipline, which Mr. Picher, Mrs. Haddon, Mr. Amboy, and Miss Grove have taken. Can you suggest ways that some of their problems might have been avoided?

If you were Miss Grove, could you at this time develop a code for discipline in the library, with guidelines for its administration? What form might it take?

What is your opinion of the role of Miss Gallitzin concerning discipline in the library? Of Miss Grove's responses to her?

Are there problems of discipline which might be resolved by arrangement of schedules for class visits? If so, how?

Using the information presented here, and adding other information if necessary, construct a library schedule that would accommodate all the problems which Miss Grove felt were obstacles in scheduling. Note which activities or kinds of periods might have priority.

19.
The Case of
the Knowing Newcomer
. . . .

Beth Meigs, a new teacher at Scioto High School, came to town a few weeks before school opened to get settled in an apartment and to get acquainted with the community. One of her first visits was to the public library, where she applied for a borrower's card and introduced herself to the librarian, Selma Ziebach. Miss Ziebach remarked that it was a pleasure to have a teacher visit in person for a change, rather than to have to get acquainted over some misunderstanding about assignments after the start of school.

"Oh, I'm sure I'll be in often. I use the public library a lot, and there are magazines that I can't afford to subscribe to that I like to read. You'll be tired of seeing me before the year is over." Miss Ziebach was to remember that blithe statement later.

On that first visit, Miss Meigs looked through the card catalog to see whether a sampling of the titles she had used before for debates were there, as well as some of the books on a reading list she had prepared the year before for reluctant freshman readers. She was pleased with what she found, and told Miss Ziebach so. Miss Ziebach commented that she would probably find most of what she needed at the high school library as well, and added, "And I'm sure that Mr. Trout, the librarian there, will purchase anything you might request."

Even before she received the form from Mr. Trout asking her what books she might like to have placed on reserve for her classes, Miss Meigs had made it a point to visit the library in the school. Since she was to be teaching three sections of freshman English and a sophomore section in

150

American literature, she checked for items on the reading lists she had used in those kinds of classes before. She indicated titles that were apparently not in the library and asked for a time when she might talk with Mr. Trout about materials available. She wanted to book some films and to see about having an overhead projector assigned to her class for the second and third weeks of school, when she would be reviewing some grammar from eighth grade.

"We can discuss all that right now, if you like," Mr. Trout said. "These look like good lists you have. Did you make them out yourself?"

"Yes, I've worked hard at getting them in this good a shape. Of course, the librarian at Greeley helped me a lot with them, and I used things like the NCTE lists and book reviews, but I've read the books myself, and I know they're the kind of thing the students enjoy. Since there have to be book reports, they might as well be on interesting books, don't you think?"

"Oh, of course, I think that. But I'm not sure I think there have to be book reports. You'll find that the other English teachers here don't require them. They go in more for book discussions, tests on books read outside of class, things like that. They vary them so the reporting doesn't get too boring."

"I like that idea," Miss Meigs said thoughtfully. "I'm not sure I have enough imagination to make it work, but maybe I'll talk to some of them and try it. Thank you."

She had turned to leave when Mr. Trout said, "Wait a minute, and I'll give you forms for requesting your reserve materials."

"Oh, I think I won't put anything on reserve. The students use anthologies as texts, and since you have so many of the titles on the reading lists, I think there should be enough to go around."

"I think, Miss Meigs, you'll find there will be a run on the most popular titles, and students will hold off doing reports to wait for books they want, then wind up with nothing on the night before the reports are due."

"Well, I'll solve that problem when I come to it. I'm going to stress that they should be reading consistently, that that's the purpose of the reports, and since I know that a lot of the titles are in the public library, I'll encourage them to use it also."

"With the freshmen, you may be right. You may be able to convince them of all that, but the sophomores will remember how convenient it was to come to the library and find all the titles recommended for outside reading in one place, behind the desk, where they're still free to borrow them for two days, instead of for the two weeks they'd tie up a copy from the general collection."

"But it seems to me, Mr. Trout, that it would be better to have them browsing in the regular collection, getting acquainted with what's there, than always knowing that they can get just what they need in one place. Isn't that what we're both trying to do—get students to find and use what's available?"

"Yes," said Mr. Trout, "but since the rest of the school will be browsing through this same collection, don't say I didn't warn you."

Miss Meigs was sure that her plan for extensive outside reading on the part of students would provide them with enough challenge to make sure they would find what they wanted and would read widely. She prided herself on being able to motivate them to get the books from one source or another. And in the first three weeks of school, the plan seemed to work well. She occasionally saw that a student had one of the books on the recommended list. She was sure they were doing the reading for which reports would be due on the fourth Friday on the school year. She was not even too concerned when, on the fourth Wednesday evening, she visited the public library and Miss Ziebach greeted her with, "Say, you must be doing a good job. Your students are driving us crazy for the books on that freshman reading list. We're coping as best as we can, but I told them that, of course, all the titles should be in the school library, and they should try there first. And I was sure it would be all right with you if we substituted as necessary. Sometimes that takes persuasion, but I'm pretty persistent."

Miss Meigs smiled and said, "Well, Friday will tell the tale." It did not occur to her that substitution of titles not on the list for ones that appeared there had been necessary. She assumed that Miss Ziebach had simply had to steer students away from one of the most popular titles on the list to others in less heavy demand. She recalled the conversation as she began to read the book reports that weekend. Of the eighty-five reports that had come in, more than twenty were on books not on the list, and in many cases she considered the substitution less than adequate. When she returned the reports to the students the following Friday, she stated that there had apparently been some misunderstanding this time, but that in the future, she would expect them to find some book on the list that could be read for a report. As she pointed out, there were more than one hundred titles on the list and just ninety students in the classes, so there should be enough to go around.

Since Miss Meigs had not "marked down" for substituted titles, there was little reaction in her classes, but as she crossed the lawn to her apartment that evening, Jane Tripp, who lived downstairs and was in one of her classes, stopped her.

"Say, Miss Meigs, we're friends, aren't we?" Jane asked.

"Why, of course."

"Okay. I thought I'd just tell you that some of the kids think we're getting a runaround about these books. Miss Ziebach says that we shouldn't expect to find everything at the public library, and I suppose that's right, but Mr. Trout says he doesn't have all the books that are on the list anyway, and that even though he's ordered them, it will be March before they come in. He says if you'd play the game like other teachers, there wouldn't be this problem. What I really don't understand is why Miss Ziebach says that, of course, all the books are in the school library, and Mr. Trout says, of course, they aren't. Why doesn't she just call up and find out? I think she doesn't believe us."

Listening to Jane, Miss Meigs caught unconscious imitations of the two librarians, and realized that the interest and courtesy she had sensed at the public library might not extend indefinitely if her classes were really a problem, and also that Mr. Trout seemed to have more than one way to bring her around to his way of thinking. She sighed as she got up from the lawn chair next to Jane and said, "Thanks for telling me, Jane. Did you have trouble getting what you needed?"

"Oh, no, not me!" Jane said with a grin. "I found two of the books on the list in my brother Mike's room and since he's away at college, I thought it was safe to take them. And I borrowed one from you, remember?"

Miss Meigs did remember. "So that makes three for you, but let me see, you reported only on—*Light in the Forest*, was it?"

"That's right. In a way, I fooled myself. That was the thinnest, so I thought it would be the easiest to review, but there's a lot to that book, you know. But I went ahead and wrote the other two reports. All I'll need to do when the next report is due is to copy one of them over."

"But you can hand in more than one at a time, if you like. For that matter, sometimes, if one book reminds you of another or has some things in common with it, you could review the two of them together."

Jane was getting cagey now. "Mm, I might try that," she said, "but it sounds like it might be complicated. So maybe next time I'll hand in these two, and I'll be one ahead. O.K.?"

"That would be okay with me. Meanwhile, do you stop reading?"

"Oh, no, Miss Meigs. That's a good list, and Jerry and I and a lot of the other kids are going to read almost everything on it, if it stays as good as it's started out. Jerry's mother went to the public library the first day we got the list at school and she has eight of the books now. At her house, they don't even worry about the books being overdue. They're pretty rich, you know."

Jerry's father, the best known of the town's doctors, was relatively wealthy, but Miss Meigs had not thought of that as being a good reason for keeping books overdue. Later, in her apartment, she reviewed her conversation with Jane, and realized that if one girl had eight of the titles from the public library, even if she shared them with friends, there were seven people who had that much less chance to get the books they wanted. She recalled, too, that she had never checked back with Miss Ziebach to learn on what basis substitutions had been made for titles. It wasn't always as simple as another book on the same period or by the same author or at the same reading level. She had included some books on the reading list and excluded others by the same authors because they lacked the depth or scope she wanted the students to get from their outside reading. One thing she could do, even over the weekend, was to discuss this with Miss Ziebach.

The public library was quiet that Saturday morning, and Miss Ziebach noted that with the high school's homecoming football game that afternoon, it would probably be a quiet day. She had plenty of time to chat. However, when she saw the direction of the conversation, she seemed a little cooler.

"Why, Miss Meigs, I'm so sorry," she said. "I've always felt that we here at the library had the confidence of the high school teachers. Most of them say on their lists, 'If you don't find a title on this list that interests you, ask the librarian to suggest another title.' We have never had any complaints."

"This isn't a complaint, Miss Ziebach. I just think there is enough range in the lists themselves—both the freshman and sophomore ones—so that other suggestions shouldn't be necessary. I also don't want to burden you or anyone else on your staff with having to spend a lot of time making suggestions when I feel sure there is enough to choose from if the students will only be a little more adaptable. I suppose some of them are greedy—or perhaps just eager—like the girl I heard of yesterday who latched on to eight of the books the first day the list was distributed."

"Oh, yes, Dr. Bennett's daughter. We've been hoping those would come back, but the overdue notice won't go out on them for another three days. I remember them because I checked them out to Mrs. Bennett myself without realizing they would be in such demand. Later, after I'd looked at those lists enough times, I remembered she was looking pretty smug when she left with them."

"Do you ever recall books in a case like that?" Miss Meigs asked.

"Why, of course not!" This time, Miss Ziebach seemed really horrified. "This is a public library. We must give equal service to all. Of course, if Mrs. Bennett herself were to drop in again, I might ask her about them, but I really don't think it's our job to call all over the countryside rounding up books for your students. You may not know this, Miss Meigs—" Miss Ziebach lowered her voice "—but the school library doesn't even own all the books on your list. Why, we probably have a better collection of them than they do, although a few of ours that are in the catalog are actually missing or at the bindery. But we, of course, don't have the responsibility that the school library has."

"What responsibility is that?"

"Why, to have every title that's recommended reading at school. Otherwise, why have a school library at all?"

Miss Meigs pondered that last question over the weekend, knowing that her next visit would have to be with Mr. Trout. Except for occasional "hellos" in the halls or nods across the faculty lunchroom, she had seen little of him since school began.

Mr. Trout gave every indication of being ready to help. He pulled out the copies of the reading lists she had given him, and showed her some markings he had added. He had photoduplicated one of the lists on which a student had noted the public library's call numbers, and had penciled next to them the call numbers used in the school library. Miss Meigs felt he was being rather patronizing when he said, "Many teachers don't think this through, of course, but I think it would be good to have the call numbers added before the lists are duplicated and distributed. In biographies, especially, there are major differences. We tend to put biographies in the subject categories where we think they will get the most use—Henry Ford in the 600's, for example, with books on automobiles—but Miss Ziebach has no patience with that. And since I understand you've been telling your students that once they understand one library and know their way around it, they know them all, I suppose that would puzzle some of them."

Miss Meigs looked at Mr. Trout to see whether he might be teasing her, but he continued unsmilingly.

"And, of course, some of the students have been disappointed that so many of the books were already on reserve for other classes. That has probably accounted for part of the shortage."

"Do you mean, Mr. Trout, that the students in my classes can't borrow, even for two days, books that are on reserve for another class?"

"Why, no. That's our policy. Otherwise, what would be the value of putting them on reserve?"

"Doesn't it sometimes happen that two teachers ask to have the same book on reserve? What do you do then?"

"Well, in a case like that, for one thing, we'd allow students in both teachers' classes to borrow it. And if we run short of reserve books, we have a policy that permits us to send a rush order for the necessary titles and, since they are duplicates, we often have them on the shelf within two or three weeks. You'll find, I think, that there are some advantages to our system of reserve books."

This time, Miss Meigs felt the librarian was being almost malicious. He seemed to enjoy her discomfiture. She blamed herself for not having investigated more carefully the ramifications of her decision not to have a reserve shelf for her class. Later, she felt that Mr. Trout's apparently casual remark about her having told her students that libraries were much alike might mean he resented the fact that she had not brought her classes as groups to the library for the orientation visits about which he had sent her a form memorandum. It had seemed to her that her plan of letting students visit the library in groups of five or six during class time would accomplish much the same thing, and, more important, stress the independence she wanted them to achieve.

Miss Meigs felt she was caught between two librarians with somewhat different attitudes. She was still concerned that she did not feel confident enough to have tried some way other than the written book reports to get feedback on the students' outside reading. Were her lists too restrictive? Was she being too rigid in not allowing librarians to make substitutions? It seemed to her that it was her teaching and her way of working with students which were really being questioned, and her assurance based on past success with a similar plan was ebbing away.

• • • • •

What might Mr. Trout have done in the initial interview with Miss Meigs to have averted some of these problems?

In addition to the forms sent from the library to teachers, to which the case refers, can you add items that might be supplied to teachers on a regular basis to avoid misunderstandings like these? Be fairly specific about their contents.

What is the role of the public library in a situation of this kind? Has Miss Ziebach performed that role?

What kinds of help and from what sources might Miss Meigs get to assist her in learning to use other methods of checking on students' outside reading? Or are any such methods desirable?

20.
The *Moonachie* Apache
Makes *Whoopee*

· · · · · · · · · · · ·

Nancy Demarest, the first girl to be editor-in-chief of the student newspaper at Moonachie High School, took her responsibilities seriously. She was determined that again this year, the *Apache* would take top honors in the state and national competitions for high school papers, and that it would also be read and respected by students and teachers. In the fall, the twenty-five-person staff had put their energies into supporting the student government drive to stimulate better citizenship throughout the school. There had been a series of "Weeks"—Clean-Up, Shape-Up, Hole-Up, and Crack-Up—which had campaigned respectively for anti-littering, physical exercise, reading, and humor. The *Apache* had the honor of announcing the room, class, and school winners of each week's contest for the best examples. In those weeks, the paper had no sooner hit the stands strategically located throughout the building than copies had been eagerly snatched up.

In the weeks between Christmas vacation and the end of the semester, the period which the dean of girls referred to as "the era of bad feeling," the *Apache* searched for a theme, a cause to carry it through the rest of the school year. When Nancy was invited, on January 4, to attend a high school press conference and workshop in nearby Newton, she went looking for a theme. She talked with other high school editors like herself, she listened to newspaper moderators pointing out the strengths and weaknesses of various papers, but it was only when one of Newton's most popular daily columnists spoke to the high school journalists in the afternoon that she felt she was getting somewhere.

"This is the Era of the Squeeze-Out," Jay Paterson, the columnist said. "You young people are being squeezed out of college by the tightening requirements for admissions. You are being squeezed dry of ideas by your teachers who are handing you the same old claptrap they've been giving out for years now. You are being squeezed out of your youth into premature adulthood, into the army, into marriage, into major responsibilities for which you are not ready. But you have to fight this squeeze. The only answer is freedom. It is up to you to see that, by seeking out responsibilities now in the areas in which you want it, you make yourself ready for responsibility when it is thrust upon you. How many of you know —yes, even know, much less are a part of—how decisions are made that affect the running of your own schools? Who chooses the textbooks? And how? Who picks out what will go on the library shelves?"

His talk went on, but Nancy needed little more. Here was a project. The *Apache* could investigate these decisions at Moonachie. There was bound to be good copy here. And, more important, they could begin to push to take part in decisions. Even as she listened to Paterson, she began to sketch out a plan for following up on the questions he had raised.

At the *Apache* staff meeting, held the following Monday, Nancy threw out some of the ideas she had picked up at the conference, and then, as a bombshell, she offered the rest of the staff the plan she had developed over the weekend. It was something that could involve them all, stimulate student interest, and at the same time contribute to the school.

"Here's what I think would be great. Herb, you interview Mr. Oradell, down in the library, just as soon as you can, and get him to tell you how things get into the library. Jean, you go right to the principal, Mr. Penn, and find out who selects our textbooks and why. And meanwhile, Tom, you can be thinking up a neat little form we can run in the *Apache* to get kids to comment on what they don't like about some of this stuff. We'll have another meeting Thursday afternoon and see what we've got. O.K.?"

"Say, Nancy, I think there's something else we can do," Holly Glencoe said. "I get really bugged at the way these teachers censor stuff they show us in class. You know, Miss Ephraim was reading a story to us in advanced comp. the other day, and we were supposed to finish it without hearing the ending. Well, right in the middle of it, she blushed like crazy and stumbled around, and later, we got the book off her desk, and found out—you know what?—the little phrase she hadn't wanted to read was about Indian women, and it referred to 'their naked, exposed breasts.' For heaven's sake, what do you suppose she thinks we are? Children? And another thing—in Mr. Key's history class, when he was showing a film last week, he held a cardboard up over the projector for about ten minutes, while the film about Eskimos showed them doing some kind of a wild dance, and then all sleeping together in their ice-house."

"Aw, Holly," said Jerry Netcong, "it couldn't have been ten minutes! The whole film lasted less than half an hour, and that was just a little bit of it—maybe two minutes, at the most."

"Well, even two minutes is too long," Holly persisted. "It's not just a matter of who picks things out for us, and how they pick them out, but what they do with them after they get them. Why, do you know that in that big collection of stories about math—what's it called, *Fantasia Mathe-matica*—the old librarian, Miss Cresskill, cut out two stories that she thought weren't suitable for young people? Yeah, she cut them right out of the book! Can you imagine what would happen to one of us if we did the same thing?"

"How do you know?" Jerry challenged her.

"I saw the book. It's on reserve for the advanced math classes, and Mr. Oradell says the math teachers were so keen to get it that Miss Cres-skill couldn't say no. But she was so disgusted by those stories she just cut them out. I say there's a story for the *Apache* there—what's being kept from us?"

"Hey, that's a good title, Holly. Why don't you play around with that? Maybe you could do the lead editorial to get this thing kicked off. Or we could do it together," Nancy offered.

The two girls concentrated on getting stories from other students about what they considered unjust censoring, and as their interest spread around the building, a number of students remembered incidents. Someone who knew a rabbi in the community told them that he had been invited to speak at last year's commencement, but that the invitation had been with-drawn after he had appeared on a local television talk show, expressing the opinion that marijuana, since it was nonaddictive and probably harmless, should no longer be illegal to possess or to sell. One of the library student assistants tipped them off to a shelf of books kept under lock and key near the collection of materials for the faculty. Several recent, sexy popular novels were there, along with a book on palmistry, another on folk medicine, and the authorized biography of the Beatles. It was a strange assortment, but Nancy and Holly made careful notes of titles and were prepared to back up their charges that some people were limiting access to books purchased for the students to use. They felt they had scored a real *coup* when Hal Hamilton, a black member of the basketball team, came to the *Apache* office to report that one of the reserve books used in his section of American history included passages referring to how happy the slaves were on the old southern plantations, and how devastated they had felt when they were freed and forced to go out into the world and make their own way.

With these and other incidents, Nancy and Holly enthusiastically went ahead with their editorial, almost forgetting what the other staff members would be presenting at the meeting later in the week. But their discoveries, too, were eye-openers. Jean reported that Mr. Penn, after breaking their first appointment, had given her lists of textbooks approved for purchase in their state, and had shown her which ones were in current use at Moonachie. Nearly all were used somewhere, and, as he had pointed out, teachers, when they were getting ready for classes in the summer, could ask for the books they wanted to see, and there usually was enough variety among them that all the books were pretty evenly used. For very different reasons, teachers sometimes had different preferences. But at no point had he mentioned the possiblity of getting student reactions to the selections.

Mr. Oradell had been similarly cooperative with Herb. He had envisioned a feature story in the *Apache* about the library program, and said it would be the first time anything about the library, aside from discipline or the new addition, had been given any publicity in the student paper. He described his efforts to get faculty members' suggestions on what to have in the library, and had shown Herb the slips on which they could make suggestions, as well as the reviewing media he used most often in deciding what to buy. When pressed, he admitted that it was these periodicals on which he relied most heavily. He, also, made no mention of suggestions from students. He had given Herb a copy of the selection policy for materials.

Tom had come to the meeting with several sheets of paper, including different drafts of the questionnaire he wanted to use. He had also made an overhead transparency of the best of these, and he projected it for the others to see and comment on. He wanted to keep the whole thing relatively simple and allow students lots of opportunity to speak out. It could be run in a double column at the bottom of page one of the next issue. It looked like a sure attention-getter.

OPERATION SPEAK-OUT AGAINST OPERATION SQUEEZE-OUT

Do some of the incidents reported in this issue of the *Apache* make you mad? Do you know of others? The *Apache* is ready to listen. Let us hear your story. Using this form, you can give us the clue to a story we can track down. Or drop into our office and tell all. Many of you may report the same thing; we will follow up on every lead, but if we don't come back to you, it may be because we are getting complete information about the same story from another source. But don't assume somebody else will report on what you know. Let us in on it now. Drop this completed form in the *Apache* mailbox, main office, or bring it to the editorial office. We will speak out for you!

WHAT HAPPENED _____

_____

WHERE _____
TEACHER(S) INVOLVED _____
STUDENT(S) INVOLVED _____
YOUR NAME _____HOME ROOM _____

Mr. O'Neill, the faculty moderator for the *Apache*, did not attend all staff meetings, but he read all copy before it was printed. The first he knew of the *Apache*'s new campaign was what he read one evening when he and Nancy were the only people still at work in the *Apache* room.

"Hey! What's this all about?" he asked. "Are you trying to wash all our dirty linen in public?"

"Oh, no, Mr. O'Neill, but it's our new thing. We didn't realize what a gold mine of information and cases there would be when we started out, but it looks like a good issue, don't you think?"

"No, I don't think," he said. "It doesn't even seem to me like it's good journalism. You're going out on a witch-hunt, so of course you'll find witches. Why, this thing on the front page will get you comments from every nutty kid in the school who's ever thought he didn't like an assignment, or has ever found a dirty word in a library book. Is that what you want?"

"Of course, it isn't, Mr. O'Neill." Nancy was puzzled at his reaction. "You were at that same meeting I was, where Mr. Paterson said to speak up and make students think. Isn't that what we both want? And I think this is the way to do it."

"I'm afraid issues like this are so big they're something you and I can't settle between us, Nancy. I'd like to talk with Mr. Penn about this."

"Are you going to censor this issue?" Nancy asked, her voice hoarse and tense.

"Well, that's the wrong word to use, if ever I heard one," Mr. O'Neill said with a chuckle. "No. I'm going to do just what I said—talk with Mr. Penn. And I'll let you know what he says."

The wary mood of the *Apache* staff was very obvious to Mr. O'Neill when he entered the room the next day. He had shown the galleys for the next issue to Mr. Penn, and had been somewhat surprised at the stand he took.

"So that's what that kid reporter was up to! Here I gave him this material myself, and he's using it against me. Makes it sound like we're running a police state or something. But one thing I'm glad to see—they do sound interested in doing something. I suppose they wouldn't be so keen on picking out textbooks if they'd put in as many hours reading and comparing them as some of the people who've served on those state committees have. And they're all wet about Rabbi Morris, of course. He turned us down after he'd said he'd give the invocation, because by that time he was in big demand on T.V. and everyplace else. I have to admit, of course, that I don't know the answer to some of this stuff, but to tell you the truth, Frank, I'd say let them run it and take the brunt of the reactions. If they want to play in the big leagues, let them find out what it is to have to field the ball as well as pitch it. Oh, you might check with Mr. Oradell, and see what he has to say."

Mr. O'Neill told the staff members they had the green light to go ahead on the issue, but he flinched as he read the sentence Nancy and Holly added to their editorial: "There was some doubt that the *Apache* would be able to report these things to you, but we are free, here at Moonachie—at least, for the present."

Mr. Oradell's reaction had all the fire Mr. Penn's had lacked. He was outraged at what he considered the duplicity of the student who had interviewed him, then written the story about the library selection policy. He was not aware of some of the instances of teachers' censoring portions of films or books, but he felt they had the right to decide those matters for themselves, and that the question did not concern the library. He chuckled at the report of Miss Cresskill's snipping out the stories. He had known of that, but as he said to Mr. O'Neill: "So what am I supposed to do? Throw out three or four copies of an expensive book because some old maid librarian decided to bowdlerize it on her own?"

As for Mr. Oradell's own purchases, which included the biography of the Beatles, he defended them, saying, "I know if I had put that book out on the general shelves, it would have been stolen or mutilated in no time. I think it's a good book to have, and for the kids who will use it thoughtfully, we've got it. Why not keep it where it will be available to them? I'd like to have your kids try to run this library for a month and see what kinds of decisions they'd make."

"Of course, we all make mistakes. I know that some of those novels I bought turned out to be much too juicy for the students, so I put them over near the faculty collection, where teachers can read them if they want to. What do they expect me to do, for Pete's sake? Burn them?"

"Tell you what," Mr. O'Neill said, "this is going to run as it is, but I promise you that in the next issue, we'll run any kind of answer you come up with. I don't know whether you'd like to write it yourself, have another interview, or maybe get one of the kids who uses the library a lot to defend it. As far as I can tell, there's no real lack of truth in anything the kids have reported. Some of their interpretations are forced, maybe, but you can answer them with your own, if you like. What do you say?"

"It seems I have no choice," Mr. Oradell said stiffly. "You're going to run this right here in our own school, and God only knows what will happen if a local paper or somebody like that nut Paterson picks it up. And I'm helpless. Who ever reads—really reads—a letter to the editor? Or an answer to an attack like this?"

The days after the next issue of the *Apache* appeared seemed more hectic than ever to Mr. Oradell. One student carried the unabridged dictionary to the copying machine to try to photocopy the full-page skeleton of man, and he submitted the fuzzy reproduction to the *Apache* with a note saying he saw Mr. Oradell frequently stop at the dictionary and turn it to lie open at another page when this picture, approximately in the middle of the book, was on an open page. A freshman girl borrowed a copy of a book on ecology, marking pages which had been pointed out to her by her father, a minister in a nearby church, which he charged were in favor of evolution. She submitted the book with her report form to the *Apache.*

Mr. Oradell had the feeling that he was struggling to put out brush fires when he should have been practicing fire prevention, but he also felt that each challenge should be answered. There was nothing that had been brought up which had not at some time been a problem somewhere, but it was the fact of having them all thrust upon him so suddenly and, he felt, so needlessly, that really upset him.

Two evenings before material for the next issue of the *Apache* was due in the editorial office, Mr. Oradell asked his friend, Fidelis Torrance, who was librarian at a high school not far away, to stop by Moonachie after school. He showed Torrance the latest issue of the *Apache*, pointing out the form for student reactions, and said, "I wanted to talk about this with someone who could be objective, but who'd understand the whole mess. I scarcely know what tack to take in my answer. I've looked at the American history book on reserve, which the black student had reported. It does have a paragraph on the pleasures of Negro slave life on southern plantations, with an illustration of a well-fed family of slaves getting into a buggy to go to church services. Bruce Ewing, the teacher who had placed the book on reserve, knew about it, of course, but he says that the book's description of the Reconstruction is the best one he knows, and that it was that section only which was included on the students' reading list. The student who objected had evidently really searched out this section of the book for himself.

"Should we have photocopied only the section the teacher wanted students to read? Are there differences in degree between books specifically reserved for classes and those in the general collection? But if I defend this one on the basis that its one section on Reconstruction is so useful that the rest of it doesn't matter, what can I say if some student then says I should cut out the pages about slave life, just as Miss Cresskill had cut out the stories in *Fantasia Mathematica?*

"I've seen the students nudging each other this week, looking at a mutilated page in an encyclopedia or other reference book. I'm beginning to think they're always assuming I've been censoring with the scissors, when the truth of the matter is that students themselves are usually the guilty ones—as you well know. In their haste or lack of concern for others, they tear out what they need—not often, but the library bears the scars. And the *Apache*, with all its fine interest in citizenship last fall, has done not one thing to help that situation.

"Was I foolish to keep books that were much too mature—almost pornographic, really—from students, and to allow teachers to use them? If I had simply discarded the books after I had read them more carefully, no one would have been the wiser. I could have discarded those darned books that Miss Cresskill had censored in her own fashion, and I could have bought other copies and no one would have known the difference.

"What really bothers me is the negative tone of this whole thing. Here we have a good policy on the selection of materials, and the students seem determined to look for issues in how materials are used or housed. It seems to me that the staff of the *Apache* and the students who are cooperating in this witch-hunt are a minority of the school, but I'm not sure how to get through them to the majority. Right now, I'm not even sure it's worth the effort to try."

•   •   •   •   •

Assume you are in Fidelis Torrance's position and have just heard Mr. Oradell's problems. What suggestions would you make to him? If you suggest persons with whom he might discuss this, indicate reasons why these persons might help, and what information Mr. Oradell should give them. Specifically, indicate what action he should take in regard to the possible response to be prepared for the *Apache*.

21.
The Case of
the Preschool Program

· · · · · · · · · · · · · · · ·

In the village of Tupper Lake, elementary school libraries had begun only
with the advent of federal funds under Title II of the Elementary and
Secondary Education Act of 1965. Because of early interest in some
kind of library program which had been shown by citizen groups, the district had provided funds for the staffing of the school libraries as they were
set up. Shannon Zane considered herself fortunate to have stepped into a
full-time position in an elementary school immediately after completing her
master's degree in library science. The school to which she was assigned,
Raeford, was one of three in the village which had full-time librarians. The
eight other elementary schools had librarians for assignments ranging
from one-fifth to one-half time. When Nan Woodruff, the curriculum director who had the major responsibility for school media programs in the
district, had described the assignments to a meeting of the librarians and
the principals, she had said, "Now, we know you librarians would all like
to be full-time in one school, and that you principals would like to have
them that way. However, we just can't swing that yet, financially. We
have special federal funds for personnel in the three schools that are 'tar-
get' schools under Title One, and we've decided to make Raeford a demonstration school for the use of media. That's why those four have full-time
librarians, but we expect that if all goes well in those schools, we should
be able to make more full-time appointments in the other elementary
schools."

Later, in a conversation with Bob Niles, the principal at Raeford, and
Mrs. Zane, Mrs. Woodruff gave them more of the background for the assign-

ments. "As I see it," she said, "if the three Title One schools, with their large proportion of disadvantaged children, were the only ones to have a full-time librarian, people could always say, 'So okay, disadvantaged children need this kind of special media program, but what does that prove about *our* kids?' And we're counting on the impact of these programs to make the voters support a bond election next spring. We want to get funds to go full speed ahead on media programs in the elementary schools. So, if we had only these part-time assignments, we probably wouldn't make a dint on public opinion. I think it's important for us to be able to point to one place that has had enough support to get a good program going, and meanwhile to give that place as much help as we can to make it really spectacular. Your school, Bob, seemed a natural for this, because the parents have been screaming for a library for ages, you seem to be an expert at getting good publicity, and, with the conversion of that kindergarten suite, you have the space for the library."

"Well, you know how proud we are to have been chosen for this," Mr. Niles said. "I think I can guarantee you that our teachers will do everything they can to make this work. We've put all the media we've had in closets and everywhere else, into the center, where the third kindergarten used to be. It may not be in the best organized way, but it's there and ready to be used."

"And it shouldn't take me long to get it organized," Mrs. Zane said. "I've looked at the filmstrips, and there are some good ones there. And I understand more are on order, Mrs. Woodruff. Right?"

"Yes, we'll be sending them along to you. But right here, Shannon, I want to say that I hope you don't make a big thing out of this matter of getting them organized. I know what people say about librarians' work being like an iceberg, with ninety percent of it under the waterline, and only ten percent of it showing. For the sake of the program in this district, I want you to reverse that figure. We're assigning a library aide to Raeford, too, and you'll be getting the materials that were ordered this summer, all processed and ready to use. The important thing is to see that they're used and used well. Don't spend a lot of time getting all the numbers to match. Get the stuff to the teachers and the kids. We want your work to be highly visible. It may be that you'll get some negative reactions even from the other librarians, who may feel bogged down in getting started, in more than one school, but you were chosen for this assignment because we think you can get it rolling. Just go your own way, and in the long run you'll do more good for the school media programs in this district than if you spent your time dotting *i*'s and crossing *t*'s on catalog cards. How does that sound?"

"It sounds challenging and meaningful," Mrs. Zane answered with a chuckle. The other two laughed with her at her use of the superintendent's favorite pair of adjectives. She went on, saying, "Oh, I want to make this thing go, too, Mrs. Woodruff. It sounds like what we were always talking about in library school. I never thought it was so possible. And at the end of the year, you and Mr. Niles are not going to be concerned about how straight the books are on the shelves, or whether every filmstrip is in the right can or not, but only with what the children and teachers think of the program by then?"

"Yes. And let's say not just the children and teachers, but the parents of this community, who have a lot of influence, and who will help decide how the bond election goes. I think I can say to you, Shannon, that we want you just to be as creative a librarian as you were a teacher, and everything will be fine."

Mr. Niles spoke up. "And while you're right here, Mrs. Woodruff, I want to say that you should feel really free, Mrs. Zane, in the decisions you make about the media program in this school. Just keep me informed, and if you want to do something really wild, check with me beforehand. But don't hold back on anything just because you don't know of its having been tried before. I think this may be our year to try what hasn't been done before, and I'm behind you, one hundred percent."

"You can't beat that, can you?" Mrs. Zane smiled at the other two. "You know, one thing I'd like to try right off, that I think might really work in a community like this, is to have a preschool story hour. I've read about schools in Oregon and North Carolina which have them, and they seem really to be worthwhile as a part of readiness for school and reading. That would be extending our program right out to the community, too, and if we had mothers accompanying the children, as it's been suggested they do, they'd see for themselves what's going on."

"Sounds good to me," Mr. Niles said. "We certainly should have enough kids for it, judging by the enrollment projections for this community."

"You see, I'm not so good with really creative, brand-new ideas, but I think I've stored up many that may work here, and I'm anxious to try them out. I think I can borrow enough ideas, and adapt them for us in this school to make them work."

"And that's just what we want," Mrs. Woodruff concluded.

Mrs. Zane sometimes felt that running the media center at Raeford was like filling a bottomless pit. The teachers' enthusiasm was genuine; the children responded with pleasure to the availability of materials and she knew they liked her, too. Mr. Niles proved to be as good as his word in giving her a free hand. Several weeks passed before she felt ready to start the preschool story hour which she had suggested. She had set up a schedule for use of the library which allowed children to come at any time and in any number. She remembered the first time a group of four second graders had come walking down the corridor, notebooks tucked under their arms. Mr. Niles had passed them, asked where they were going, and then followed them when they had identified themselves as a library committee. He had stayed in the library while they divided themselves up to look for the definitions of various words carefully lettered on their papers. One list had read:

POLLUTION

BLIGHT

SMOG

BUDGET

CONTROL

Nelson Olmstead, who had that list, had explained that the words were ones Miss Ridge had put on the board. They were going to see a film about pollution, and these words were in it, so they were each to be ready with definitions from the library dictionaries. Mr. Niles had been both amused and delighted at their efficient way of going about their tasks and at the kind of assistance Mrs. Zane gave them. He had asked her later how typical that kind of activity was, and she had replied, "Well, Karen Ridge is really a great teacher, and she gives them something specific to get when they come. That works best, but, of course, the other teachers are catching on, so it's working out. What I like best about this flexible schedule is that I really can give the kids who come the time and attention they need right at the time they need it."

It was in that same conversation that Mrs. Zane asked for an okay to send a message home with the children about the preschool story hour. She wanted to get it under way with time enough to have six weekly sessions before Thanksgiving. That would mean starting no later than the third week of October. The story hour was set for Monday afternoons, and parents were to be required to stay with the children. Mrs. Zane's reason for that was to get some carryover for the kinds of reading readiness activities that would be included in the hour's program. Also, it would mean the mothers would be on hand to take the children home after the story hour. For the forty-five-minute period set aside for this program, the center would be closed to children in the school.

Response to the first announcement was prompt and enthusiastic. Mrs. Zane began to wonder whether the center would hold all the children who might come. She had carefully worked out a program in which she would alternate the telling of a story from a picture book with the playing of a musical recording to which the children could play a simple game. She was prepared with rhymes, finger plays, and pictures to show and to encourage the children's comments. One of the reports of a program like this which she had read indicated that a major value for the parents should be the opportunity of seeing how their children participated in listening, playing games, and talking in a group of other children of the same age. Since Mrs. Zane had set firm minimum and maximum ages of three and five for the children who would attend, she was certain that for most, this would be their first experience in a group outside of their own families. Her own anticipation was as keen as the children's.

Twenty-three children arrived for the first session. Fifteen would have been ideal, Mrs. Zane thought, but she had wanted to avoid seeming to discourage attendance by setting up any kind of registration, and there would probably be dropouts over the six-week period. It had been announced that no new children would be admitted after the first week. This, too, fitted with one of Mrs. Zane's impressions—that preschool story hour, if it was to help make children ready for school, should encourage regular attendance, with the idea that stories and activities could be selected to build on what children had done the preceding week. The twenty-three children in attendance were a charming and varied audience, from the pixie-like little girl who never left Mrs. Zane's side from the moment she came in and took off her coat, to the large, blond boy who refused to leave his mother until he became interested in a story, but who inched his way across the floor to the rest of the group as he became more and more interested, then walked back to his mother after each story. A few of the children greeted each other like long lost acquaintances, surprised and overjoyed to find playmates in this distant place called school, but others knew no one and watched shyly till it was time for some of the action games. Mrs. Zane realized she had been wise to choose recordings that would allow children to participate as actively and as independently as they wished.

The pixie-like girl compared almost everything with her favorite children's television program, remembered one story from it, and thought Mrs. Zane's chair was just like the one the lady on television used. She announced these findings in a firm, clear voice. Barry Onslow, whom Mrs. Zane recognized from his likeness to his older brother in school, pushed the others on in every kind of participation. He said, "Oh, you can do it. You've just got to try, see?" to a friend next to him. The friend promptly tried and did better than Barry in touching thumb and forefinger, forefinger and thumb, as they followed Mrs. Zane in "Eensy-Weensy Spider."

Mrs. Zane had prepared a set of clear sketches of children's clothing, which she had cut from her daily paper and pasted on half sheets of typing paper. She had printed the name of each article below the picture—"dress," "mittens," "shoes," "shirt," "cap," "coat." As she held up each one, she said, "Now, we are going to think a minute and then we are going to say the name of what is on this page. And I will show you what it says under it." The children then responded with the name of the piece of clothing, and Mrs. Zane went on: "So, under this, I have printed, 'dress.'" The children watched and listened through the set of pictures, and then she repeated it, holding up a picture and saying, "Now what did I put under this?" Aside from some confusion over whether the cap was a cap or a hat, the mittens mittens or gloves, the children remembered well.

Then, Mrs. Zane explained that she would ask each one of them to pick out a picture from a magazine or newspaper, or perhaps even draw a picture, to bring to school next week. They were to be sure what it was, ask their mothers to print the name under it, and each of them would then come up to the front, hold up his picture, and have the other children name what it was. The mothers listened to this assignment as attentively as did the children, and when they were leaving, the children busily reminded their mothers not to let them forget to bring their homework. Especially for those with older brothers and sisters in school, Mrs. Zane sensed this homework loomed as important activity for the week to come.

On the whole, Mrs. Zane was pleased with the story hour. Mr. Niles had looked in once or twice just to see how things were going, and he looked happy about it, too. Mrs. Zane also saw Hazel Chamberlain, one of the kindergarten teachers who had given her some valuable tips on working with children of this age. Hazel had looked in the glass-windowed door for several minutes, smiled at her, and had gone on. Something they would try to work out was whether attendance at these story hours would affect children's progress in kindergarten. Mrs. Zane wanted some kind of evaluation aside from regular attendance and interest, and she and the kindergarten teachers had discussed somewhat vaguely what they might look for in the following year.

The use of the cards with pictures had been Miss Chamberlain's idea, and she had explained this was a fairly simple means of encouraging reading readiness. It prompted the children to thinking of names of ordinary things, then to associate those names with the words printed below the picture. Mrs. Zane thought the idea had worked well, and that it would be relatively simple to follow through, with pictures of toys, household appliances and furniture, and other easily recognizable objects.

Later in the afternoon of the first story hour, Mrs. Zane was surprised to look up and see Mr. Niles escorting Judy Caddo, the children's librarian from the nearby branch library, into the center. Mrs. Zane had met her on several of her visits to the library, and remembered how helpful and interested she had been in the plans for the center at Raeford. They had talked about her coming to visit sometime, but no time had been set, and Mrs. Zane had not pushed the matter. After a few minutes of showing Mrs. Caddo the features of the center which he most enjoyed, Mr. Niles excused himself and left.

Mrs. Zane asked whether there was anything Mrs. Caddo would especially like to see, but the children's librarian simply held out eight or ten gay posters announcing a series of film showings for children, to be held in the branch library on Wednesday afternoons. "I think there's one for each grade level," she said, "but I can bring more if you think they'd be used. We just didn't want to overwhelm you with one for each room. Will you get them around to the teachers?"

"Yes, of course, I'll be glad to," Mrs. Zane said. "This looks like something the children would enjoy. Do you do this every fall?"

"No, we missed last year, because we were so short staffed, so I hope we can pick up enough interest this year to keep it going. If we get a good core group of, say, fourth graders, who are old enough to remember about the programs, and young enough to be interested in all kinds of things, we usually do pretty well. I do hope it goes well. I've previewed all the films, and I know they're good. We'd be glad to have you come, too, if you'd like."

"Why, thanks. I'd like to, if I can. Perhaps I could just stop on the way home, and get an idea of what our children from Raeford do at the public library."

"Oh, they're some of our best customers, I can tell you. We love to see them coming. And then, perhaps, you'd let me visit one of your story hours?"

"Why, of course. Come any time. But I guess you mean our class visits. We are pretty flexible about those, but I could let you know when we'll be doing something interesting, and you could come. O.K.?"

Mrs. Caddo seemed somewhat embarrassed, but she went on. "No, I mean your story hours. The ones for the preschool children. We heard about the one this afternoon from Mrs. Onslow, who's a great friend of the branch librarian's. I guess I should tell you we were—are—rather concerned, because we've always considered the preschool story hour a public library program."

"Yes, I knew that most of the preschool story hours were in public libraries, at least judging by what I've read. But I didn't know you had one."

"We haven't had one for the last several years. Frankly, we just gave up when the matter of registration, holding children to the age limits, and getting mothers to come with them seemed to make the whole thing too complicated. And the same budget cuts that did away with all special programs last year ruled out the preschool story hour as well. But we've been thinking of going back to having it, and I think, Mrs. Zane, that it is the public library, not the school, that should serve the preschool child. After all, your job is related to instruction in the school, and we see the preschool story hour as something that is unstructured and refreshing for the children, not just sugar-coated reading readiness."

Mrs. Zane was somewhat taken back. Under Mrs. Caddo's pleasant manner, she sensed a real strain, and she was sure neither of the cause nor of what she could do to relieve it. She said, "We'd be glad to have you visit the preschool story hour. Believe me, I didn't think of there being one kind of activity for you to provide, and another that would be exclusively ours. It seems to me, for example, that we use films regularly in instruction and that's no reason for you not to schedule them for afternoon showings for the children. I don't see that as competition."

"But maybe you would if you'd been as hard hit with budget cuts as we have. Mrs. Zane, I haven't had an assistant for more than a year, and we serve your children as well as those from three other elementary schools where there is no kind of library program. We have no relief in sight since the bond election we'd hoped for was delayed because the school's bond election comes up this spring. Competition may not be a very nice word to use, but I'm afraid that's what it is—not just competition for the children's interest and time, but for the taxpayer's dollar."

"Yes, I see what you mean," Mrs. Zane said. "But if you are short-handed and everything, doesn't it make more sense for us to give the children the best we can, that's available here?"

"No doubt it does to you. But then, why not really serve all of the school children's needs first? Why reach out to preschoolers? Oh, I know what fun they are to work with, but you surely don't think you've taken care of all the other children in this school today? If you had, they wouldn't come flocking to us at 3:30, when you close your doors and go home."

Mrs. Zane bit back a comment about when she really went home each day because she realized Mrs. Caddo was really upset now. She wanted to soothe her, to convince her of the value of the program at Raeford, but she also needed to sort through her own reactions. She knew the coolness or, worse, hostility of a group like the public library staff could be serious in terms of the bond election. Without seeming to make an issue out of this, she felt she needed someone else's support and advice. More than any-thing, she wanted to be able to show Mrs. Caddo what this new center did, what its objectives were, but it seemed sad to have to try to describe them when they were standing right in the center which, at this moment ten minutes before dismissal for the afternoon, was deserted and quiet.

22.
Views of Reference
· · · · · · · · · · · · ·

Kenny Snyder bounded into the library one Tuesday morning with a friend, went straight to the librarian's desk, and greeted Marie Blount, the librarian on duty, with: "Hi, Miss Blount. You know everything. What're Winston Churchill's dates?"

"Born, 1874, died, 1965. I don't know everything, Kenny, but he was the same age as my grandfather, who died in 1963, so I'm not likely to forget."

Kenny turned to his friend, Rich Saluda. "See, she's good, isn't she? So we can use him all right."

"What are you going to use him for?" Miss Blount asked, with mild interest.

"Oh, we've got to write a paper for social studies, and it's got to be about somebody who overlapped the nineteenth and twentieth centuries. I wasn't sure Churchill was born long enough ago, but I thought he'd be great, because he's practically modern, and most of the kids can really remember something about him. He'll be a lot more fun than Pershing, Woodrow Wilson, or some of the other guys the kids are picking. Well, let's go, Rich."

Miss Blount looked after the two enthusiastic boys with a smile. Kenny pushed Rich toward the encyclopedias and busily showed him how to make the best use of the indexes, then went to the card catalog to begin his own search for materials. Just then, Pat Sneed, the head librarian, who had been revising some filing in the card catalog, walked back to the desk.

"Kenny's right, Miss Blount. You're good. I'm rather glad I happened to overhear this little exchange, because I'm concerned about some things I've been hearing about you from the faculty. Several of the teachers have told me that you're too quick on the draw for our students, that you give them answers right off the top of your head, and that—"

"But, Mr. Sneed, that's the best service I can give. Why play around looking something up when I really know the answer?"

"I'm not sure that using the wealth of reference materials we've built up over the years is 'playing around,' Miss Blount, but this may be a more serious point than you realize. I hadn't wanted to comment on this habit till I observed it myself, but I think this was a good example of it."

"You're usually very fair, Mr. Sneed, and I think we've gotten along beautifully. Are you really going to pick on me for telling kids what I know as a fact?"

"Let's say that part of Kenny's assignment was to ascertain the dates of the person he wanted to write about. Aren't you doing part of his work for him?"

"If that were true, I think Kenny probably would not have asked me. He gets too much enjoyment out of working things out for himself. He's one boy I love to watch at work. He really grinds away, under that gay exterior of his." Miss Blount was as disturbed at the implied challenge to Kenny's integrity as she was at what she considered the unfair accusation leveled at her. She realized she was in danger of losing her temper.

Mr. Sneed, who was a sensitive person, reacted as he saw her strain. "This may be something we should have discussed long ago. Why don't you take your coffee break now, though, and I'll take over at the desk? I'll go later, because I want to stop by room 301 on the way and see whether Abner has it set up for that film showing during the second lunch period."

Gratefully, Miss Blount excused herself and left. She was sure this matter would come up again, but she wanted it to be at another time and some place other than the public desk. When she ran into Frank Dyer at coffee, her spirits lifted.

"Hi, Marie," he greeted her. "What's with you? Are you burning the candle at both ends, or working too hard?"

Miss Blount laughed. Since they had first met in September of the previous school year, when they were two of the seven new teachers at Hancock Junior High, she and Frank had been friends. She was not sure now, though, whether to answer in the same teasing way he had used, or to cry on his shoulder. "As a matter of fact," she said, then laughed at her choice of words, "as a matter of fact, would you believe I'm just depressed because I've been corrected for giving out a matter of fact?"

Mr. Dyer chuckled. "And you a librarian! What did you do?"

"What I did was tell Kenny Snyder the dates of Winston Churchill's birth and death."

"So that's it? What are they—classified? Or maybe he's still alive?" Mr. Dyer was clowning to cheer her up, and Miss Blount laughed with him.

"Oh, Frank! The thing is, evidently somebody's been complaining to Mr. Sneed because I answer questions without always checking references for them, and I did that today. I knew the dates, and I just told the boys what they were."

"Then I'd say that Sneed is just jealous. He wouldn't have known, and he resents a lot of things you do that really help to make the library run more smoothly. You don't suppose the boys had asked him, and he didn't know, so he thought you were showing off for his benefit? Could it be something like that?"

"Oh, no. For one thing, the boys had come roaring in from class—you know how Kenny hits the library whenever he has a chance. And for another, Mr. Sneed is certainly not small like that. He really loves it when people compliment me, and he's proud of what we accomplish in the library. I'm proud of all that, too, and I just feel that, with all our teamwork, we may have hit on a stumbling block here that could really upset things."

"That bad, eh? Well, don't let it get you down for the day. I'll see you tonight at the math meet, right? And remember, good timekeepers have cool heads. That's why we want you."

Miss Blount smiled after him as he left the teachers' lounge. She was reaching for a magazine on the coffee table, when Alta Morris, one of the best English teachers in the school, came over and sat in the lounge chair next to her.

"I'm sorry, Marie. I wasn't eavesdropping, but I heard your conversation with Frank, and I think I should tell you that I'm probably one of the teachers Pat Sneed was talking about. I wasn't really registering a complaint, but one evening, we were at the same party, and I was saying that the students were making a sort of game of it to ask you who wrote what, what period a given writer was in, that sort of thing—as you must have noticed. And I also just sort of wondered out loud whether the library was making them lazy. You're popular with the students, and I'm sure it's because you're interested in so many things they do—like being timekeeper at the math meet, for instance—and they respond to that. But I don't think they should take advantage of you. Nor do I think you should do their work for them. As far as I'm concerned, I don't care whether you give them the answer without checking in a book or not, but I wonder whether perhaps you give them too many answers, just as a matter of course." The older woman had leaned forward and spoken earnestly and quietly to Miss Blount, who was touched that she was so quick to assume responsibility for the anonymous complaints which Mr. Sneed had mentioned.

"Thank you, Mrs. Morris. I'm glad to know that the comment was as informal as that. And I think this may all blow over. I'll think over what you said about doing too much of the students' work for them. I really don't think I'm guilty of that, but you've given me something to think about. See you." The two women left the lounge together.

Mr. Sneed was in a hurry to get off when Miss Blount returned, but he handed her a reading list on which he had been noting call numbers from the card catalog. "Here," he said, "I thought this was something we could do while keeping an eye on the desk. It's a list Mr. Codington brought in. I told him we'd check it to see what we have in the library, and then pick four or five of the titles that are in and check them out to him. He'll pick them up after school this afternoon. There's no rush, but you might as well finish it while you're on the desk. O.K.?"

Miss Blount sensed that Mr. Sneed was pleased to have something specific to talk to her about. This relieved the tension between them, but she was still sure he would want to discuss the problem he had raised earlier. She went over to the card catalog as he left the library.

"Hey, Miss Blount!" Kenny Snyder had come up beside her at the catalog, and he spoke almost in a whisper. "I'm sorry, Miss Blount, if I got you in trouble."

"Oh, Kenny, what makes you think you got me in trouble?"

"Well, you know, I was still working around here, and I heard what Mr. Sneed said to you. He bawled you out for helping us. I just don't get it! I'm always telling other kids, like Rich, that they should ask the librarians for help—that that's why you're here. Then somebody like Mr. Sneed comes along and acts like a fink about it. Well, I guess I know how to find my way around the library if I have to. It'll take me longer, but I'll leave you alone. I promise you that. Oh, I'll still talk to you and all that, but I won't bother you any more, not if it's going to cause you trouble with him. He's the boss, isn't he?"

"Yes, Kenny, he's the boss. And a very good one, very fair. I think we're going to be talking some more about this, and I'm not going to take it too seriously." Miss Blount laughed, partly in gratitude as she thought of the boy's straightforwardness and concern, partly to reassure him. "You didn't get me into any trouble, at least not something that can't be fixed. But tell me something, Kenny, do you think that when I give you an answer without looking it up in a book or somewhere else, that keeps you from learning how to use the library? I'd just like to know."

"Oh, no, Miss Blount. As a matter of fact, I think I use the library better than anybody else I know, and the reason is that I'm used to asking for help. You give me a start, like you did today, and then I can go on my own. That's just the way I like it."

"I see. Well, thanks, Kenny. And don't worry."

Kenny returned to the table where Rich was working, and Miss Blount continued to check for the items on the principal's reading list. It was a strange list, she thought, including some recent novels, few of which were in this junior high library, one or two of Catherine Drinker Bowen's biographies, several books of general background reading in several sciences, and five or six novels for teenagers. Of these, two or three had been considered too sophisticated or too frank for their library collection, but she was pleased to note they had the others, as well as about half of the books in sciences. As she finished marking the call numbers in the left margin, she noticed initials at the bottom of the second page: LMH:rs. Of course! She should have recognized it at once. These were books that Lydia Marshall Hand was going to be reviewing in a luncheon series sponsored by the local branch of the American Association of University Women. She remembered seeing a reference to several of the titles in the AAUW monthly calendar, but since she knew she could not get away for the luncheon meetings, she had paid little attention. She smiled to herself. So Mrs. Codington had handed the list to her husband to get him to pick them up at this library, where the other ladies would not have a chance to get them, and here were herself and Mr. Sneed working away to keep the principal's wife informed and active as a cultural leader in the community.

Something nagged at Miss Blount's mind as she searched the shelves for the titles that were available, checked them out to the principal, and placed them on a ledge under the desk with his name on them. She tucked the list into the book on top. When Mr. Sneed walked through the library on his way to his office, her concern focused on their earlier discussion.

Suddenly, she resented the fact that she had spent perhaps fifteen minutes of school time on a personal errand for the principal. And on the same day, she had been corrected for being too ready to help students. It didn't seem to make much sense.

At times during the day Miss Blount thought of her encounter with Mr. Sneed, and she was not surprised when he suggested, at 3:40 that afternoon, that she stop in his office for a few minutes. It was just as well to settle this matter, to the extent that it could be settled, as quickly as possible.

Mr. Sneed began carefully. "I didn't want to upset you this morning, Miss Blount, and I'm sorry if I did. But we are, after all, two reasonable, mature adults, and I think we should be able to work this out. I had thought before of mentioning to you the criticisms I had heard, but I didn't want to do so until I had observed it personally. And when I did, just by chance, I guess I moved too quickly. I don't think this is a major difference of opinion, but I do want to know whether you now see things my way. The point I should have made this morning is that the library is a part of the instructional program of the school. We are not here to hand out, indiscriminately, what people want; we are here to help people use the materials more effectively, and that means encouraging them to search for themselves. Of course, there may be times when you would work right along with them, but we are not just dispensers of information. We are teachers."

"And teachers aren't dispensers of information?" Miss Blount asked innocently.

"Oh, now, Miss Blount, don't try to trap me. We've worked too long and too well together for that. I realized that today when a memo about your contract for next year was in my mail box. You're the first assistant who's weathered a full two years here, and you are, as you know, eligible for tenure. I think that we make a good team, and it is wonderful, let me tell you, for me to look forward to another year when we can continue to work together and really build a stronger program here. I'm anxious for us to move faster into the area of nonprint materials, and next year, with Jack Woodbury back, we should be able to do that. But now, what about this little matter?"

"I'm sorry, too, Mr. Sneed, but the more I think about this, the more I think this isn't a little matter. I guess we've either just been lucky—or perhaps terribly unlucky—that we haven't run head on into this before, but

I'm beginning to think that we operate on two different philosophies about service. I don't see how I've missed seeing it before. But you seem to think, 'whatever teachers want, teachers get; whatever students want, make them grub around for.' I realized that today when I was gathering those books for Mr. Codington. Oh, there he is now!" She stood up and went to the desk, which she could see through the window of Mr. Sneed's office. Mr. Codington smiled as she handed him the books.

"Oh, five of them! Great!" he said. "I surely appreciate your getting these together, Miss Blount. And thank Pat, too. I probably should stop in more often and tell you some of the good things I keep hearing about the library from the teachers. But you both know I know you're doing a good job. Thank you. Good night." He left with the books under his arm, and Miss Blount returned to Mr. Sneed's office.

"You know what that was all about?" she asked. "Those books are ones his wife wants to read so she can go eat chicken salad and hear Lydia Hand discuss them. That's one of the things that began to get to me, Mr. Sneed. We dropped everything to round them up for him, because he's the principal. His wife could get them at the public library, or even buy some of them in paperback, very easily. But I'm not supposed to answer a simple reference question without making it look complicated. I just think that looking everything up, when it's perfectly obvious all the time, is the way old-fashioned librarians develop a mystique about how difficult it is to work in a library."

"Did Mr. Codington tell you why he wanted the books?" Mr. Sneed asked.

"No, but I belong to the AAUW, and I recognized the list, which is the one they're going to be reading from. You do see, don't you, Mr. Sneed, that I'm talking about preferential treatment for teachers? I'm beginning to think that you and I have lots of different points of view about service, and they've just never come to light before. I never thought of it until you talked with me today."

"But, Miss Blount," Mr. Sneed leaned forward with a smile, "you're the one who's being unfair now. You leap to the conclusion—again, you see, that impatience and assurance that keep you from consulting a reference before you give someone an answer—that because you know the source of that reading, that Mrs. Codington is the one who's going to use it. It just could be that Mr. Codington came across it, and thought it would be a good way to keep up with what young people are reading. And I might say that's one of his strong points as a principal—he's very interested in young people, and he seems to read everything. But this is somewhat beside the point anyway. You think I give—and encourage you to give—preferential treatment to teachers, over students. I suppose I do, at that. I see our service to teachers as being more like that of a special library. We compile bibliographies for them, we check lists they have, we gather materials for their classes, we give them unusual loans. But with the students, we fill more of a teaching role. We need to teach them to be self-reliant in a library. I'm sure I've told you that one of the highest compliments I've ever received came from the public librarian after I'd been here several years. She said she could always tell our students because they can operate on their own. I'm not just proud of that for the sake of the public library. I'm proud for the students' sake, for their self-respect. And Ouida Winner at the high school says the same thing. Our students can cope with what they need to use in that library, which is much larger than this, and they fit right in."

"I know," Miss Blount said wearily. "I like that, too, but part of the reason they use the library well is because they like it. We help them, but we don't spoon-feed them, if that's what you call the other extreme. And I don't think I do, either. Really, Mr. Sneed, no other librarian has told you the students have gotten lazier in the time I've been here, has he?"

Mr. Sneed's smile answered her own. "No, of course not. But I don't see why you're making such an issue of this. Perhaps I didn't realize what a strong habit of yours this was, because I hadn't observed it myself. It may even be helpful on occasion, but please, Miss Blount, let us just say this afternoon that from this point on, you agree that when you are on duty at the desk, you will not rattle off answers without checking them for accuracy. I won't even ask you to promise not to jump to conclusions about why people like the principal want specific books, but I think that, too, is part of an ethic, if you don't mind such a highflown term."

"What I can do, Mr. Sneed, is to agree that I will double-check, or even triple-check anything I'm not sure of, and, if there's lots of time, I will always verify an answer. But I really believe I would be doing a disservice to the students of Hancock Junior High School if I said I'd never again give them information that was more accessible in my brain than in a book."

"Well, we seem to have reached an impasse. Perhaps we'll both be aware of this difference in practice and policy and discuss it another time." Mr. Sneed was moving his plastic folder of papers to one side of his desk.

That was his signal that he was getting ready to leave for the day. Miss Blount realized the conversation was over, and she felt a mixture of relief and disappointment. She felt that nothing was really resolved. They would each go his own way, although she would try to keep the promise she had made. But the most disturbing thing was that Mr. Sneed did not see that these supposedly minor incidents and differences of opinion perhaps indicated a basically different philosophy. She was not sure she could continue to work with him for an indefinite period of time if these differences increased. If she had discovered so many today, there might be more and more each day. Better to leave, she thought, before the two of them turned out like the mythical librarians who had refused to use each other's reference materials and had administered service from either end of the school library. She was sure the story was an old one, based on little or no fact, but the prospect of being watched and somehow evaluated by Mr. Sneed, and of continuing to differ with him, somehow chilled her.

23.
The Case of
the Committee Chairman

· · · · · · · · · · · · · · · · · · ·

Helen Spinard had been librarian at Glendale High School since it had opened, fifteen years ago. She managed to keep in close touch with the needs and interests of faculty and students, and to develop a library collection which usually satisfied their requests. For the past two years, she had been assisted by John Ralston, a teacher who had a state certificate as an audio-visual specialist. They had divided the work load fairly equitably, Mrs. Spinard felt. Both of them served on the reference desk, assigned times for use of audiovisual equipment and materials, and shared such responsibilities as orientation of classes to the library. Mrs. Spinard was definitely in charge, but she valued Mr. Ralston's willingness to learn, and the good communication they had achieved. With the enrollment at Glendale leveling off at 2,500 students, both staff members sensed a renewed zest and interest in the high school on the part of members of the community and teachers at the school. The reason for this seemed to be that, with school buildings no longer so crowded, and with the families now looking toward college for their children, there was growing concern for academic excellence.

Some time earlier, Mrs. Spinard suggested at a faculty meeting the idea of a library faculty committee, and, with the endorsement of George Douglas, the principal, the committee was established. There were five members, one each from the three largest departments—English, social studies, and science—and two from the rest of the faculty. This year, the two appointed by Mr. Douglas, at Mrs. Spinard's suggestion, were Joan Ramsey, a home economics teacher, and Henry Melbourne, an industrial arts teacher, who was chairman of the committee. Mr. Melbourne accepted the chairmanship cheerfully at his first meeting. Since he was known on the faculty as a bright, ambitious teacher, active in the education association of the school district and taking courses in educational administration, everyone present realized how pleased he was to accept this responsibility.

What no one predicted was the enthusiasm with which he would enter into the chairmanship. One of his first acts was to visit the small professional library in the workroom and to select several books on school libraries. On that visit, he commented to Mr. Ralston that he thought the library committee should meet more regularly and initiate more suggestions, rather than simply react to ideas offered by the librarians. Mr. Ralston repeated this comment to Mrs. Spinard, who assumed it was typical of Mr. Melbourne's interest in organizations and committee work.

Mrs. Spinard realized the seriousness with which Mr. Melbourne had approached his chairmanship when, about ten days later, she received this memorandum in her school mail box:

To: Miss Perrine, English Department
    Mr. Naranja, Social Studies Department
    Mr. Haines, Science Department
    Mrs. Ramsey, Home Economics Department
    Mrs. Spinard, Librarian
    Mr. Ralston, Librarian
    Information copy to Mr. Douglas, Principal
From: Henry Melbourne, Chairman, Library Faculty Committee
Subject: Plans for action by this committee

As members of the Library Faculty Committee, you are probably as anxious as I am to get to work. Knowing that all of us have many responsibilities, I suggest that you mark your calendars for meetings of this committee at 7:30 a.m. on alternating Thursdays, beginning Thursday, October 1. If the committee has no business to take care of on those dates, you will be notified no later than Tuesday afternoon that the committee meeting has been canceled. I think it is important, however, that we meet regularly to discuss library problems and progress, and that we follow an agenda. I will be glad to receive your suggestions for agenda items.

The meetings will be in the industrial arts drafting rooms, and will usually last fifty minutes, so you will have ten minutes to get to your first class. I will arrange to have coffee and rolls ready for each meeting, and Mr. Douglas has agreed that we can finance this modest cost from the school fund, since this is official school business.

I know you are just getting into the swing of things for the school year, so I will suggest a topic for discussion at our first meeting on October 1. It is the possibility of having the library collection divided on a departmental basis. This is a practice that seems to be spreading in a number of high schools comparable to ours in size, and if we follow this pattern, we will be a good model and pacesetter for other high schools in our immediate area, which seem to be slower to accept the idea.

As I understand it, departmental libraries are located near the teaching areas of the appropriate departments. In industrial arts, for example, this might mean we would have a collection in the drafting room, which is large and central for the rest of the classrooms in our department. Since there is always a lot of movement in this room, having students come to borrow materials would be no great distraction even during class time. Also, it would mean that these materials could be used more easily along with the books on drafting, which we have always kept in the drafting rooms and which were bought with departmental funds, rather than as library materials.

It might be that a large department, such as English, where students are expected to read on a broad range of subjects and to consult many of the encyclopedias, and other reference works which are in the library, would not require a departmental library. Instead, the English department might prefer to have a specialized library, for example, a journalism collection in the *Snapper* [school newspaper] office, instead of a single large collection. To be sure all this meets with the approval of faculty members, this is a topic which might first be discussed at individual departmental faculty meetings. If your department has a meeting scheduled between now and October 1, perhaps you could sound them out then and come prepared for discussion.

After reading the memorandum, Mrs. Spinard asked Mr. Ralston, who had been reading his copy while standing in the library between classes, to join her in the workroom. She opened the conversation by saying, "John, did you know that anything like this was happening? Apparently he's already gotten Mr. Douglas behind him, since he's cleared that bit about coffee with him. And he's presenting this idea to the committee as though it's something we have to do to keep up with the Joneses. Of course, he hasn't gone into it in any depth, and he doesn't have the vaguest idea how much this would cost in duplication, additional staff, and all that. Did you know he had those drafting books down there in some kind of special collection? What do you think, John?"

John Ralston smiled as he answered, "You want me to answer that last question first, Helen? I think we finally have a livewire committee chairman who won't be content just to come into the library once a month, have a cup of coffee with you, and decide there's no need to have the committee get together. Maybe you don't like it?"

Mrs. Spinard was a bit flustered. It occurred to her that Mr. Ralston might be a co-conspirator with Mr. Melbourne. She decided to take a different tack.

"Well, he is rather high-handed, isn't he? Why didn't he come here to talk this over? For every article he can find recommending departmental collections, I can show him three pointing out some of the problems involved and giving reasons why some schools have avoided them like the plague and why others are dropping the idea and going back to centralized collections. Has he considered the costs? Of course not!"

"Henry? No, he probably hasn't. He's a real idea man, and you know it. But he gets things done. I worked with him on that committee to get the school district to give the education association rented space for an executive office in the administration building, and he went at it in about the same way. The funny thing was, by the time he'd won his point, the superintendent was being patted on the head by the school board for having been so foresighted and progressive as to set up something like that. You could come out of this the same way, if you handle it right."

"You mean make it all sound like it was my idea? Why should I do that? You act as though there is nothing we can do to stop him!" Mrs. Spinard said nervously.

"What I was thinking was that some of the things you and I have discussed—the idea of locating more of the equipment nearer the classrooms to cut down on all this carting around we have to do, for example—could be accomplished this way, and the faculty would be convinced we were doing it to make things easier for them, rather than for ourselves. And you've often said yourself that if the faculty would really support the need for more staff, we'd get it. Don't you think they'd be more likely to do that, if they thought it might mean someone, even on a part-time basis, assigned to their own departments?"

"Of course, Mr. Melbourne's already gone over our heads—right to Mr. Douglas and the members of the committee. Right this minute, Miss Perrine is probably talking to Mr. Parker about the possibility of a departmental library in the *Snapper* office. And that's a good example! Mr. Melbourne evidently would put these collections in the most active, least supervised areas. We'd lose thousands of books a year, and it would look like the library's fault. And all the time, we'd have to be duplicating more titles. Has he thought, for example, about how much overlap there is between English and social sciences, in the materials they use? Has he thought about the student who may want to spend one study period on math *and* industrial arts and science, and who would have to run all over this huge building getting materials if they were scattered all over the place?"

Listening to her own voice, Helen Spinard realized that she sounded panicky. Mr. Ralston's equanimity was all the more galling, but he continued: "Helen, I'm very sure that Henry has not thought of all those things. He's stumbled on to an idea and he's ready to carry the flag for it, that's all. But he's not necessarily acting in bad faith. I think he'd love to talk all this over with you—but tomorrow would probably be better than today. To him, the natural thing is to get out a memo to all members of the committee and the staff liaison for it. That's the way he works in the education association, and he's just following the same plan. I think he'd love to have you call or go down to ask to discuss this with him. I'll go with you, if you like, but I think we should know what we're doing and what we want, first. O.K.?"

"Yes, okay, I guess," Mrs. Spinard answered slowly.

"What I'm driving at is this—are you angry about what he's doing or about how he's doing it? Remember how dull old Miss Montrose used to run these committee meetings last year? They got to be such a bore that half the committee members never showed up, and the ones who did always came late because she started them late and had nothing planned to discuss. Of course, she did always check with you in advance. But what should the library committee be? A reactor panel or a change agent?"

· · · · ·

What is your reaction to the roles played, to date, by Mr. Melbourne, Mrs. Spinard, and Mr. Ralston?

With whom should Mrs. Spinard next discuss this problem? With Mr. Douglas? Mr. Melbourne? The entire library committee?

Assuming that Mrs. Spinard meets with Mr. Melbourne, prepare an annotated listing of articles or references about departmental collections which might be helpful to her. Suggest ways in which she might use such a list. Suggest points she might wish to cover at such a meeting.

What facts, unknown in this situation, might have bearing on the problem?

What is your reaction to Mr. Ralston's final question about what the library committee should be?

24.
The Case
of Modular Madness

· · · · · · · · · · · · · · · ·

Henry Canton, director of the media center at Lapeer High School, was one of the most enthusiastic proponents of the school's transition to modular scheduling. He had had the opportunity to visit several high schools using this system of scheduling, and, although he was sometimes disappointed that the library programs he saw were not as innovative as he might have wished, he sensed the promise this kind of scheduling could hold for his school. The 1,800 students at Lapeer, and the faculty and staff were equally enthusiastic. Mr. Canton attributed much of this enthusiasm to the planning, discussion, and ideas for evaluation offered by Howard Kent, the principal, and his younger assistant, Tom Roscommon. Mr. Roscommon had the responsibility for instruction, in general, and was Mr. Canton's immediate superior.

There were problems when twenty-minute modules were tried for several weeks in the spring semester. Some of these were predictable. Graduating seniors, accustomed to forty-five minute class periods and feeling more casual about classes in the last days of school, took pride in being the biggest "goof-offs," spending their unscheduled modules lounging on the patio near the lockers or leaving the school campus when they thought they would not be missed. Ninth, tenth and eleventh graders, however, entered the experiment with gusto and were dismayed, but not unduly upset, when their individualized schedules led them into classrooms already filled to overflowing with students or left without a teacher, because of problems with the computerized schedulemaking. Their pride in being at the one school of the four in the township to try this new kind of scheduling, however, led their spokesmen in the student council to be very positive about the values they saw in modular scheduling. Mr. Canton was somewhat disappointed that the spring tryout did not lead to any noticeably better patterns in use of the media center. Staff members in the media center met together to pool reactions before the all-day faculty meeting at the close of school, at which Mr. Roscommon was to lead discussion of the problems and strengths of modular scheduling. This center staff included Harold Herring, Joan Mason, and Selma Wayne. As a teacher, Herring had had problems with discipline which led to his being relieved of a classroom assignment, but his ability to organize work was well utilized in the center. He scheduled staff and student assistants, handled many of the routines such as fines and overdues, and acted as liaison between the staff and teachers in the making of graphic materials and scheduling of media in classroom instruction. Mrs. Mason, a recent library school graduate, did most of the reading guidance and reference work with students, and also was responsible for completing orders for materials and checking in materials as they were received by the center from the district processing office. Mrs. Wayne, who was a college graduate with business experience and artistic talent, was, if anything, apparently overqualified for her work as graphics specialist and general clerical assistant.

Mr. Canton considered his own greatest strength lay in making the best use of this varied staff, which included keeping Mr. Herring free of discipline problems, Mrs. Wayne uninterrupted while engaged on lengthy production projects, and Mrs. Mason scheduled flexibly in her different tasks so that she did not feel the behind-the-scenes work pressing when she should have been working with students. Besides maintaining most of the communication with teachers and other staff, Mr. Canton relieved Mrs. Mason on floor work and offered most of the library instruction or orientation. He was proud of this staff's work, and was anxious to hear their reactions to modular scheduling.

The meeting began somewhat unpropitiously with Mr. Herring's question, "Well, after these four weeks, who'll transfer to bedlam with me?"

"Has it been that bad, Harold?" Mr. Canton asked.

"Oh, I'll go along with it, Henry, but I really think it's a disaster. The kids who come into the center don't know why they're here or what they're supposed to do. They're simply not ready to handle this kind of responsibility. And, of course, when we get into this full-time and on a permanent basis, it will be worse. We'll have to give up the student assistants program, I'm sure. It's ridiculous to think that students can get anything done in twenty minutes, either on the circulation desk, or delivering stuff to classrooms. I don't know how I'll ever manage without them, but I guess we'll all just have to cope."

"It seems to me we're giving up something pretty valuable if we give up the student assistants program," Mrs. Mason said. "Can't we keep trying it anyway? I realize it's your job rather than mine, Harold, but the kids are so proud of their service to the school, I'd hate to see it dropped. What surprises me is how much commotion there is all the time in the library. With big turnovers of kids every twenty minutes, and with their being free to come and go as they please in between, it's like trying to be a reader's advisor in an airport. And at that, since it's spring semester, we haven't had nearly as many class groups coming for orientation."

Mr. Canton said, "Well, I think this spring has been the time when students and teachers have gone all out for emphasizing the twenty-minute modules. As things shake down next fall, I think we'll see the real value of modular scheduling. Teachers will use two or three modules together for a class, and students will realize that they just have to make better use of what they've considered free time this spring. The whole idea is to make them more aware of being responsible for their own work and for going ahead in real independent study. I think we can work it out, all right." Mr. Canton knew that this was a time when his own convictions and enthusiasms could lead the rest of the staff on, even though they were not really convinced by his judgments and decisions.

They went on to discuss details of scheduling that might be changed in the future. Mrs. Wayne offered a suggestion.

"It seems to me," she said, "that we're not going to have a chance to do anything except track down kids if this schedule keeps up the way it has. If there was one phone call from the main offices today, asking whether so-and-so was in the library, I'll bet there were fifteen. And, each time I stopped and went around the reading room and conference rooms looking for whoever it was, it probably took five minutes. Do you remember that school we visited where students put their identification cards in racks as they visited the library? If we had something like that, we could check the rack for attendance and find out who was here."

"What I don't like about that," Mr. Canton answered, "is that it becomes a sort of variation of the pass system, which we've always tried to avoid. I noticed there were a number of calls for individual students today, but I think a lot of them were for seniors to come in about their graduation pictures. There will be less of that in the fall."

"There's more to it than that," Mr. Herring put in. "We're now trying to treat students like adults while still keeping track of them like children. Parents call because they know they can always catch a student at school and that he'll be sent to the office to take the call. With a school this size and with all the complications of this new schedule, I think that's a luxury we just can't afford any more. Dr. Kent will have to tell the parents that students can be reached only during the first or last modules of the day—or something like that."

As the meeting went on, Mr. Canton found it ironic that the supposed flexibility of modular scheduling seemed to be leading the staff toward more inflexible ideas about keeping track of students, scheduling groups into the library, and giving up such programs as the volunteer assistants. All of them went on to the faculty meeting at which these and many comments from other faculty members were reviewed. The problem of locating students during the day, however, was brushed aside. Mr. Canton felt that teachers, who would have, at the absolute most, seventy-five students in a large group presentation, simply did not understand the problems of the media center with the prospect of seating as many as 120 students in the reading room and conference rooms, and with none of the students regularly assigned there. He pursued the matter with Mr. Roscommon later.

"Henry, I've always felt that the media program here was one of the things pushing us toward more flexibility and individuality. Now, here you are, raising questions about implementation of modular scheduling, which is supposed to achieve that for us. I can assure you that it's potentially much more upsetting to teachers, who are having to revise many of their preparation and presentation techniques, and who aren't used to turning the students loose so much. You wouldn't want us to put in an attendance roster just for students using the library, would you? Don't you remember the little old lady in tennis shoes who went around with the clipboard checking initials in little blocks when we visited Keweenaw? You thought that was as funny as I did."

Mr. Canton remembered the librarian who had seemed to spend more time checking students in than providing any kind of service, and he did not want to be, even jokingly, put in the same class with her. He was determined that the media center should remain in the lead in this new pattern of scheduling, but he was also aware that, with other negative reactions beginning to drift to Mr. Roscommon's attention, it might be his job alone to resolve the problems of the center. During the summer, he reviewed his notes of schools they had visited and realized that in his interest in modular scheduling, he had often overlooked the fact that the library program some-times did not relate to the flexible schedule.

In one center, the director had said: "Modular scheduling has made no difference to us. We receive students from the study halls and one of the monitors goes back to report on who is in the library during the module. Of course, this takes a lot of time, because it has to be done every twenty minutes, but a monitor does it, so it's not library time." Another had com-mented: "Our relations with the faculty were so good under traditional scheduling that we have found them quite adaptable to this new scheme. The teachers still make appointments when they want to bring their classes to the library, and we accommodate them. We tell them we can't let classes in for only one module at a time, and they accept that. There is no prob-lem."

Mr. Canton saw that there was no problem in instances of this kind, but he now wondered whether there was any innovation. Was the media program operating on one schedule, the rest of the school on another? He regretted having spent so much of his time visiting the media centers or libraries themselves. What he had was the librarians' views of modular scheduling, with little or nothing of the teachers' or students' views of the libraries or centers.

His own instincts were to keep as many features of the present pro-gram—the use of student assistants, the system of having no passes, the scheduling of orientation and instruction sessions—as he could, working within modular scheduling. His decision might not be popular with the media staff, but he was sure they would accept it for another trial period in the fall.

The surprise in the fall was not the extensive use of the center, but its comparative lack of use. Although the staff had never kept attendance records, the center at almost any time of day included many empty seats, some students lounging near the periodical shelves, and perhaps sixty stu-dents scattered at tables and carrels throughout the reading room. In spite of this, the frequent noisy exits and entrances of students bothered Mr. Herring, whose position at the circulation desk or just inside the workroom allowed him to see and hear all the distracting activity. He often was brusque or impatient with students.

Mr. Canton's own schedule changed somewhat. In response to his memorandum suggesting orientation sessions for ninth-grade English classes in the media center, several teachers had asked him to present, instead, a series of three large-group presentations in the assembly hall. They scheduled modules back to back, so that in nine forty-minute presentations he had presented information about location of indexes, use of the catalog, and brief introductions to outlining, skimming, and related skills, to the 600 ninth graders.

Joan Mason's schedule and pattern of work had changed also, and not to her liking. One day when she returned to the reference desk in the reading room, she said to Mr. Canton, who had been on the desk in her absence, "Well, are you getting a taste of what it's like to try to do, one by one, all the orientation that used to be done right here in the center?"

He recalled that there had been, during Mrs. Mason's break, several ninth-grade students who had seemed to be completely at sea and whom he had helped to find various nonfiction sections and other areas of the center. Had this responsibility increased as the result of having the orientation sessions elsewhere? Mrs. Mason stressed that it had. "Why, not only that," she said, "but look what it's done to keep kids out of the center. You go to their classes and they treat you like a visitor. It doesn't dawn on them that the next step is for them to use what you've taught them right here in the center—or maybe the teachers are just so confused by trying to keep up with these schedules themselves that they aren't giving the students the right assignments. Something is keeping the students away. But why worry about that, when we have to work about three times as hard with those who do come, just because they don't know where to begin."

Mr. Canton thought that he should have anticipated that the savings of his own time in orientation probably would work hardships elsewhere. The usually placid Mrs. Mason was the first staff member to confront him so openly with her objections, but the next one came soon. Mrs. Wayne was waiting for him at the door of the workroom.

"I'd like to show you something," she said, walking over to the tilted work table where she made transparencies. "This is a job that used to take me ten minutes at the most. I've just scraped the dry glue off this overlay for the second time, because each time I've been ready to press it on the template, I've been called to the phone. Once it was to round up a boy who had walked off the basketball court with a broken wrist. The coach was nearly out of his mind trying to find him, because he wasn't due at any class for another hour and twenty minutes, and he'd gotten away while the coach was busy with something else. I must have walked miles in this building trying to find him, and when I did, he was leaning up against his locker just about to faint. Now, I don't mind that, because it was an emergency and the office said the three secretaries down there were running their tails off this morning anyway, with all those visitors here, but the other interruption was the last straw. I ran all over this library looking for a girl wearing a brown wig, because her mother wanted to get the wig from her in time to wear it to some luncheon. When this job gets to be a cross between a telephone operator's and a baby-sitter's, you can count me out—and it looks like it won't be long."

Mr. Canton knew that Mrs. Wayne would not make such a statement lightly, and he was concerned by it, even as he was half amused by the mischances of the morning. "But couldn't one of the student assistants have done some of that running around?" he asked.

"Ask Mr. Herring about that!" Mrs. Wayne snapped, as she clicked on the fluorescent light over her work table and sat down. Mr. Herring was obviously in a bad mood when he entered the work room pushing a projector cart loaded with two tape recorders and an overhead projector.

"Mr. Canton, I can't go on like this," he said. "I've just picked up equipment that was in use three modules ago, and I'm late getting the other stuff out for this module. If teachers were making use of materials the way they were at this time last year, I wouldn't be even this far along. As it is, since they have so little time with any one class, they're mostly using media just incidentally. You've noticed, haven't you, that our requests for films from the university center are down to about twenty percent of what they were last year? But even so, with my doing all the fetching and carrying, I can't keep up with the requests we do have."

Glancing over Mr. Herring's shoulder, Mr. Canton saw two girls working at the circulation desk. They were the only student assistants in sight, and they were busy with files and cards. They were the same two he had seen on duty almost an hour ago. He wondered whether Mr. Herring's reluctant agreement to "go along with" things this year had simply covered up the fact that he would let the student assistants program die a natural death. But this did not seem to be the time to ask Mr. Herring what was going on in that program. What Mr. Canton felt he needed most was to sort out his own ideas and reactions and then, with the staff of the center and perhaps Mr. Roscommon, to review where they were now and what the impact of modular scheduling was on the center—as well as vice versa.

· · · · ·

Indicate major topics which Mr. Canton should have for the agenda for this discussion meeting. Note topics on which he will need to have more information before opening the discussion. Select one topic, provide information on it which is not included in the case, and provide one or more suggested solutions including the means of implementing or encouraging acceptance of those solutions with staff.

Mr. Canton probably should alert Mr. Roscommon to some of the problems to be discussed. Prepare notes for a memorandum for him, pointing up the aspects of the problems which are most directly related to the school's instructional program.

25.
Sore Point
at Sharp Corners
· · · · · · · · · · · · ·

Vernon Coos had come to Sharp Corners as superintendent of schools, to succeed an elderly educator who was much respected in the town, but who had deferred many decisions on new suggestions and activities during his last years before retirement. The school board had taken its responsibility for choosing a successor seriously, and had hired a team of three consultants from the department of education of the nearest university to solicit and screen applicants from many parts of the country. The stability of the town was one of its prides, and the board indicated firmly it was looking for a superintendent who would settle in and become the community leader his predecessor had been. All of this had appealed to Mr. Coos, whose experience as curriculum consultant, principal, and teacher in several suburban communities made him anxious to put his own mark on a small school system.

The system included the high school, accredited by the state but lacking regional accreditation because of its severely limited science curriculum; the junior high school, which occupied the building vacated by the high school when its new facility had been built a decade or more ago; and four elementary schools. The elementary schools were almost paired. Two served the east and west sides of the town and had enrollments of approximately 400 students; another was twelve miles north of Sharp Corners and had become part of the school system only when the smaller community of Ferndale had reluctantly given up its own school district in order to affiliate with the new Sharp Corners High School; the fourth school, improbably named Empire, was seven miles southwest of the town, and when Mr. Coos spotted it from the highway on his interview visit to Sharp Corners, he realized the small building was one of the state's oldest school buildings. On a later visit, he had seen how the former one-room school had been partitioned and extended so that three teachers, one of them acting as head teacher, worked with two grades each in the recently refurbished, well-lighted classrooms. Enrollment remained fairly constant at seventy-five to eighty in the six grades which made up the school.

At Mr. Coos' interview with the school board, the critical questions seemed to relate to the high school's needs in science, the necessity for a kindergarten program, and the desirability of some kind of library service for the elementary schools. One member of the board, Emily Faribault, was especially vocal about this third program. Her husband drove forty miles to the state capital to his job in the state library, and she had run the small public library in Sharp Corners ever since she and her husband had returned to the community to take over her parents' home some years ago. The variety of library experience she had acquired elsewhere had convinced her that every school district should provide service within each school. She pointed out that her own credentials as a librarian were superior to those of the high school librarian who had taken enough library science courses to get a state certificate after a number of years of teaching. It was a rare meeting of the school board when Mrs. Faribault failed to present other members with photocopies of articles about the total inadequacy of elementary schools which did not have libraries, or with what Jim Emsworth, the chairman of the board, characterized as her husband's propaganda pieces from the state library about the need for better local library service. Her conviction and drive carried weight with the other board members, but Mr. Coos realized that any action of his would have to be carried out simultaneously on all three of the major issues raised by the board. It was not a matter of correcting one shortcoming, then moving on to the others. And in the meantime, there were the many neglected details of running the school district which had accumulated during the last year when the ailing former superintendent had postponed decisions.

Mr. Coos realized that a key person in the school district, and one who could become his strongest ally or most jealous watcher, was Evert Barnes, the high school principal. Barnes had been passed over for consideration as superintendent because, at sixty, he would be with the district only five years till retirement, but his following within the school district was strong, and he encouraged the speculation that he might leave at any time to teach administration in the small teachers' college where he had taught every summer for thirty years. The message, as Mr. Coos read it, was that Evert Barnes' loyalty and support were worth having, but they were not to be taken for granted by any newcomer-superintendent. Their first task together was to tackle the problem of the science courses in the high school, and Mr. Coos appreciated the frankness with which the principal approached the problem. During one of these discussions, he asked Barnes about the possibility of having Henry Duryea, the high school librarian, visit the four elementary schools and report on ways of initiating a program of library service. He was unprepared for Barnes' reaction.

"Well, as far as I'm concerned, you're welcome to use Henry, but he's not the most imaginative or thoughtful guy in the world. If he were, we'd have a better program in the high school than we do. I'm proud of the library because it's one of the choice spots in the building, but nothing much happens there. You know, I get around a lot to meetings and conferences, and I've seen libraries in poorer facilities that would put ours to shame. But, Vernon, you know how it is—you can't get rid of a guy for doing a lackluster job, and, for that matter, maybe old Henry will come through, if you lay a little flattery on him. But there's another thing—he *is* the high school librarian, and I don't see that he has any more business getting involved in shaping up the elementary schools than, say, our coach would have going out to show the grade school teachers how to supervise their playgrounds. If you need him for a day or two, fine, but that's the limit."

Mr. Coos was aware that Barnes was being honest, but that he was also testing him. He had no desire to see the high school weakened by having any of his teachers' energies directed into other channels in the school district, and he was making his point now. And Coos wanted to show him his own good faith. He called Henry Duryea later that morning and asked him to come in to the office after school the following day. At that time, he gave him a number of the materials that Mrs. Faribault had given to him earlier. He stressed the informality of this visiting of the schools and waved aside the question of a written report. Coos himself would call the four schools to let the principal or head teacher know that Duryea was coming, and it would be up to Duryea to set the time for each visit at his convenience. When he had visited all four, he was to report back to Coos with his notes, and that would be the end of his responsibility. Recalling the caution expressed by Barnes, Coos stressed this latter point.

He sensed, however, that Duryea was flattered to have been asked to take on this new responsibility, and the librarian opened up in conversation.

"Mr. Coos," he began rather awkwardly as their interview seemed to be at an end, "I want you to know that I care about those grade schools. I may not go around on a soapbox like Emily Faribault or some other people, but I've got kids at Empire and I see how many things they miss out on that these town kids take for granted. My wife and I have always considered that we have to pay the price for living out in the country where we have the kind of life we like by making up to our children what they may miss by not being able to walk to a library. It happens to be fairly easy for us to do that, because I can take stuff home from the library to them. No other father in our neck of the woods can do that. But, if they could have a library right there, that'd be great. And if you're willing to get the ball rolling on this, Mr. Coos, I'm for you. I'll help in any way I can."

The superintendent was impressed with Duryea's evident sincerity and with the way he went about his visiting. When Mr. Coos talked with the three principals and the head teacher the next day, their enthusiastic reactions also encouraged him. At Ferndale, Harriet Edwards, the principal, pointed out that they would like to show Mr. Duryea how the children were already using their library. Mr. Coos might have missed seeing it on his visit, she added, because it was open only part of the day, but part of the all-purpose room was screened off when the room was not in use as a cafeteria or gym, and a different mother came in every day to teach the children how to use the library and to help them find what they wanted. The books? They had come from the Parents Association, either as gifts, or bought with proceeds from their fund-raising activities. Miss Edwards did not hold with having parents run the school, but she was all in favor of their really carrying through on one activity, and the library was a good thing for them to work on.

Jake Girard at East Side was more skeptical, There were a dozen things they needed more than a library at his school, he pointed out. He'd be glad to have Henry drop by, and he'd show him around, but everyone knew that libraries, which had been the big thing in the 1960s, were out. The thing to get going was a real center for individualized learning. He had been to a conference where a listening center was displayed; it was port- able and could be brought right to the individual classroom for an hour or two. That was what he and the teachers saw as the next thing to get. They had plenty of books already and their kids could find just about anything they had to have right in their public library. As for the teachers, they felt pressure enough just getting through the textbooks they had to cover. Why stir up a hornets' nest?

So it went. Vernon Coos almost wished he could accompany Henry Duryea on his visits, but he had turned the matter over to him and he wanted to see how Duryea handled things. He learned that one of Duryea's first moves had been to call the state school library consultant, Phyllis Berwick, because she telephoned Mr. Coos before the week was out.

After introducing herself, she said, "As you know, Mr. Coos, we don't usually come into a district without an invitation, but since you're a new superintendent, I'd like to stop by to meet you—perhaps Wednesday, when I'll be driving through on my way to an in-service meeting in Dravosburg. I want you to know I'm delighted to hear you're ready to move on elementary school libraries. That's been a sore point about Sharp Corners for years. And since you're starting out, you have the opportunity of really doing this the right way, right from the beginning. I'll be interested to know what Henry has to say after he visits the schools, because I've never been to any of them, but when you're starting from scratch, you can't go anywhere but up. Is it all right with you if I stop by your office then?"

Mr. Coos tried to shake off a feeling of annoyance at Miss Berwick's assumption that he was really ready to move and her implication that Sharp Corners was some kind of neanderthal land without elementary school libraries. Was she also, perhaps, implying that she or someone else, not Henry Duryea, should have been making this survey? He might have thought of asking for assistance from the state department of education, but he had felt that by asking Duryea instead, he would find out more about this school district and its staff, and that Duryea would have suggestions to make based on his own experience and related to the community's needs and interests.

Miss Berwick came on Wednesday, and she was armed with many of the same materials that Emily Faribault favored. She spread them out on the table and offered them to him one by one. Mr. Coos was reminded of a fortune-teller offering cards.

"I'm sure you'll agree, Mr. Coos," Miss Berwick said, "that there's no point in reinventing the wheel just because you're starting a new program. You know, the elementary schools of this state probably have the best library programs because they have not repeated the mistakes of the high schools. They've started fresh, and right from the beginning they've become materials centers, where everything related to media is all in one place. Why, in your four schools, I bet you'd find that the principal, the secretary —if there is one—and the teachers are all having to carry some of the load that should be part of the library program. In a really good library, with a good librarian, there'd be listening areas, previewing areas, a good collection of professional materials for the teachers, and a lot of the teaching about study skills, like skimming and outlining, that teachers probably have to do in their classrooms right now. Oh, you'll be glad you made this decision."

Feeling somewhat overwhelmed, Mr. Coos observed, "The only decision I've made so far, Miss Berwick, is to have Henry Duryea visit the schools. I'm interested in what you have to say, but where would you fit all those activities into a three-teacher school like Empire?"

Miss Berwick paused. "Oh—that charming little old school you can see from the highway? Well, I don't know of any really strong library programs in schools that size, because there just aren't that many schools that size in this state. Most of the existing ones are due to be phased out in the next few years."

"I don't see Empire being phased out, since I've read some of the history of attempts to close it when the enrollment was much lower than it is now. It's a matter of pride to people like Henry Duryea, for example, that they do have their own school and they're not likely to give it up. On the other hand, I feel a kind of responsibility to have things be spread as evenly as possible among the schools, and I realize there's just no way to have even a library room at Empire—at least, in the near future."

"You know, Mr. Coos, the route some school districts have taken is to begin the development of elementary library programs almost on a demonstration basis. Start with your most promising school—the one where the teachers are enthusiastic about a library—and give it everything it needs—a full-time librarian, a classroom, at least, to start with, and a good-sized collection, and then let the others see what happens. I think they'd be clamoring to have one—and perhaps figuring out ways to get it that would not occur to you or me, sitting in this office—or even to Henry on this little survey he's making."

"Yes, I've heard of approaches like that. In fact, at Manning, the neighboring district to Whitney, where I worked last year, they had a gal who came in, divided her time between two schools, and built them up, two at a time, organizing two each year, then turning those two over to be run by a library aide while she moved on to the next two. With their eight schools, of course, it took four years, but this year, as I understand it, she's a coordinator or something for the district, and she just sees that they all keep running."

"That's Sharon Gaffney, and she has done a good job. There's just one problem at Manning—they've insisted on using library aides instead of librarians, and they'll pay for that kind of penny-pinching in the long run."

Mr. Coos was amused. "You librarians do stick together! That's the same thing our library consultant in Whitney used to say. But what Joe Honea at Manning says is that it was impossible, when they started, to get qualified librarians, and it was this or nothing."

"Yes, I know what Superintendent Honea says. But in most places, you could find teachers who are already almost qualified for school librarianship and you could push them to go on for whatever course work they needed. I can see the value of aides, but only when they are working directly under a librarian."

"But isn't that what they're doing in Manning?"

"Well, they're responsible to Sharon, of course—but I mean working under a librarian in the same building, and there's a big difference."

"But if you had to choose between that and nothing, what would you choose?"

"That's a hard choice, of course, and if every district had a Sharon Gaffney, they might get by all right, but they don't."

"Yes, and we don't, either, I guess," Mr. Coos said thoughtfully.

Miss Berwick hurriedly gave him the rest of the materials, suggested that he, Henry, and some of the principals or teachers, visit some of the school districts in the state that had strong programs, and encouraged him to call her any time when she might be of help. Then she left to drive on to Dravosburg.

Henry Duryea telephoned on Monday of the following week to report that he had completed his visits, had spent the weekend sorting out his notes and checking up on some things he didn't know about elementary school libraries, and asked when Mr. Coos could see him. With the fall meeting of the state teachers association scheduled for the end of that week, they agreed on Tuesday afternoon.

Duryea came in with considerably more assurance than he had shown during their first conversation. He had carefully typed notes in a manila folder, and he offered a copy to the superintendent. There was one sheet for each school, and, with comments about the location of rooms, kinds of books in evidence in classrooms, and suggestions made by the principal or head teacher of each school, it was virtually a written report.

Mr. Coos put his copy to one side, leaned back in his chair, and said, "You can be sure, Henry, that I'll read this all over very carefully, but right now, I'd like to know just what you think I should do. You've undoubtedly got some ideas about this. What do you say?"

Henry was obviously confused. He was ready to discuss his report, not to engage in imagining or offering suggestions for the future, but he took up the challenge.

"Well, for one thing, I'd make it clear to people that we *are* going to have elementary school libraries. That's one of the reasons the board wanted you, isn't it? You can't have principals really picking and choosing among things they want or don't want for their schools. I'm more convinced than ever of the need for libraries right in the schools, and I thought you'd be interested in something I might have heard, but hadn't realized, before. A lot of the elementary teachers have nice little classroom collections from the public library. On a teacher's card, they can get as many books as they have children, plus five—for example, thirty-two books for twenty-seven students. And for all Mrs. Faribault's talk about wanting us to get started on school libraries, that's one of the reasons many of the teachers are pretty casual about whether or not they ever have a library in their own school. And another funny thing—this system is really pretty unfair, because unless a teacher lives in the public library district, which isn't as large as the school district, he's not entitled to this service. What that really means is that teachers have to exchange a lot among themselves, but basically, they seem pretty satisfied."

"No, I hadn't known that," Mr. Coos commented.

"Of course, the best setup I saw was at Ferndale, where the kids really use that little library. The mothers up there are evidently very faithful about coming, and it really seems to work. It should be fairly easy to have that same kind of thing in every school, and not too costly, either. Now, whether Jake Girard would even be interested or not, I don't know. He's all excited about some kind of phonograph-on-wheels, but that's terribly unrealistic for a community like ours. I say start slowly and build."

"Start slowly and build? Is that the gist of what you have to say?" Mr. Coos picked up Duryea's last statement, and the librarian hesitated.

"Well, yes, sir, I guess it is."

"And who would build it?"

"Well, Mr. Coos, of course you'd want someone who really knows his way around libraries, someone who understands this community and what the kids need and want, and that means knowing schools, too. Then, I'd say start with something like one of these collections in each school." Duryea produced a sizable volume and handed it to the superintendent. "That's a basic collection, recommended by national experts, for elementary schools. You can buy every book that has first priority in it, and have every one delivered, cataloged and ready for the shelves, for 4,500 dollars."

"Mm, and that's an investment of 18,000 dollars for the district." Mr. Coos, who was accustomed to rapid mutiplication of costs on a per school basis, saw Duryea falter at the figure.

"Yes, but it would be worth it. And I'd start just with books. There's time enough later to go into other things. I did make notes of what kinds of things there are in the schools, like recordings and filmstrips, but that's probably only the visible part of the iceberg, because I didn't poke into closets or anything. But much of the equipment I saw seemed to be little used, so there's no point in throwing good money after bad. Right?"

Mr. Coos' first impression of Mr. Duryea as a fairly conservative librarian was coming back. Even Barnes had described his running of the high school library as "lackluster," but the other impression that was coming through to Mr. Coos was that the librarian was really interested in this problem. Duryea's description of the person to solve it fitted himself fairly neatly, although he was far too modest to suggest himself more directly. Based on the rest of the conversation and the first reading of Duryea's report, Mr. Coos wondered whether more responsibility and opportunity might help the librarian grow into a good organizer for the elementary school libraries.

A disquieting note came when Mr. Coos met Jake Girard at a civic club meeting Wednesday evening. Mr. Girard said, "Well, I guess old Henry's told you what he thinks about us by now."

"Yes, I talked with him after he'd visited the schools."

"He's a good enough guy, Vernon, but he doesn't know elementary schools. Why, I went into one classroom with him and he was surprised to find the kids discussing sets in mathematics. He's hardly set foot in an elementary school. He may know libraries, of course, but we are different, and he needs to keep that in mind if he's going to be giving you advice on this stuff."

Mr. Coos took this comment at face value, but he was unprepared the next day when a telephone call from Mrs. Faribault indicated she questioned whether Duryea knew libraries.

"I'm glad you're moving on this, at last, Mr. Coos," she said. "I don't mind telling you that, since you've been here three months now and nothing has happened, some of us are getting a bit anxious. I'll say more about that at the board meeting next Monday, of course, but for now, I just want to say that it's probably no good at all to send somebody like Henry Duryea around to get facts and ideas. He wouldn't know an idea if he fell over one. And the only library he knows is that dead place in the high school, where nobody ever goes. Now, I want to give you credit for making some move, but what I really called to say was that I'll be ready, at next week's board meeting, to call attention to the fact that nothing's been done yet about elementary school libraries, and to ask for a report from you, in some detail, at the next meeting. Between friends, that's fair warning, isn't it?"

26.
Consultant's Choice
. . . .

The public school district of Glen Lyon had been increasing its staff in the central administration building on a fairly regular basis, and the fifth consultant employed in the curriculum department was Paul Farrell, who was to have responsibility for the media program in all of the twenty-three schools in the district. These included three high schools, seven junior highs, and thirteen elementary schools. The junior highs were in the process of being converted to middle schools, which would house grades five through seven, rather than grades six through eight, which had been the junior high grades. This meant that for two or three years the senior high schools would be crowded, probably beyond actual capacity, but, as the superintendent explained to the preschool staff meeting in the fall, the school board was gambling on some evidence of decreasing school enrollments in the future, and did not anticipate building another senior high school. Dr. Ithaca, the superintendent, was well aware of the seriousness of the gamble, and he made this clear at a meeting of the staff of consultants and administrators in the central building.

"This is the kind of situation where we are, in a sense, putting our careers on the line. I'm speaking just for myself, of course, but I know that if, in two or three years, the high school enrollments level off as we anticipate, and we can keep going with grades eight through twelve in our present buildings, with no double shifts and no wild schedules, we'll all be big heroes. On the other hand, if we get caught with a new subdivision or a switch to younger or bigger families which no one has predicted or planned on, we'll be caught right in the squeeze. We have enough land for a new high school out on the west side of the district, but if we end up having to build there in four or five years and under emergency conditions, we may have to spend two or three times the amount we would spend if we began building today. I am telling you all this because we may be heading for tense times in these years, when we're pushing a wider range of students together into the high school buildings. We have studied the idea of the middle school, and we believe in it as an educational concept. We are moving in that direction now, even though it may make things tight in the high schools for the time being.

"Why do I tell you all this? Because you're the ones of this staff who may be caught in the crossfire. Teachers and parents may give you some static. I count on you to clear up what you can. I suppose everything would be great if the timing were different—if we could open a brand-new middle school and make it a prestige thing to have one, as they did in Belleville two years ago. But we're stuck with a commitment to the idea and no good physical plant or anything of that kind to use as a pilot school. I am asking you to be prepared for the crunch of taxpayers' and even teachers' reactions over what may be a rough two- or three-year period."

At the end of the meeting, Paul Farrell stayed to talk with several of the consultants about a forthcoming workshop on reading which they were planning. As Dr. Ithaca walked past, he said, "Oh, Paul, if you have a minute, there's something I'd like to discuss with you."

Dr. Ithaca gestured toward the rear wall of the room used for open meetings of the school board as well as for staff meetings of this kind and other meetings sometimes scheduled at the administration building.

"One thing I'd like you to get started on is a professional library for this staff. I found out when we were trying to get background information about the middle school idea that we really are in a bad way when it comes to finding anything, even from education periodicals, in any very orderly way. I was fortunate that Miss Eddystone, who was my secretary then, was interested and willing to go to the public library and the college library to look through their indexes, but I've noticed that several of the consultants have little clutches of books in their offices. I know that some—maybe not all, or even most—of them were purchased from school funds, because I've signed the orders. I'm sure that many of them would be useful for more than one person, and I'd like you to get the ball rolling on combining them into a professional collection for this building. I'll be glad to give up whatever

I may have in my office, and that includes some recent periodicals, too. You can look through what's there and take what you think other people can use. Occasionally someone borrows something from my shelves, but all too often, they don't even know it's there, or they're too embarrassed to come in and interrupt me or something. I want those things accessible, and I want you to work up some kind of budget for periodicals and other things we may need to make this work. I remember hearing you tell the other librarians at that meeting at Dupont last spring about how you built up the professional collection at the high school. You teased teachers into giving up these little clutches of books by offering them more from the central collection than they could hope to get together on their own. So, how about trying that technique with us? Oh, and you can check back with me, say, in two months or so—does that give you time enough?—to let me know how it goes."

Mr. Farrell had hoped to present almost the same kind of proposal to the superintendent as soon as he was more settled in his new job, and he was glad to have this assignment. He returned to the little group that was still planning the reading workshop.

"The way I see it, we should stress this as being for the people who really want to make waves. If we could get by with it, I'd like to offer this without even giving in-service credit for it, because that way, we'd keep out all the teachers who'll come to anything here rather than trek off to an extension course in the evenings. We should attract the teachers who want to take hold in reading. I guess that naturally means the elementary teachers should have some kind of priority, but we want a mix from the middle schools and high schools, too. And our plan calls for just fifty participants. We've practically guaranteed the speakers that's all we'll have, and they're suggesting small group discussions and lots of feedback, so we want to keep it small enough to house it in this room." Rachel Alisal, the curriculum director, was holding forth on the overall plan.

"Sounds good to me," Jerry Reedly, the language arts consultant, answered. "I'll be delighted if we get fifty good people, frankly. I assume we'll publicize this in the usual way, in the newsletter, then narrow the list down, if we have too many applicants. I'd like to believe we'll be overwhelmed, but I really doubt it. There are too many other things going on. And, of course, we do have to offer in-service credit. That's part of our agreement with the state, which is funding it."

"Yes, of course." Mrs. Alisal agreed. "But I think you might follow up that newsletter announcement by encouraging some key teachers to apply. I see this workshop as a real breakthrough. We're going to push them into real individualization in the reading program, and we're going to give them more information about how to spot serious reading problems much earlier than we've been catching them. I keep hearing from the teachers in special education how many of the kids might have been helped, maybe with just a remedial reading teacher, or perhaps just a more perceptive classroom teacher, if they had been spotted early enough, before the reading problems led to psychological blocks about learning. We need this workshop to beef up the reading program, which, we should admit, hasn't been all that strong."

"Hear, hear!" said Rose Perris, the consultant for special education and remedial programs. "If you can put us out of the remedial business by making every teacher a better reading teacher, I'm all for it. I really like this idea of our working on this together. Paul, what are you going to be doing?"

"Well, I'm going to encourage the librarians to apply. They're really in the position to spread the word within their schools, and I'm sure we'll have more of these as time goes on. And, of course, I'll help with any of the arrangements as we get moving."

"Now, that's what I like to hear!" Mrs. Alisal smiled at him. "It's really great to have you here. We've needed someone like you on the consultant staff."

The talk turned to arrangements for sending out notices, compiling the programs, and other details. Mr. Farrell participated in the discussion, as he did in the next meeting of the group. By that time, the applications from interested potential participants were in, and the group studied them. Mrs. Alisal gave the summary.

"Well, we certainly can say they're interested. We have forty-five applications, which means we could accept every one. However, two of the elementary schools have no representatives, and we'll get after them to come up with two or three each. It could even be that they're just delayed in the school mail, and will turn up. However, I'm disappointed that there aren't more new teachers who want to come. Maybe they think this is not for them, since they're just out of school, or perhaps they've even been discouraged by their principals. Jerry, could you nudge some of the ones who'd benefit from this? We need them, and they need this, so encourage them to come. And if you want any lessons, Paul here might tell you how he conned thirteen librarians into applying. That must be almost all of them, isn't it?"

"No," Mr. Farrell replied. "There are actually twenty-one, two at each of the high schools, one in each middle school, and eight in the elementary schools, some of them serving two of the smaller schools. But thirteen is a good showing, I'd say."

"Indeed it is," Mrs. Alisal said. "Now, I'll have to ask you to go through the applications and suggest which ones we should accept. We don't want such a heavy proportion of librarians. Maybe you could get it down to seven?"

"But why?" Mr. Farrell asked. "We have room for all of them, don't we? You're looking for other teachers to fill it up to fifty, and at the same time, you're saying let's hold down the number of librarians. If they're interested, why can't they come? Is that the only group you're cutting down on?"

"Yes, it is," Mrs. Alisal said. "But we're doing it because we want to get to more teachers."

"It may seem clear enough to you, Mr. Farrell, but we have a commitment to the state to use this program to benefit classroom teachers, and filling it up with librarians is not the way to do it." Jerry Reedly spoke crisply. Mrs. Alisal handed Mr. Farrell the thirteen applications, and the discussion went on to another aspect of the planning. The issue seemed to be closed.

Later, as Mr. Farrell went through the applications from the librarians, he reviewed what he knew about each of them. One of the first tasks he had set for himself as consultant had been to visit each of the schools. In the case of the small schools, he had made it a point to be there when the librarian was in the building. They seemed to have appreciated his interest, and several had commented on their fear that a "downtown consultant" would remain some distant supervisor with little or no knowledge of what their daily work was like. At the Ross Elementary School, Selma Folsom had told him of the chaos she had found in that small school library, which she had attributed to the year-long assignment of a substitute during the past school year. The substitute, a Mrs. Saranap, was a friend of the principal, she explained, and although the district had never given Mrs. Saranap a contract because of her erratic work record and poor references, the principal often managed to get her in as a long-term substitute.

Two weeks after his visit, when Miss Folsom had had an emergency appendectomy, Mr. Farrell had been prepared for the principal's suggestion that she would be able to "get one of our good parents who has substituted for us before from time to time" to keep the library open for a week or two. Mr. Farrell had countered with the suggestion that, since he had never worked in an elementary school himself, he would run the library for the first few days and see how things went. He explained his position to Dr. Ithaca, who had been rather dubious, but who had agreed to the arrangement in the light of Mr. Farrell's offer to keep up with his own desk work by remaining late in the evenings or coming in on weekends.

"Actually," Mr. Farrell had pointed out, "I think this may give the librarians more confidence in me. They know I've had nothing but senior high school experience, and I want to show them what I can do. I'm sure the word will get around."

The word had indeed gotten around. Lorna Ryan, a junior high librarian who had stayed on when her school was converted to a middle school, had called him after his eight-day stint at Ross was over, and said, "I hear you're giving a helping hand in the schools. Can I be next? You remember we agreed to send over to the high school any of the books which we thought, because of grade level, might not be useful in a middle school. Well, I've done a preliminary sorting, but I combined it with a good weeding, which we've needed for a long time, and the shelves really look bare. I'm afraid Mr. Brinkley will blow up when he sees what I've done, and, anyway, I'd like your okay on some of the decisions I've made. Will you come?"

Rather pleased that Miss Ryan, with many more years' experience than he had himself, would ask for his help, Mr. Farrell had agreed to go. Like many of the jobs he found himself doing, this turned out to take more time than he had anticipated. The two of them had worked through the whole collection, and since they did not finish on the Friday he had set aside for the school, they had agreed to work as much of Saturday as was necessary. The work was done, and the books were arranged on the shelves so that no glaring gaps were obvious, when Mr. Brinkley, the principal, who had been working that same Saturday, stopped by. He commented on the neatness of the room.

"I've always said you you don't need the most books to have a good library. As long as we have what we need, that's fine with me. The whole place looks better with a lot of those tattered old books out of the way. We surely do appreciate your help, Mr. Farrell," Mr. Brinkley had said.

Mr. Farrell thought the librarians with whom he had worked most closely might expect him to support their applications for this workshop, if there were competition. He chose Miss Folsom and Miss Ryan, and kept grouping the other applications. What he was not sure about was whether to encourage the less experienced librarians by selecting them for the workshop or to offer it, in a sense, as a reward to the ones with more experience and competence. As he made selections, he was aware that the division of his own time had to be made on the same basis. He had been invited, for example, by Orlen McFarland to attend a middle school faculty meeting. Mr. McFarland, one of the newer principals, was anxious to have the best middle school in the district, and the meeting really had been a brainstorming session about how the library could be more effective in the school. The teachers were, for the most part, more imaginative than Elana Downey, the young librarian. They were eager to transform the school library into a real media center, and Mr. McFarland felt that, by emphasizing the needs to the parents in the community, they could get the support they needed to make a strong start. He was plainly trying to push Mrs. Downey into a more active role. She was competent enough, but afraid of overextending herself or, as she put it to Mr. Farrell, "We could get lots of things started, and maybe even be a showcase, as Mr. McFarland wants us to be. But I'm not sure I could keep it up. Why can't he give me another year to be sure of what I'm doing now? Or even some help?"

The help that Mr. McFarland felt prepared to offer was really from Mr. Farrell, whom he had known for some years. "I tell you what, Paul, if you could just give us some more of your time, come and visit the classrooms, see what really happens in the library in the course of a day, and even listen to me some and give me your ideas, we could be a model resource center for you, so you could trigger the rest of the district by letting them visit us, too. What do you say?"

Mr. Farrell, still catching up with work that had accumulated while he was out at the Ross School, had demurred. He kept in touch with Mr. McFarland and Mrs. Downey enough to know that they were gradually developing a stronger program, but McFarland was becoming impatient, and Mrs. Downey seemed to be becoming stubborn and discouraged. Things there were not going too well, and Mr. Farrell wondered whether part of the blame was his. Mr. McFarland had found out that he had spent most of one school day at Oxnard High School, and he commented, "What are you supposed to be, Paul—a consultant or a troubleshooter? If I did my job as principal by just taking care of the problem teachers and never encouraging the good ones who could get better, I'd soon have nothing but problem teachers on my hands. I just hope you don't make that mistake."

Reviewing the reasons for spending the day at Oxnard, Mr. Farrell wondered whether that had been the mistake he had made. He had gone because Dick Banning, the librarian at Oxnard, had told him the library program was going down the drain because of the school's overcrowded conditions. Study halls were now scheduled regularly in the library, Dick had reported, and he felt the library was misused. Mr. Farrell had visited and, although there was little he could do about the scheduling, he had been able to suggest some changes in seating arrangements, to allow classes to come with teachers for library lessons or for other use of the library, which could go on without interference from the students under the supervision of the study hall monitor. By a minor change, the library was still free for use by individuals during these same periods. As Mr. Farrell had pointed out when Dick Banning was profusely thanking him for his help, it probably was not that he knew any more about what to suggest, but that the study hall monitors were more willing to listen to suggestions from an outsider, and he was in a position to follow up on the suggested changes of arrangement of furniture by checking with Jim Redding, the director for buildings and grounds, on his men's work assignment at Oxnard.

It occurred to Mr. Farrell that Elana Downey might be a good person to get into the reading workshop. He looked for her application, but there was none from her. He wondered if she were just disappointed about any hope for assistance, or perhaps simply too overwhelmed with her own work at this time. He went on making selections as fairly as he could. He finished late, and, as he was leaving his office, he met Dr. Ithaca in the hall.

"Oh, Paul, I'm glad to run into you," the superintendent began. "I thought of you at the board meeting the other night. I noticed that nothing's been done about getting any professional books into that room. You haven't forgotten our little conversation, have you?"

"No, sir, I haven't, but, well, I guess I've just been too busy with the day-to-day stuff."

"I've been wondering about that, Paul. I don't see why you have to go out and pack books in boxes for Lorna Ryan. One of the custodians could do that, but John Brinkley told me you even gave up a Saturday to do it. I didn't mean to set any precedents by letting you work at Ross that time. You're a consultant, and we pay a premium for you. We need to make the best use of you—for your sake, as well as for the district's sake. Every consultant here has his own pattern of work, and they decide for themselves how much time they spend in the schools, but I've never held with the idea that you help the teachers best by standing at their side all the time. You can help them from right here at your desk just as well. And I hear you're working on this reading workshop. Mrs. Alisal is pleased about that, but frankly, it's getting to be a pretty expensive workshop if it takes lots of your time, when Mrs. Alisal and two of the other consultants are already working on it."

"I suppose that's true. I'd thought it was important to show the link between reading and the library, and it was natural for me to want to do my share. As a matter of fact, I seem to have oversold the workshop to the librarians, and I've just been selecting the ones who'll be allowed to participate."

"Well, that's a switch!" the superintendent said with a smile. "But if they're so eager that they have to be selected to participate, why do you have to put time in on it, too? I see you as a consultant, not just for the schools and the librarians, but for this central office staff. And I thought I had made clear that it was important for you in your role as consultant, to develop that professional library. Try to get to work on that, will you?"

"Yes, I will, Dr. Ithaca. I do wonder, though, how to set priorities sometimes. No one else on the consultant staff really has a comparable responsibility, it seems to me, if you see me as a sort of professional librarian for the staff in this building. Jerry, for example, doesn't have to teach anybody reading."

"That's true," the superintendent countered. "But remember, Paul, he also has several hundred teachers working in some area of language arts, and you have—how many?—a couple of dozen librarians. Quite a difference, right there. But I'm in a rush now. You know your job description, and I don't doubt you're doing it, as you see fit. But maybe the two of us, perhaps with Mrs. Alisal, should go over it in the next few days and put our ideas together. Remind me, will you?"

27.
The Case
of Extended Evenings

· · · · · · · · · · · · · · · · · ·

The school district and the public library of Torrington served the same population. Both had been affected by the consistent growth of population, the increased demands for a variety of materials required for instruction, and the problem of local finance with many young families purchasing their first homes and facing the prospect of taxation to provide necessary community safeguards and amenities. Sometimes considered a bedroom community for the nearby city of Stoughton, Torrington had some small, "clean industries" and numerous businesses of its own.

Three senior high schools, grades ten through twelve, six junior high schools, grades seven through nine, and eighteen elementary schools, grades kindergarten through six, comprised the school district. Two elementary schools, one junior high, and Northpoint High School had been built in the past two years. This capital outlay had increased the financial problems of the school district.

The addition of one permanent branch library to the present public library arrangement had long been contemplated. One central library, built more than twenty years before, and staffed for the first years of its existence by women from a local church who were anxious to provide free library service to all, and two storefront branch libraries in rented quarters in busy shopping centers, were the only public library agencies.

Charles Chatom, the superintendent of schools, served as *ex officio* member of the library board, and had become increasingly concerned at frequent reference in board meetings to the problem of the "deluge of students" using the public library. Library staff members stated that many adult patrons were driven away because at the central library and its branches, residents of the community felt they had little chance of visiting and selecting books in an atmosphere of leisure and quiet during the evening hours. Each of the branches had seating for approximately fifty people at tables for four, in the browsing area near the periodical section, and on some window seats. An evening visitor might, however, find all these seats taken, and students standing to take notes at the card catalog or in the reference section.

The situation at the central library was even worse. The overcrowded stack area, with the growing book collection, had encroached on the formerly limited seating area. A maximum of seventy-five persons could be seated, even when six chairs were arranged around tables designed for four. Staff members had become accustomed to receiving telephone requests from adult patrons asking to have specified books placed at the charging desk so they could just run in and pick them up, rather than contend with the outdoor parking problem and the indoor seating problem. Commenting that the students often used the library as a meeting place, and that some materials, such as encyclopedias and back issues of periodicals, received extremely heavy use while many other items were rarely touched, members of the library staff expressed the view that they sometimes felt they were running a study hall or dating bureau rather than a library program.

Mr. Chatom discussed some of these problems with the committee of three school librarians, one for each level of school, and with the assistant superintendent for instruction, who had direct responsibility for the library program. The librarians volunteered to visit the public libraries several evenings during the next two weeks, to assess the situation for themselves. The senior high school librarian, Mrs. Uvalde, who often acted as spokesman for the librarians, said that her efforts to find out what assignments were made and what materials were likely to be in demand had met with little success. She was willing to guess, in advance, that most of the young people using the public libraries were from her school or from the two other senior high schools, and she took this opportunity to point out the desperate need for more staff and more materials at all three of the high schools. She reminded Mrs. Bullock, the assistant superintendent, of a survey she had shown her earlier about the increasing spread of extended-hours programs in the evening and on weekends in various high school libraries. She asserted that the library at her school, Eastwood, would have sufficient materials and space to be used in this way, as would Westbrook Senior High.

She was less certain about Northpoint, where the new collection of materials was more limited. Since the library there was built as the school's inner core, where more than ninety percent of the students came by school bus, in contrast with the sixty percent at Westbrook and Eastwood, there were problems of access in after-school hours, she thought.

When the same group of five met again in two weeks, Mr. Chatom had become even more anxious to resolve what he considered something of a crisis. He had attended a library board meeting at which the disparity between public librarians' and school librarians' salaries had been discussed (occasioned by the resignation of a fine children's librarian from one of the branch libraries, to become the librarian of one of the elementary schools at a salary for ten months which was thirty-five percent more than her former salary for twelve months.) He had also been visited in his office by the director of the public library, who presented statistics on the mutilation and loss of materials and showed that all but a few of the titles or sections destroyed were on high school reading lists. Miss Henry, director of the public library, indicated that this, and other evidence of the disproportionate attention and service provided for students, was seriously undermining the library's "real role" of service to the entire community.

The three school librarians reported that they had observed that probably seventy-five percent of the persons using the public library between 7:30 p.m. and the closing hour of 9:00 p.m. were senior high school students. Junior high school students were also there during those hours, and a few adults. They pointed out, however, that a surprisingly large number of the high school age students could be identified (by their notebooks, blazers, or textbooks) as students from the two private schools located in the district, where school library facilities were much more limited than in the public schools. In the hours between 3:30 and 5:00, the librarians agreed that the heaviest use of the library was made by elementary school students, with the great majority of them from public schools, some few from the two parochial and one private school in the community. Since no complaints had been made about elementary school students' preempting space and services in the evening, the librarians had agreed among themselves that extending hours of opening for the two high school libraries, Eastwood and Westbrook, would go a great way toward solving the problem.

Mr. Chatom was impressed with the librarians' report, and it fit what he had had in mind for some time. The discussion then turned to the means of staffing and maintaining the library—what regulations and policies should be established, how hours should be determined, and other decisions. Principals of the two high schools and the two professional librarians at each of these schools met to lay out some ground rules at this time. One recommendation was to schedule the librarians for extra hours at extra pay, with an "evening clerk." Mr. Chatom reminded them of an earlier regulation of the school district which prevented additional pay for additional hours of the same kind of work. This had been drafted when the question arose about having athletic coaches receive extra pay for hours worked in practice or at games. In their case, their employment for the summer months had been arranged to compensate them for the additional hours during the school year, while it was understood that they would put in shorter hours during the summer weeks.

The librarians became wary and hesitant at the thought of leaving the library each evening in the care of a teacher who could be recruited for additional hours, since this would not be his regular assignment, but they also agreed that they themselves should be scheduled during the school day when use of the library, visits by classes, and conferences with teachers were part of the established pattern. On a trial basis, it was agreed that teachers would be employed on an hourly basis to man the libraries, which would be open from 7:00 to 9:00 p.m. One library aide, or paid student assistant, would work the same hours, and maintenance staff would be deployed for the evening hours so that one or more would be available if needed for an emergency during the evening.

Because students had been accustomed to borrowing reserve books at 4:00 p.m., when the library closed, it was decided that this practice could continue, but because of the limited staff in the evening, no books or other materials would be circulated during the evening hours. Another reason for this decision was to establish the fact that the school's students and faculty could borrow materials, but the evening periods would be times when all residents of the community could use the resources of the library without the privilege of borrowing. To provide for building security, entrances, exits, and public rest rooms near the library were to be kept open, but the library was isolated as completely as possible from other areas of the building.

Gabriel Pike, a social studies teacher, was on duty the first evening at Eastwood when Mr. Chatom dropped in to see how things were going. Mr. Pike was chatting with several boys at one of the tables, but he walked over when he recognized the superintendent.

"How goes it?" Mr. Chatom asked.

"Everything's just fine. I threw a few of the boys out about eight o'clock because it was obvious they didn't come here to study, but the rest seem to be getting along well. How does it look to you?"

Mr. Chatom looked around the library. Perhaps thirty students were working in the large reading area, where ninety could have been seated. He walked around, chatting with some, observing others at work. He guessed that some had come because they wanted a quiet place to work, others because they were using library materials, and still others for the novelty of the experience. He had intended to stay only a few minutes, but as he walked past the circulation desk, where Mr. Pike was standing, he paused to listen.

"Can you help me find some government documents? I'm supposed to use at least one for a reference in my report," a student was asking.

"Didn't the card catalog help you?" Mr. Pike asked.

"No, sir, and I don't know the titles of any anyway. I thought they might be in those drawers over there." The student pointed toward the pamphlet file.

"Well, you can look if you like, but if I were you, I'd come back tomorrow when one of the librarians is here to help you. Or have you tried the public library?"

As the student wandered away, Mr. Pike turned to Mr. Chatom and said, "These kids are just going to have to learn that I don't have all the answers they want. After all, I'm not a librarian."

Mr. Chatom left after making a mental note to himself to look into the possibility of some kind of in-service program for the teachers working the evening hours. He was not sure how this could be arranged, in terms of the librarians' hours and the teachers', but he realized that if all the students whose needs could not be served in the school library were referred on to the public library, reaction from the staff and public there would be more negative than before.

Before the first week of the extended hours schedule was out, Mr. Chatom had had two telephone calls and one conference about the service. The principal of Northpoint had made an appointment to express his distress at Northpoint's having been excluded from the plan. Mr. Chatom explained that the decision was no adverse reflection on the school, but had been made in consideration of the new school's limited collection, the special problems of its facility, and the fact that its location was remote, even for many of its students. James Faulkner, the principal, was not satisfied with this reply.

"Look," Mr. Faulkner said, "when you asked me to take this new school—and I agree I was delighted and pleased to have the chance, though I knew there'd be problems in a new community like that—you and I both knew what the community was like. These people are aggressive and enthusiastic. On the whole, they're wealthier and older than the people in the other two neighborhoods. They're accustomed to getting the best. They're farthest from any of the three public libraries, but they're looking forward to the new branch planned for the area. They know we have a long way to go with our library collection, but after all, the reference materials are what students would use most at night anyway. What better way for them to realize how great the needs are than to have community access to them? Is it too late now for us to get into the act?"

Mr. Chatom described the unusual arrangements he had had to make to divert funds for additional staff for the trial period at the other two schools, but agreed to think over the matter of adding Northpoint to the libraries open in the evening. After Mr. Faulkner had left, the superintendent wondered whether he would be so anxious to participate in the plan if he knew some of the problems already arising. Two major ones had been called to Mr. Chatom's attention.

The first call had come from a woman in the Westbrook area. She protested that her teenage son had been denied permission to borrow a book from the high school library. It was a book her husband had been unable to borrow from the Stoughton Public Library; it was not in the Torrington Public Library, and it was essential for her son's report in his eleventh grade social studies at the Izard Boys' School, one of the private schools in the community. Mr. Chatom responded by repeating the regulations for the use of the school libraries in the evening, and he mentioned the limitations of staff, collection, and other factors, especially during this trial period. The woman, who did not wish to give her name, was angry. She was a taxpayer in the community and she had offered to show the teacher on duty her tax receipts, but he had been firm. Mr. Chatom tried to point out that, by permitting her son the use of the high school library in the evening, the service available to her was being increased, not limited, but she paid little attention to his explanations and concluded the conversation by saying, "Well, you may be as far as I can go in the school system, but you haven't heard the last of this!"

As though to keep things balanced, Mr. Chatom's third comment came from a parent in Eastwood. This was a father who had dropped his ninth-grade daughter off at the library one evening and agreed to pick her up at nine o'clock. When he arrived, he had noticed some older boys loitering around the parking lot and recognized one of them as a boy recently suspended from the high school after having been picked up on a narcotics charge. The man's tone to Mr. Chatom was friendly but firm. He wanted to know whether the school district intended to provide adequate safeguards for students and others using the library in the evening. When he asked whether a suspended student would be allowed to use the library which was, theoretically, open to the whole community, Mr. Chatom realized this was a question that had not been faced in planning. He thanked the man for calling some potential problems to his attention and agreed to keep him posted.

Leaving the office at the end of the day, Mr. Chatom commented to Mrs. Bullock: "We're having our headaches with this evening hours schedule for the libraries, but none of them is insurmountable. Anyway, it should pay off in community good will and in good relations with the public library."

With some pride, Mr. Chatom attended the next meeting of the library board, but instead of the commendation he had expected or hoped for, he was greeted with questions from other board members about when the school libraries would open in the evening. He explained the plan was already in operation, and even showed statistics on attendance, indicating averages of forty-five students at each of the two libraries each evening. One or two of the board members smiled approvingly, but one asked why the plan had been kept top secret if its purpose was to serve the public. Another, a frequent user of the public library, said, "So, great! You're handling maybe a hundred kids on a busy night, but I can tell you, the public library is still overrun with them! I've been in all three of the public libraries in the past two weeks, and I can tell you they're as crowded as ever. Maybe all you're doing is uncovering a whole new public."

Mr. Chatom recalled comments from teachers working the evening hours, indicating that many of the library users were junior high school students, and he wondered whether this might indeed be the case. The school libraries were not actually assisting in the "student problem," but were uncovering a new public. Since one of his next responsibilities was to draw up a plan for some kind of continuation of this program, if it was indeed of value to the community, he left the meeting, still mulling over the problems associated with the extended hours program.

• • • • •

What steps in planning might have averted some of the problems encountered?

How can a program of this kind be objectively evaluated? When and how should the evaluation procedures be established?

What policies and procedures might be established if the program is continued?

What indications are there of the relationship between schools and public libraries in this community? How might they be improved?

Are there aspects of instruction or administration underlying some of the problems encountered in this plan, which might be handled or solved by this or other programs? If so, how?

Betty Rice experienced conflicting reactions as she started to prepare her recommendations on the work assignments for the first library technicians to be employed in the Manistee schools. Her tireless emphasis on the need for assistance with the nonprofessional aspects of library work seemed to have paid off. In the secondary schools, there had developed a good working arrangement, with high school students in the distributive education departments coming in to do typing, filing, and handling of the circulation routines. The same program had provided students to handle the distribution of films on loan, operation and minor repair of projectors, and production of some graphic materials for teachers. In her descriptions of this program, Mrs. Rice, as the district specialist for instructional materials, had always been proud of the fact that the school was using and training its own students, yet not exploiting them as volunteers, but transferring funds from the library budget into the distributive education fund, from which the students received their pay. She knew of no better arrangement.

The elementary schools, however, had presented a different problem. She felt that the materials specialist in each school was seriously handicapped by having so much behind-the-scenes work to do, while, for the most part, remaining responsible for a heavy schedule of classes. The fact that ordering and processing of materials was done at the district level cut off some of the work, but, as the elementary specialists pointed out to her, there was still a lot to do when materials arrived at the school. Each of them kept her own record of budget, and from her occasional examination of them, Mrs. Rice knew these were likely to be weird and wonderful things. They ranged from the neat bookkeeper's record maintained by Liz Ingham, to the raft of small slips thrust into one red clothespin from which Anna Vernon seemed always to be able to make some kind of sense. From her visits, Mrs. Rice also realized that the housekeeping tasks like simple mending of materials, storage of posters, or organizing additions to the vertical file varied greatly with the individual specialist's abilities, interest, and available time.

It was typical that she had thought of Miss Ingham and Mrs. Vernon and their way of keeping records. She enjoyed the variety they offered to the group of eight elementary librarians, who frequently met together as an in-service group. Miss Ingham had come to work in Manistee's elementary school libraries straight from library school, but in the years between college and library school, she had worked overseas in various government posts. Her office experience was unusual, but at forty-two, she'd had enough glamour for a lifetime, and she wanted to put down roots in a community like this one. She had been engagingly honest, pointing out to Mrs. Rice that she had found much of library school a bore, that she was sure she would never be able to tell stories, but she knew she could read them well, and pointing out that her experience as an office supervisor and occasional interpreter should make it easy for her to teach children how to use library materials. She had taught school for a year or two after college, so the elementary school was not really strange to her.

Anna Vernon might have been her *alter ego*. Mrs. Rice had known her when she was one of the most creative kindergarten teachers the district ever had. The children in her classes produced original plays, made murals, sang and danced in every school performance. For many of them she seemed to light a spark in the joy of creating or enjoying beauty that stayed with them always. She was a favorite teacher in her school, but one day she had come to Mrs. Rice's office to talk about what she should do to become a school librarian.

"I love these kids," she said, "but I don't want to think like a kindergartener all my life, and I don't want to stick with this until I get bitter. As you know, Joe and I have no children, so I guess I'll be teaching all my life. I look at our librarian, and I think, 'Now, she's doing all the things I really enjoy most, and she's doing them with all the kids in the school.' I guess that's just the kind of action I want a piece of. So what do I do?"

Mrs. Vernon had taken some courses, like children's literature, by extension in Manistee, and had completed her work by spending a summer in residence on the university campus. She had gritted her teeth to get through research methods and bibliography of the sciences, but as she reported to Betty Rice later, "I just kept thinking, once I get through this I can go back and do what I know I can really do well, so it's worth it. And I made it."

These were the two librarians to whom Mrs. Rice was going to assign the first two of the library technicians. She felt strongly that if the first technicians went to schools where the librarians had the strongest programs already in operation, they would be recognized from the beginning as essential in every program, not just as assistants for the less capable materials specialists. The new program for library technicians had gotten under way at the community college less than three years ago. In her file, Mrs. Rice had a copy of the brochure announcing the program and listing the courses. She read it again:

First Semester	Credits
Written Communications	3
Survey of World Literature	3
Introduction to Libraries	3
American Institutions	3
Psychology of Human Relations	3
	15

Second Semester	Credits
Library Procedures I	3
Typing I	3
Speech	3
Library Resources I	3
Modern Literature	3
Technical Terminology	2
	17

(Summer work experience may be taken for 3 elective credits.)

Third Semester	Credits
Communications Media I	3
Library Resources II	3

Library Procedures II	3
Survey of World History	3
Introduction to Humanities	3
Science Elective	3
	18

Fourth Semester	Credits
Economics	3
Communications Media II	3
Library Services for Children and Young Adults	3
Introduction to Data Processing	3
Electives	6
	18

Mrs. Rice herself had served on the advisory committee for the community college program, and she was anxious for its first graduates to make important contributions in their first positions, so the program would prosper. It was almost five years since she had received the form which the librarian of the community college had used to survey the libraries in the community and see what the prospects were for employment of library technicians. She had a copy of the sheet, with her replies on it, before her:

Name of employer   *Manistee City Schools*
Number of library staff members   *14 professional*
   8 other (equivalent of part-time help)
Type of library   *8 elementary schools; 4 secondary schools; 1 processing center*

Please comment, as fully and frankly as possible, on the kinds of job assignment you might give if graduates of a two-year program in library technical assistance were available for employment. How many might you employ initially? Eventually? What skills would be most helpful to your library? Would salary funds be readily available for this kind of personnel?

Our major reason for wanting nonprofessional assistants in the materials program would be to free the specialists to do the unique things for which they were employed. Qualified technical assistants might

*complete processing of materials within the individual school; handle
other records, e.g., circulation and budget; assist with or conduct inventory; route materials to teachers; supervise student helpers; arrange
displays; repair materials; prepare reports for the district office when
necessary; carry out other responsibilities as designated by the materials specialist with whom he would work. We would have to employ
such assistants at first on a pilot basis, perhaps two or three of them.
Our eventual goal might be to assign a library assistant to each specialist. This would mean 14 or more. At the present time, there is no
salary item for this. First assignments would probably be paid at the
rate now paid to secretaries in the district office, to cafeteria assistants,
or to other supporting staff. Salaries would be commensurate with
academic background and experience.*

Name of person providing this information   *Elizabeth W. Rice*
Title   *District specialist, instructional materials*
Telephone   *382-0578*

At the time of completing the form, Mrs. Rice had discussed it with
Vincent Luce, the superintendent, then in his first year in the district. He
had approved the information she had provided, and had asked about the
direction in which she wanted the materials program to develop. He was
interested in the program, and during his years at Manistee, he had proved
to be an excellent administrator. He had expressed to her that day the
reason for much of his strength and his high standing in the community.

"You know, Mrs. Rice, I think that what can happen with really
good people and good materials in an elementary school is just about the
most exciting thing in education. To me, this kind of library means freedom, and not just freedom to read or look or listen to lots of different
things, but a free kind of place within the school. I'm getting around to
the schools gradually, and I like what I see. You're not stamping the
libraries out like cookies. You're letting each library or materials center
or whatever you want to call it, develop its own style. To me, that's important. As you can tell, I hope, I feel the same way about the style of
principals, the atmosphere of schools."

"Yes, and I think that's why our honeymoon period with you goes
on and on," Mrs. Rice said with a smile.

"Say! Now, that's what I like to hear! Thank you. But one of the big things we have to keep thinking about is how we sell this sort of thing. I'm always working on two levels—trying to figure out what this staff, these kids, this community, want and need, and, on the other level, how to sell that idea to the board of education, the voters, the power structure, if you will. It's that two-way stretch that wears a guy out."

Mrs. Rice had often recalled that conversation, because there had been times when the tension of the two-way stretch was terribly obvious. But on the whole, Dr. Luce was still considered an asset to Manistee. One of the pleasures of working with him was that he wanted the staff, especially those in district offices, to participate in this two-way stretch too. His own quizzes about requests for new programs, new expenditures, were grueling, but they frequently resulted in a firmer idea, on the part of the staff member, about what he really wanted and what kind of difference it would make. Sometimes, too, this kind of discussion led the individual to withdraw an idea, to rethink it or evaluate it more carefully. Mrs. Rice had had both experiences. As a result of this kind of effort, she made it a point to involve more of the librarians in the planning of new activities.

For example, she had asked Mrs. Vernon and Miss Ingham to prepare statements about how they would use a library technical assistant if one were assigned to them. Their memoranda in reply were typical of the two women. Mrs. Rice considered Miss Ingham's a model of neatness and logic. She wrote:

To: Mrs. Rice
From: Liz Ingham
Subject: Job assignment for technical assistant

Having reviewed the literature and my various notes about use of assistants in materials centers, I have attempted here to incorporate those suggestions into the things which most need to be done here. I understand that such an assistant would have had courses in some basic library skills, some aspects of working with children, and some general office skills. What I most need is someone who will be able to work independently but cooperatively. I need someone who can complement the work I can do best and most efficiently. Although I realize that some of these assignments would take time and experience before they would be performed really well, I believe that even an inexperienced assistant who is interested in children could perform them capably. In this way, I would be freer to plan with teachers, to organize the collection better, and to investigate ways this center might expand its program, especially in becoming a center for more of the varied kinds of materials, e.g., models, which our teachers would use if they were available.

The initial responsibilities would include some of the following. Others listed here might be added in time, or substituted if some of the first-named ones seemed inappropriate. I would wish, of course, to be flexible about this.

1. Tell stories to the primary grades.
2. Select materials on specific topics at teachers' requests.
3. Assist children during the center's browsing periods.
4. Arrange displays in the case and posters in the hall and in the center.
5. Work with small groups of children in gathering materials on special projects or in discussing materials, either during regular class visits or at other times.
6. Type and duplicate materials needed for instruction in use of materials.
7. Assist children while they are working on these assignments.
8. Supervise the work of each class's library helpers.
9. Prepare and distribute to teachers, lists of new materials, items of news about the center, suggestions for free materials available, etc.
10. Supervise the center in the absence of the specialist, which, for example, would allow us to keep the center open during lunch hours and perhaps before and after school.

Anna Vernon's note had come in on her own monogrammed stationery, and it was obviously written hastily by hand at home. Anna herself had delivered it the morning after the deadline Mrs. Rice had suggested, and she had dropped it off on her way to school, saying breathlessly, "Here you are. I hope I don't miss out on getting an assistant just because I'm late with this. Oh, do I need one! Well, just read that and see for yourself."

Her note read:

Dear Betty,

Oh, do I need an assistant! I find myself thinking of all the things I could do that I'm not doing at all, or all the things I'm doing poorly that I might do well, if I could just have help—and I mean HELP. Just to take a typical day, I think how nice it would be if somebody had the books which the kids return first thing in the morning all slipped and shelved before our first class came in. The kids now do some of this themselves, and I'd want them to keep on, but an assistant could do the pick-me-up things that don't get done otherwise. I think our fish, Polycarp, would like an assistant who would change his water and feed him more regularly than either the custodian or I manage to do. Between us, we've killed off seven fish in two years, and I think the kids must hate me for it, but they'd hate me more if we didn't have a fish.

Today, for example, it would have been lovely if an assistant could have laid out the refreshments for the faculty meeting, always held in the center, and I could have stayed in the all-purpose room that much longer getting a skit on National Library Week ready for the parents next week. You'll tell me the faculty could do without coffee, but when they have it, they stick around afterwards or come early and talk, and I get a lot of ideas and feedback then.

Now, Betty, you're probably thinking I'm not giving very *professional* reasons for needing an assistant, but, darn it, these things are important and, at the present time, I have to do them at the expense of letting other things go, so I think they are something to consider. But to get to something perhaps easier to defend, here's just a list of things I did *not* get done this week, that could have been done perfectly well by an assistant:

1. Unpack, check cards and order, and get ready for the shelves two cartons of books, received from the center. (I did root through them twice, looking for specific titles, but that time would have been saved, too, if I'd been able to spend the two hours probably needed for each carton.)

2. Change the bulletin board. (Would you believe we still have Abraham Lincoln up there?)

3. Shape up every file and record in the place—from the notes about things requested which I'd like to order, to the budget, which I've struggled with for far too long, and perhaps even devise a way of keeping our circulation file so that all the books borrowed by kids

in the same class can be easily located, as well as the things along the same subject—a problem I've never solved.

4. Type a second set of book cards for many of the primary books which teachers borrow for a whole classroom, so they can use the second set of cards to loan the books to individual children.

5. Round up from teachers their requests for films, filmstrips, and equipment for classroom use for the coming week, and get their reactions to what they have used. (I manage to keep my head above water on the requests, but I never seem to be able to track down or follow up the request that can't be filled right away, or the item which proves to be unsatisfactory. It's all a matter of time, I know, but I can't think of anything I could give up to do this better.)

I'd have thought there'd be dozens of things I could list, but let me assure you that, given the opportunity, I'll find them. One of the best things, as I see it, would be just to have another person in this building whose main concern is this center, and on whom I could bounce off some ideas and get some reactions. Don't think I'd be gabbing to an assistant all day, but this is an important thing, I think.

If I think of more, I'll call you. Please keep my name in the pot when you're passing out assistants.

Cheers!
Anna

Mrs. Rice laid out the notes from Miss Ingham and Mrs. Vernon alongside her own first ideas, as reported in the survey, about what a technical assistant might offer. About the only task on which all seemed to agree was the responsibility for bulletin boards, displays, etc. It was clear to her that each of the specialists was really searching for someone who would complement herself. Anna Vernon would be appalled to think of a technical assistant telling stories in the center where she worked; Liz Ingham had once remarked to Mrs. Rice that she could run two or even three libraries perfectly well if she only had a good assistant, not necessarily trained in librarianship or media, to work with the children. Their points of view, like their interests and abilities, were diametrically opposed.

What concerned Mrs. Rice, as a result of all this, was how she could defend, or whether she wished to defend, great disparity in job assignments for these first two assistants. One of the things the advisory committee had discussed at the community college was the necessity of stressing that even the best of assistants coming out of the program were not to be used in lieu of librarians, and that there should be definite lines drawn between the responsibilities of the professional and of the technical assistant. Mrs. Rice had expected that one concern, once assistants were assigned to schools, might be their eagerness to take on what were really professional responsibilities. Now, looking at the two specialists' suggestions, she began to wonder whether those professional responsibilities were, in fact, as well defined as they might be. She smiled grimly to herself as she wondered whether the freedom and individuality which she had encouraged among the materials specialists might turn out to be a complication in this instance. Of course, it was quite possible that in this year's crop of technical assistants, available from the community college, there might be individuals with exactly the right characteristics and qualifications to fit the niches which Mrs. Vernon and Miss Ingham had described. But in prototype assignments, would that mean that from this point on, every materials specialist could just ask for an assistant who would be the other side of the coin for him? If every assignment were so individualized, how could she defend the great difference in salary which was to exist between the specialists and the technical assistants? And would she have to face a future in which assistants and specialists would work as teams, where there would not be the flexibility of assigning assistants in terms of where they were needed, because they would have to be assigned to specialists whose abilities complemented theirs? To Mrs. Rice, of course, the more basic problem was how or whether to defend the great variation on assignment of the first two assistants, and, with that, what position to take in making the specialists aware of how individually their own jobs had apparently developed.

29.
The Case
of Considering a Center
· · · · · · · · · · · · · · · · · ·

At the request of Dr. Stephen Lorain, the associate superintendent in the Hardin school district, Mrs. Charlene Campbell, Hardin's library supervisor, made a survey to determine interest in, readiness for, and potential of centralized processing of instructional materials for her own district and the six others within the county. Hardin, with twenty-five schools, was the largest of the seven districts, and the only one with a library supervisor. Two districts, Brownsville and Paris, had coordinators for instructional materials with district-wide responsibility, and the other four smaller districts had high school librarians who assumed some responsibility for the library program in their districts. It was to these six people that Mrs. Campbell sent a brief questionnaire. One was returned, without having been filled out, by Helen Henderson, librarian at Altamont High School, in a district with five other schools, three of them elementary and two junior high. Miss Henderson had added a handwritten memorandum:

> Charlene—as you know, half the reason I'm here is to get away from the regimentation and red tape of a big system. Count us out of any plan for centralized processing. We don't have libraries in our elementary schools and at the rate we're going are not likely to. The junior high librarian and I share cataloging tools and keep in close touch, and neither of us would give up the chance to know what's in the new books. If there's anything else we can help with, let us know, but on this, count us out. See you soon, Helen.

Mrs. Campbell compiled the information received from the other

236

school districts to get a composite or profile to share with Dr. Lorain. Simply using the first letter of the district name, she identified them in columns with their responses to her questions. She used "n.a." for answers "not available," and left blanks when no response was given. This was the profile which emerged:

	H	B	P	W	T	D
Number of schools	25	12	10	6	6	3
Schools with centralized library collections	25	12	10	2	4	3
Total number of librarians in system	18	6	4	1	2	1
Total number of other media personnel	12	5	3	1	2	1
Number of these who are para-professional	10	3	2	1	2	1
Extent (in percent) in which the following are used in processing materials:						
Purchased sets of cards	60%	n.a.	40%	40%	75%	90%
Commercial processing of materials	10%	n.a.	20%	40%	10%	0%
Original cataloging at district level	25%	n.a.	30%	15%	0%	0%
Original cataloging at school	5%	n.a.	10%	5%	15%	10%
Approximate number of items processed annually	18,000	10,000	9,000	2,000	5,000	750
Percentage of these in each of these formats:						
Books	90%	85%	90%	100%	93%	100%
Filmstrips	5%	10%	8%	0%	5%	0%
Tape recordings	5%	5%	2%	0%	2%	0%
Estimated cost of processing per item	$1.13	n.a.	$.85	$.50	$.45	$.35
Number of times major orders are placed each year	10	6	1	1	2	1
Usual means of selection of materials:						
Teacher recommendation	x	x	x	Ha!	x	x
Published reviews	x	x	x	x	x	x
Personal examination or preview	x	x				

So much for the straight statistical answers, Mrs. Campbell thought, as she reviewed the neat sheet she had compiled. They told everything except what was happening and what was likely to happen. Brownsville, which appeared to leave a number of questions unanswered, was the place where Ed Shelby headed up the materials program. Almost every day since he had received the questionnaire, he had called her to see how the plan was going. He was so anxious for some kind of central processing, he said, he could taste it. The librarians in Brownsville, some of whom had two or three elementary schools to which they were assigned, were anxious to get about doing their own work and they wanted to be relieved of repetitive processing. He simply could not guess at the costs that must be involved when the librarians sometimes repeated the same task in three schools in one week. He had offered to go with her to plead the case to Dr. Lorain, but she had laughingly suggested that, since Dr. Lorain must be interested or he would probably not have suggested the survey, he should save his enthusiasm and energy for convincing other librarians if the plan was to be further discussed.

Floyd Murray in Walworth was one of the ones who would have to be convinced. He had the look of always being exhausted or on the ragged edge, but he prided himself on having centralized the libraries both in the junior high and senior high in Walworth, with extensive assistance from student assistants. He was cynical about teachers' interest or concern for the library, but he loved the students. Mrs. Campbell was sure that his estimate of the cost of processing, like those from Tionesta and Davison, was based on the cost of supplies such as cards, rather than on anything like the costs in terms of time of staff members, space devoted to processing, and other items. She was well aware that the figure of $1.13 per item, which she had estimated for her own district, where more processing was done centrally, was, if anything, conservative because the school budget did not charge items such as lighting, heating, or use of office machines to the processing center which was located next to her office. She smiled ruefully, thinking that the economies promised by centralized processing looked as though they were nonexistent if one compared her figure with those from the other districts.

An important factor which was not determinable from the answers she had received was the extent to which the other districts were developing a total approach to instructional materials. Again, Ed Shelby's point of view was most like her own, and this was reflected in the percentages given for different kinds of materials. Although she had had one or two other formats listed in the survey, the numbers of them added or organized into any of the collections was so small that she had not included them on the summary sheet. If anything, she was sure that Brownsville, Paris, and Tionesta had overestimated the percentage of new materials which were other than books, but still, what the survey did not show was what would happen if the nonprint materials, which were already in the schools, were processed in one central place. There had to be more than were reflected on the answers to her survey. If so, could the projected processing center offer retrospective service, processing what was already on hand? She was willing to predict that each of the districts would, fairly soon and fairly rapidly, be incorporating more nonprint materials into the library collections, and she was almost certain the problem of handling, housing, and processing them would be greater than with the book materials with which she was, at least, more familiar.

The other thing that glared up at her from the summary sheet was the infrequency of ordering in most of the districts. This was one of the reasons she heard grumbles from frustrated teachers in the other districts, and why many of them willingly changed jobs to get into the Hardin district. It seemed ironic to her that the largest of the districts, where supposedly there would be more red tape associated with ordering, was the one which placed orders most frequently. But associated with this were a dozen other questions: Would librarians or those responsible for ordering in the other districts welcome the opportunity to order more frequently, or might they consider it a continuing chore? If the Hardin center were enlarged to accommodate the multidistrict processing venture, would they have to reduce the number of ordering periods from the current one a month to, perhaps, six a year, the number which Ed allowed in Brownsville?

Mrs. Campbell noted one item of information she had neglected to get from the districts. She should have asked the source of most of their orders. She was not sure how reliable their estimates would be, but it would have been helpful to know the extent to which they ordered from jobbers, direct from publishers, or from bookstores or other agencies. Nor did she have any idea of the variety of processing they might use. She was doubtful that any of the districts used paperbacks as extensively as her own, but it had taken more than a year of experimentation and struggle before Hardin had arrived at the practice of using abbreviated Dewey numbers and author's last initials for paperbacks. She tried to remember, from her visits to the other schools, whether they used labels or lettering to mark their books, but her memory was not that good, nor was she sure how consistent they were, in any case.

The logic of centralized processing still appealed to her, but Mrs. Campbell wondered what her own district's responsibility was to other districts. Already, she was devoting time and thought to the plan which might not benefit her own district significantly at all. She recalled a firm statement from *Standards for School Library Programs* (American Library Association, 1960) about the necessity of centralized processing when a district comprised three or more schools. That had been part of the rationale on which Hardin's district processing center was based. She had lost her office copy of those standards, but she reached for her fresh copy of *Standards for School Media Programs* (American Library Association and National Education Association, 1969).

"Mm, two entries on Processing, Centralized," she noted. One simply referred to the district director's responsibility for supervision. The other was headed, "Organization of Materials," and she read the brief section carefully. This was not as strong a statement as she had recalled. Reasons for centralized processing were briefly stated, followed by a comment on the usefulness of commercial processing, possible use of computers in processing, development of book catalogs, and the potential of cataloging at the source by publisher and producer. Perhaps these new possibilities were diminishing the need for multidistrict processing such as she was envisioning. Mrs. Campbell realized she herself spent a lot of time on processing, including interviewing, supervising, and working with the staff of the center. They were a good team, and she was unsure what their reactions would be to enlarging the scope of the center. There was no doubt about it; if they moved in that direction, it would be necessary to tighten up many of the procedures, get more careful figures on costs, and probably at the same time permit some flexibility among the various schools which would participate. Perhaps at this time they could simply extend the center's services by offering them at some predetermined cost figure to Brownsville. She was sure that if they did that, however, the smaller districts, which often resented the leadership and size of the larger districts, would be that much more reluctant to become associated with the processing center. Then, too, if Brownsville were not satisfied or if there were problems, as her instinct told her there would be, the others might abandon the idea entirely.

Charlene Campbell was aware that there were many bridges to be crossed, but the first one, for her, was preparation of this memorandum and report to Dr. Lorain. She appreciated his interest as well as his objectivity and she felt they would both benefit if he could be given as much information on the pros and cons of this operation as she felt she had before her now. If he decided to move ahead, it would be her responsibility to plan the step-by-step implementation of the plan. She also wanted to make some notes for herself about what areas of the processing operation might currently be different in the different school districts and how these might be accommodated in one plan. Her work seemed to be cut out for her, but even as she approached it, she felt a twinge of guilt at the things that were going undone as she applied herself to what might, after all, be a hypothetical problem.

• • • • •

Compare the statements in the two publications of standards referred to in this case. In what ways do you see they differ from one another? To what reasons or events do you attribute these differences?

Comment critically on the questionnaire Mrs. Campbell prepared. Indicate items you would have included which she did not include. Indicate ones you would have excluded which she included.

Comment on Mrs. Campbell's attitude toward possible cooperation with other districts and the expenditure of her time and that of others on this project.

Do you think a consultant might have been helpful in this situation? If yes, in what ways? What should his qualifications be? At what time would a consultant's assistance have been most helpful?

Prepare an annotated list of books, articles, or other items which you think would give Dr. Lorain the information he needs to continue this discussion with Mrs. Campbell. Provide synopses of the articles as you might for him and indicate what you consider their relative significance.

Note, as you would if you were Mrs. Campbell, areas of the processing operation which might currently be different in the different school districts. Indicate how you think these might be accommodated in one plan.

Outline, as though you were Mrs. Campbell, the steps required to implement the plan for a multidistrict processing center if the plan is approved.

30.
Two Heads
versus One
· · · · · · · · ·

Nine of the ten teachers who had signed up for the series of six in-service training sessions on utilization and production of nonprint materials were on hand for the fifth session. Cosette Muncie, audiovisual supervisor of the Gloversville school district, paced the group as she had in other weeks. She talked for about forty-five minutes on various ways of evaluating materials before purchase or use. Perhaps because she had stressed the desirability of previewing before use, three of the teachers went to the small group room to view a 16mm film to which she had referred in her talk. She had given them the review cards usually filled out by central staff members, and suggested they make comments on the film.

The form was fairly simple:

Title of Material:

Format:

Features (color, stereo, etc):

Publisher/Producer: Date: Price:

Appropriate grade level: Subject area:

Comment by teacher/staff member (noting reasons for evaluation, possible uses, etc):

Signature: Date evaluated:

The other teachers were working in the production area. Two of them had brought materials to drymount, and the rest were continuing work on the transparencies they had started to make the preceding week. Miss Muncie moved among them. One of them, Harvey Pedro, stopped her and said, "I keep wondering whether it was a good idea to start all this. I've made stuff I'm sure I'll never have a chance to use at Higgins. You know that tape I made the first week? I sent two of my kids to the library to listen to it, and Mrs. Brunswick told them they couldn't listen to it there because it wasn't 'library material.' I can fight that one through with Mr. Montgomery, my principal, but it's a headache. Or maybe you were just trying to make us all more frustrated?"

"You're pretty shrewd, Harvey. I don't want to make you frustrated, but one of the ideas behind this in-service course was that if we had ten teachers out in the schools who knew how to push for all the possibilities in the equipment and materials already there, we'd have a nucleus of leaders to stimulate others. It may be that one of the people you'll have to stimulate is Mrs. Brunswick, the librarian."

John Gary spoke next. "Oh, that's about par for the course. But it seems to me, Miss Muncie, that it's the librarian who's being caught in the squeeze. Sure, we can press them out in the schools, and you and Mr. Middlebury are pressing them from down here, but there's nobody to help them. If they call Mr. Middlebury about some of the equipment, he refers them to you, or maybe just passes the message along, but they're really mixed up about this so-called unified program, when it has two heads."

"I can give you an example of what happens, Miss Muncie," Harvey Pedro said. "You remember you advised us to get those carrels with the work space on the left extending out a little farther, so kids could put previewers or cartridge projectors on them? The idea was that the back of the carrel would make a good screen. Great, but Mr. Middlebury, as the library supervisor, had the final say on all that stuff, and he ordered carrels with really dark backs to them, so that now, if and when a kid fights through to get a projector and a filmstrip or something, he's got to pin a sheet of paper to the back of the carrel in order to see it."

Miss Muncie was going to comment on this interesting revelation when Joan Field called to her from the small group room. "Miss Muncie! Would you settle an argument for us?"

Miss Muncie excused herself and joined the three teachers who had just seen the film. "Do we really have to fill out one of these forms?" Mrs. Field asked. "Clint says that since the film's already in your collection, nothing we say will make any difference. What I wondered was, why should we make an evaluation, just because we happen to be here, that might affect whether someone else, at some other school, could even get the film? And I just thought this would be a good chance to ask."

"Oh, there's no need to fill out the form. It is the same one we use when teachers preview a film before purchase. It's just that, when I have a chance to get more opinions from people like yourselves, I like to take advantage of it. Sometimes a film becomes dated, or even just scratched, or the sound is affected by splicing, and these things are not reported when the film is returned."

"I guess I'm guilty of that," Clint Darby commented. "By the time I go through the effort of selecting a film from that monstrous catalog, and getting the librarian to request it, and all that, I'm not likely to complain if it has a few scratches."

Miss Muncie picked up just one point. "Surely you aren't still using that bulky old book catalog of audiovisual materials? Why, cards for all items in the central collection went out to every school library last fall, even before school began."

"Yes, I heard that, but our librarian doesn't plan to file them till summer, when she has two weeks to work on her contract after school closes. She says that it wouldn't be too hard to file them, if they'd been sent in some kind of order, but that this way, it's just too big a job. Mr. Middlebury told her it would have been easy to sort them into order when they were all together down here, but now every librarian is stuck with the job."

The in-service session was over at six o'clock, and Miss Muncie was aware that the other teachers were gathering their things, getting ready to go, so she did not continue the conversation. She wondered whether it was by chance that the several problems mentioned seemed to stem from lack of one supervisor with overall responsibilities for the media program. She and Mr. Middlebury maintained, she thought, a good cooperative working arrangement, although she knew there were many decisions about purchase and storage of equipment, location of carrels, arrangements for loan, which she might have made differently if she were responsible for the entire media program in the school district. Until this evening, she had not thought that lack of a media supervisor would have much effect on teacher or librarians. Now she wondered whether she should make the suggestion, documenting it with some of the things she had heard this evening. If she did, and went to her superior, the assistant superintendent, he might wonder whether she was "empire-building," seeking the position for herself. She was not sure what might happen if she went to Mr. Middlebury first. He might think, as he often did, that she was seeking reasons to criticize the library program.